WORLD POPULATION TRENDS AND THEIR IMPACT ON ECONOMIC DEVELOPMENT

Recent Titles in
Contributions in Economics and Economic History
Series Editor: Robert Sobel

Lost Initiatives: Canada's Forest Industries, Forest Policy and Forest Conservation
R. Peter Gillis and Thomas R. Roach

Friedrich A. Sorge's *Labor Movement in the United States*: A History of the American
Working Class from 1890 to 1896
Kai Schoenhals, Translator

The Coming of Age of Political Economy, 1815-1825
Gary F. Langer

The Reconstruction of Economics: An Analysis of the Fundamentals of
Institutional Economics
Allan G. Gruchy

Development Finance and the Development Process
Kempe Ronald Hope

Bridging the Gap Between Rich and Poor: American Economic Development Policy
Toward the Arab East, 1942–1949
Nathan Godfried

Rethinking the Nineteenth Century: Contradictions and Movements
Francisco O. Ramirez, editor

Textiles in Transition: Technology, Wages, and Industry Relocation in the U.S.
Textile Industry, 1880–1930
Nancy Frances Kane

Threats of Quotas in International Trade: Their Effect on the Exporting Country
Gerard Lawrence Stockhausen

A Slippery Slope: The Long Road to the Breakup of AT&T
Fred W. Henck and Bernard Strassburg

The Suppression of the Automobile: Skulduggery at the Crossroads
David Beasley

New Perspectives on Social Class and Socioeconomic Development in the Periphery
Nelson W. Keith and Novella Zett Keith, editors

WORLD POPULATION TRENDS
AND THEIR IMPACT ON
ECONOMIC DEVELOPMENT

EDITED BY DOMINICK SALVATORE

Contributions in Economics and Economic History, Number 82

GREENWOOD PRESS
New York • Westport, Connecticut • London

Library of Congress Cataloging-in-Publication Data

World population trends and their impact on economic development /
  edited by Dominick Salvatore.
      p.   cm.—(Contributions in economics and economic history,
  ISSN 0084–9235 ; no. 82)
    Bibliography: p.
    Includes indexes.
    ISBN 0–313–25765–5 (lib. bdg. : alk. paper)
    1. Population.   2. Economic development. I. Salvatore, Dominick.
II. Series.
HB849.41.W67   1988
338.9—dc19   87–32266

British Library Cataloguing in Publication Data is available.

Library of Congress Catalog Card Number: 87–32266
ISBN: 0–313–25765–5
ISSN: 0084–9235

First published in 1988

Greenwood Press, Inc.
88 Post Road West, Westport, Connecticut 06881

Printed in the United States of America

The paper used in this book complies with the
Permanent Paper Standard issued by the National
Information Standards Organization (Z39.48–1984).

10 9 8 7 6 5 4 3 2 1

To Rosa

Contents

Figures   ix
Tables   xi
Preface   xiii

1. Population Trends and Economic Development:
    Introduction
    Dominick Salvatore   1

Part I: Population Growth and Economic Development   **11**

2. Determinants and Consequences of Population Theories
    Göran P. Ohlin   13

3. Population Growth versus Economic Growth (?)
    David E. Horlacher and *F. Landis MacKellar*   25

4. Population Growth, Aggregate Saving, and Economic
    Development
    Andrew Mason   45

5. Population Growth and Human Carrying Capacity in
    Sub-Saharan Africa
    Dennis J. Mahar   59

**Part II: Migration, Population Growth, and Economic
Development**   **77**

6. Internal Migration, Urbanization, and Economic
    Development
    Dominick Salvatore   79

7.   National Urban Policies and the Costs and Benefits of
     Urbanization
       Harry W. Richardson   95

8.   Population Growth and International Migration
       Gurushri Swamy   107

9.   Guest Worker Emigration and Remittances
       Robert E. B. Lucas   125

10. International Labor Migration and Development
       Thomas Straubhaar   139

**Part III: Population Size and Growth, Technical Change,
           Status of Women, and International Responsibility   163**

11. Population Density and Farming Systems: The Changing
     Locus of Innovations and Technical Change
       Prabhu L. Pingali and *Hans P. Binswanger*   165

12. Development and the Status of Women: Indicators and
     Measures
       Mary G. Powers   187

13. The Economic and Social Performance of Small Nations
       Clive Daniel   199

14. Values, Population, and International Responsibility
       John J. Piderit, S. J.   211

Author Index   225
Subject Index   231
About the Editor and Contributors   235

Figures

2.1 Declining Per Capita Income Growth with Population Growth   17

2.2 Increasing Per Capita Income Growth with Population Growth   18

4.1 Impact of Change in Price of Children   52

4.2 Impact of Shift in Demand for Children   53

4.3 Demand for Children in Industrialized versus Developing Countries   56

6.1 The Effect of Rural-Urban Migration on Real Wages and Productivity   84

11.1 Toposequence and Soil Type   171

11.2 A Comparison of Labor Costs with the Practice of Hand Cultivation and Animal-Powered Cultivation   176

14.1 Interdependent Growth   221

Tables

5.1 Food Production and Population Growth in the Ten Most
Populous Countries of Sub-Saharan Africa, 1970–1982   65

5.2 Potential Population Carrying Capacity Ratios in
Developing Regions   68

5.3 Sahelian and Sudanian Zones of West Africa: Actual and
Sustainable Numbers of People, 1980   71

6.1 Estimates of Average Annual Growth Rates of Total,
Urban, and Rural Population in Various Regions,
1950–2000   80

8.1 Gross Permanent Immigration as a Percentage of Total
Population Growth   108

8.2 Permanent Emigration as a Percentage of Increase in
Population of Emigrants' Countries   109

8.3 Emigrant Labor (legal only) as a Proportion of the Labor
Force in the Emigrant Country   111

8.4 Workers' Remittances and Export Earnings, 1980   119

8.5 Skill Composition of Temporary Migration   121

10.1 Empirical Performance of Our Simultaneous-Equations
Model   149

10.2 Short- and Long-Run Performance of the Model,
1963–1984   153

10.3 Simulated and Actual Averages for the Real Income Per
Capita and the Unemployment Rate for Greece, Italy,
Portugal, Spain, and Turkey, 1963–1984   156

11.1 Food-Supply Systems in the Tropics   167

11.2 Causes and Consequences of Increased Population
     Density   169
12.1 The Status of Women: Indicators and Measures   190
13.1 Correlations between Growth of Trade and Growth of
     Gross Domestic Product   202
13.2 Correlations between Structural Changes and Growth   204
13.3 Correlations between the Level of Development and the
     Provision of Social Services   205
13.4 Correlations between GNP in 1984 and the Growth Rate
     of GNP between 1965 and 1984   207

Preface

This volume arose from a session I chaired in 1987 at the Annual Meetings of the American Economic Association on population growth and economic development. It brings together a number of renowned population specialists from the United Nations, the World Bank, the East-West Population Institute and universities, and deals with some of the most pressing development problems of the day relating to population growth and economic development

The study of the relationship between population growth and economic development dates back to at least the seventeenth century and to Thomas Malthus. But recently, many new developments have taken place that brought the field to the forefront of the study of development economics. Many previously accepted principles have been questioned, and recent research has suggested new directions in the field. Today, more than ever before, population growth is closely examined for the contribution that it can make to economic development and for the difficulties to which it may lead.

Recent reports by the Working Group on Population Growth and Economic Development of the National Research Council, the World Bank, and the United Nations seem to reach somewhat conflicting conclusions regarding the effect of population growth on economic development. But they all raise some interesting questions and point to the need for more study and research. These are some of the reasons for the present volume.

WORLD POPULATION TRENDS AND THEIR IMPACT ON ECONOMIC DEVELOPMENT

1

Population Trends and Economic Development: Introduction

DOMINICK SALVATORE

The United Nations' 1987 *State of the World Population Report* opens by stating:

In 1987, world population will pass five billion. It is growing at a rate of approximately a billion every 12 years . . . every year by over 80 million. Ninety percent of this growth is in developing countries. How did such rapid growth become possible? Is reaching five billion a triumph for humanity or a threat to its future?[1]

It concludes by stating:

Beyond five billion, the path is dictated neither by chance nor by rigid fate. One path leads toward a balance between nature and human beings which will build a future to safeguard succeeding generations. The other will lead to difficulties which might degenerate into disaster if fertility decline is too long postponed.[2]

From the time of Thomas Malthus to right after World War II, the generally accepted view was that rapid population growth hindered economic development. This belief, however, was based more on impressionistic evidence than on careful empirical research. During most of the postwar period, it was thought to be more or less self-evident that unchecked population growth in the face of limited natural resources would soon lead to diminishing returns and declining, or at least stagnant, standards of living in most developing countries. Improved technology would slow down the harmful effects on economic development resulting from rapid population growth, but it would be unable to reverse the process because a great deal of the new technology being developed is very capital intensive, and most developing countries are capital poor. While many researchers and international institutions would not entirely reject this assessment of the problem today, they are questioning these beliefs and subjecting them to rigorous empirical tests. Ideas and beliefs that seemed only too evident a few decades ago are now accepted with reservations and sometimes even reversed. Be that as it may, the field of population growth and its relationship to economic development has entered a new and exciting period of research and development. Evidence of this renewed interest is the work sponsored by the National Research Council on this topic.

A recent report of the Working Group on Population Growth and Economic Development of the National Research Council formulated nine important questions to which it provided tentative answers based on the results of past and current research. It also pointed out areas where additional research is needed.[3] The basic questions asked and the tentative answers provided are as follows:

1. "Will slower population growth increase the growth rate of per capita income through increasing the per capita availability of exhaustible resources?"
   Because of the possibility of substituting more for less plentiful resources resulting from price increases for the latter, the report concludes that concern with exhaustion of non-renewable natural resources has been exaggerated.

2. "Will slower population growth increase the growth rate of per capita income through increasing the per capita availability of nonrenewable resources?"
   The report concludes that slower population growth can retard the decline of labor productivity and the degradation of common resources, since institutions that might resolve these problems do not adapt as rapidly as needed in most developing countries.

3. "Will slower population growth alleviate pollution and the degradation of the natural environment?"
   The answer given by the report is that slower population growth might allow more time for developing countries to implement policies and develop institutions necessary to protect the environment.

4. "Will slower population growth lead to more capital per worker, thereby increasing per worker output and consumption?"
   While slower population growth does seem to lead to more capital per worker, the report concludes that this does not seem quantitatively very significant.

5. "Do lower population densities lead to lower per capita incomes via a reduced stimulus to technological innovation and reduced exploitation of economies of scale in production and infrastructure?"
   The report concludes that lower population growth does not seem to have a negative effect on productivity, either in industry or in agriculture.

6. "Will slower population growth increase per capita levels of schooling and health?"
   The report indicates that slower population growth is likely to result in a lower student/teacher ratio and that this may result in improved test performance.

7. "Will slower population growth decrease the degree of inequality in the distribution of income?"
   Some evidence is reviewed in the report which seems to indicate that slower population growth will decrease income inequality by increasing the rate of return to labor, relative to returns to other factors of production.

8. "Will slower population growth facilitate the absorption of workers into the modern economic sector and alleviate problems of urban growth?"

The answer provided by the report is that rural-urban migration plays an important beneficial role in the development process by making relatively high wage employment, more education, health care, and other services accessible to an increasing proportion of the population. Reducing the excessive public sector subsidies to urban resident and urban-based economic activities is likely to be more effective in alleviating the problems of urban growth than is slower population growth.

9. "Can a couple's fertility behavior impose costs on society at large?"
   The report concludes that unwanted births result in welfare costs to the family and society, but drastic financial and legal restrictions on childbearing are not warranted.

The overall qualitative conclusion of the report is that slower population growth would be beneficial to most developing countries. A quantitative assessment of the benefits, however, is difficult and depends on the situation in the particular developing country under study. The report points out that the major difficulty facing most developing countries is not rapid population growth but inefficient policies. A fundamental solution to these developmental problems, therefore, lies in better policies outside the population area. These conclusions seem to be somewhat at variance with those of the World Bank, which in its 1984 Annual Report seemed to take a more positive view regarding the need to slow down population growth in developing countries and of the developmental benefits that would flow from such a policy. The World Bank Report concludes that: "population growth at the rapid rates common in most of the developing world slows development . . . (and) failure to address the population problem will itself reduce the set of macroeconomic and sectoral policies that are possible, and permanently foreclose some long-run development options."[4]

The United Nations' position regarding the relationship between population growth and economic development seems at times closer to the position of the World Bank and at other times closer to that of the Working Group of the National Research Council. The 1987 State of the World Population Report examines three propositions regarding the relationship between population growth and economic development. One is that rapid population growth leads to increased resourcefulness and ingenuity, which resolve any problems created by the rapid population growth. The second is that population growth is economically neutral and does not affect the rate of economic development. The third is that population growth is environmentally neutral. The report counters each of these propositions and concludes that rapid population growth hampers economic development. While population growth in developing countries has started to decline (from 2.0 to 1.67 percent per year from 1970 to 1985) and, in some, fertility has declined faster than was previously thought possible, there is still a need for more vigorous efforts to slow undue population growth.[5] The 1987 World Monitoring Report on World Population Trends and Policies, however, takes a more cautious position. It concludes that:

The net impact of population growth on . . . socioeconomic variables . . . appears to be, in general, rather limited. This does not mean that population growth does not matter, but that it is but one of many interrelated influences on the process of social and economic development.[6]

While the Report of the Working Group of the National Research Council, the World Bank Report, and the State of the Population Report qualify their arguments, the first (the Working Group of the National Research Council) seems to grudgingly acknowledge that rapid population growth can slow down development, the second (the World Bank) seems to grudgingly acknowledge that rapid population growth might not be as harmful to economic development as previously thought, and the third (the United Nations) seems to take one position in some publications and the other position in other publications. Even though there seems to be some disagreement in emphasis among these reports, they all raise some interesting questions and point to the need for more study and research. These are some of the reasons for the present volume.

Part One of the volume deals with some important but general aspects of the relationship between population growth and economic development. The first chapter, by Göran P. Ohlin, examines the determinants and consequences of population theories. Ohlin begins by pointing out that the rapid population growth during this century involved an extraordinary social transformation, and so it is not surprising that much attention has been devoted to it. What he does find surprising is how little agreement there is on this phenomenon and on the policy prescriptions relating to it. The reason for this, he believes, is that the causes and effects of population growth are simultaneously determined, and so it is not very fruitful or enlightening to study the effect of population growth on economic development without, at the same time, examining the effect of economic development on population growth. There is, in short, no real theory of population. Even so, there is general agreement that the very rapid population growth and urbanization that has occurred during the past few decades in the developing world have brought political and administrative strains to the system.

David E. Horlacher and F. Landis MacKellar offer the thesis that the relationship between population growth and economic development is relatively uncertain. They examine the relationship between population growth and the growth in per capita income, capital formation, natural resource development, economies of scale, technical advance, nutrition, and agriculture, and they conclude that population growth does not seem to play a decisive role in development. The main contribution of population interventions may be to give planners and policymakers more time and a greater range of options in pursuing their goals.

In his chapter, Andrew Mason examines the relationship between population growth, aggregate savings, and economic development. He presents a model that devotes more attention than other models to the link between the number of children and expenditures on childrearing, and to the effect of the latter on aggregate savings by using a variant of the life-cycle model. He shows that the dependency effect has a greater impact on savings in rapidly growing than in stagnant developing economies and that the effect on savings depends on the factors that account for the fertility decline.

In the last chapter of Part One, Dennis J. Mahar examines the relationship between population growth and human carrying capacity, with special reference to Sub-Saharan Africa, one of the poorest and most stagnant regions of the world. Mahar starts by clarifying the meaning of the concept and its operational usefulness. He concludes that, while the concept of human carrying capacity sheds little light on the forces determining technological change in agriculture, the possibility of nonfarm employment, and declines in birth rates, such calculations are useful because they provide an early warning signal to government of impending economic, social, environmental, and political disasters.

Part Two of the volume deals with internal and international migration and their impact on economic development. In the first chapter of the section, the editor presents some data on population growth, internal migration, and urban unemployment in developing countries in order to provide an overall view of the dimension of the unemployment and underemployment problems that these nations face. Since rural-urban migration is an important contributor to the unemployment and underemployment problems in developing countries, various models of rural-urban migration are presented, evaluated, and reformulated. Finally, various policies are advanced and evaluated for dealing with the urban unemployment and underemployment problems in developing countries.

In the second chapter in this section, Harry W. Richardson examines national urban policies and the costs and benefits of urbanization. He reaches several important conclusions, among which are: (1) the costs and benefits of urbanization can only be measured very narrowly; (2) the investment requirements of urbanization are substantial and place a heavy burden on the scarce capital resources of most developing countries; (3) high urban absorption costs per capita implies that there is a big payoff from successful rural absorption or fertility-reduction strategies; and (4) the recent shift in emphasis in national urban policies away from spatial strategies toward macro and sectoral policies that affect urban development is probably appropriate.

In the third chapter, Gurushri Swamy examines population growth and international migration. The paper provides an analysis of past and present day international migration, the nature of the constraints on the free international movement of people, and the costs and benefits to sending and receiving countries. One of the conclusions reached is that while temporary and permanent migration may be very important to a few developing countries, they have only a limited role to play in reducing the work force of the developing countries as a group. The author also points out that the net benefits of emigration are likely to be higher when emigrants are unemployed and unskilled because the loss of output or human capital is then small and the propensity to remit is high.

The fourth chapter by Robert E. B. Lucas examines the decision to emigrate and to remit, considers certain aspects of the demand for guest workers, and evaluates the economic consequences for the labor-supplying countries. One important conclusion is that emigration probably leads to some short-term national production losses in some developing countries, but in the long run, emigration also leads to increases in domestic production through the accumulation induced or made possible by remittances. The short-run production losses that may arise from labor migration in the developing country of departure depend, in part, on the ability of the country to switch production techniques. These possible short-run production losses, however, must be weighed against the long-run capital accumulation resulting from remittances.

In the last chapter in Part Two, Thomas Straubhaar develops a simultaneous-equations model of international migration and tests it for migration from Greece, Italy, Portugal, Spain, and Turkey to France and Germany from 1960 to 1984. He finds that a composite attractivity index, as used in the Todaro model in the context of internal·migration, is a very powerful explanatory variable for international migration. Contrary to expectations, however, he finds that job turnover in the destination country (proxied by the labor force employed in the industrial sector of the destination country) was not a statistically significant determinant of international migration. From simulation exercises, the author concludes that international migration contributed up to 10 percent of the growth of the country of emigration over the period examined.

Part Three of the volume deals with technological change, the role of women, and the economic and social performance of small countries; it closes with a philosophical piece on values and international responsibility. In the first chapter of this section, Prabhu L. Pingali and Hans P. Binswanger examine population density and farming systems and the changing locus of innovations and technical change in agriculture in developing countries. The chapter discusses (1) the determinants of the intensity of land use, emphasizing the consequences of population concentration and improvements in transport infrastructure; (2) farmer-based innovations in response to agricultural intensification; and (3) the role of science and industry-based innovations in achieving a rapid increase in agricultural output.

The second chapter, by Mary G. Powers, deals with indicators and measures of the relative status of men and women in the process of economic development. Powers discusses (1) the change in development emphases giving rise to increased concern for the status of women during the past two decades; (2) some conceptual and methodological issues underlying efforts to measure the status of women; and (3) a series of indicators of the situation of women developed as part of a large ongoing project at the United Nations Statistical Office.

In the third chapter in this section, Clive Daniel examines the economic and social performance of small nations. Daniel reminds us that since the end of World War II many small and some very small nations became independent. Spokespersons for these nations make socioeconomic development one of their primary goals. Yet the economic viability of some of these tiny nations remains in doubt. In this chapter, an attempt is made to compare the relative performance of some of these small nations as they try to stimulate growth and provide improved social services to their populations.

The volume closes with an essay by John Piderit, who takes a philosophical view of population growth and international responsibility. Piderit starts by pointing out that population growth in some developing countries is deemed excessive by the countries themselves as well as by developed countries. The normative question of what ought to be done is explored within the context of a standard model of international trade. Since the utilitarian ethic takes the number of individuals as given, that approach is not useful in handling population issues. An approach which emphasizes primary values is developed and applied to the problem of excessive population growth. One interesting result is that, under certain circumstances, it is reasonable for developed countries to put conditions on the aid offered to underdeveloped countries. This chapter provides a fitting conclusion to the volume.

NOTES

1. United Nations, *The State of the World Population 1987* (New York: United Nations, 1987), p. 1.

2. Ibid., p. 11.

3. National Research Council, *Population Growth and Economic Development: Policy Questions* (Washington, D.C.: National Academy Press, 1986).

4. World Bank, *World Development Report* (Washington, D.C.: World Bank, 1984), p. 105.

5. United Nations, *The State of the World Population 1987*, pp. 6–11.

6. United Nations, Department of International Economic and Social Affairs, *World Population Policies: 1987 Monitoring Report* (New York: United Nations, 1987), p. 559.

REFERENCES

Bhagwati, Jagdish N. (1976). *The Brain Drain and Taxation*. Amsterdam: North-Holland.
——— (1983). "The Economic Analysis of International Migration." In J. N. Bhagwati, *Essays in International Economic Theory*. Vol. 2, *International Factor Mobility*, edited by R. Feenstra. Cambridge, Mass.: M.I.T. Press.
Birdsall, Nancy (1980). "Population Growth and Poverty in the Developing World." *Population Bulletin* 35 (December): 3–37.
Bloom, David E., and Richard B. Freeman (1986). "Population Growth, Labor Supply and Employment in Developing Countries." National Bureau of Economic Research Working Paper No. 1837, February.
Campano, F., and D. Salvatore (1987, 1988). "Income Inequality and Economic Development." United Nations Working Paper No. 4 (May). Revised and reprinted in the *Journal of Policy Modeling* (Spring).
Coale, A. J. (1986). "Population Trends and Economic Development." In J. Menken, *World Population and U.S. Policy*. New York: Norton.

Demeny, P. (1984). "A Perspective on Long-Run Population Growth." *Population and Development Review* 10(March): 103–26.

Gosh, P. K., ed. (1984). *Urban Development in the Third World*. Westport, Conn.: Greenwood.

Greenwood, M. J. (1985). "Human Migration: Theory, Models, and Empirical Studies." *Journal of Regional Science* 25(November): 521–44.

Harris, J. R., and M. P. Todaro (1970). "Migration, Unemployment and Development: A Two-Sector Analysis." *American Economic Review* 60(March): 126–42.

Henderson, V. J. (1985). "Industrialization and Urbanization: International Experience." Background Paper prepared for the Working Group on Population Growth and Economic Development, Committee on Population, National Research Council.

King, T., and A. C. Kelley (1985). *The New Population Debate: Two Views on Population Growth and Economic Development*. Washington, D.C.: Population Reference Bureau.

Lam, D. (1986). "The Dynamics of Population Growth, Differential Fertility, and Inequality." *American Economic Review* 76(December): 1103–16.

Lewis, W. A. (1954). "Economic Development with Unlimited Supplies of Labor." *Manchester School of Economic and Social Studies* (May): 139–91.

Mason, A. (1985). "National Savings Rates and Population Growth: A New Model and New Evidence." Background Paper prepared for the Working Group on Population Growth and Economic Development, Committee on Population, National Research Council.

McNicoll, G. (1984). "Consequences of Rapid Population Growth: Overview and Assessment." *Population and Development Review* 10(2): 177–240.

Merrick, T. W. (1986). *World Population in Transition*. Washington, D.C.: Population Reference Bureau.

National Research Council (1986). *Population Growth and Economic Development: Policy Questions*. Washington, D.C.: National Academy Press.

Rodgers, A. (1984). *Poverty and Population: Approaches and Evidence*. Geneva: ILO.

Salvatore, D. (1980). "A Simultaneous Equations Model of Internal Migration with Dynamic Policy Simulations and Forecasting." *Journal of Development Economics* 7(June): 231–46.

——— (1981a). "A Theoretical and Empirical Evaluation and Extension of the Todaro Migration Model." *Regional Science and Urban Economics* 11(November): 499–508.

——— (1981b). *Internal Migration and Economic Development*. Washington, D.C.: University Press of America.

———, ed. (1988). *Population Growth and Economic Development*. Special Issue of *The Journal of Policy Modeling*, Spring 1988.

Simon, J. L. (1981). *The Ultimate Resource*. Princeton, N.J.: Princeton University Press.

Sjaastad, L. A. (1962). "The Costs and Returns of Human Migration." *Journal of Political Economy*, Supplement 80(October): 80–93.

Todaro, M. P. (1969). "A Model of Labor Migration and Urban Unemployment in Less Developed Countries." *American Economic Review* 59(March): 138–48.

——— (1971). "Income Expectations, Rural-Urban Migration and Employment in Africa." *International Labor Review* (September/December): 387–413.

——— (1976). "Urban Job Expansion, Induced Migration and Rising Unemployment." *Journal of Development Economics* 3(September): 211–25.

Turnham, D. (1971). *The Employment Problem in Less Developed Countries*. Paris: Development Centre of O.E.C.D., pp. 47–63.

United Nations (1987). *The State of the World Population 1987*. New York: United Nations.

United Nations, Department of International, Economic and Social Affairs (1987). *World Population Policies: 1987 Monitoring Report*. New York: United Nations.

United Nations, Department of Technical Cooperation for Development (1984). *Report of the International Conference on Population*. New York: United Nations.

United Nations, Economic and Social Council (1978). *Concise Report on Monitoring of Population Policies*. New York: United Nations, pp. 27–28.

United Nations, Population Division (1985). *Migration, Population Growth and Employment in Metropolitan Areas of Selected Developing Countries*. New York: United Nations.

United Nations, Population Division (1980). *Patterns of Urban and Rural Growth*. New York: United Nations, pp. 11–14.

World Bank (1984). *World Development Report*. Washington, D.C.: World Bank, pp. 51–186.

PART ONE

Population Growth and Economic Development

2

Determinants and Consequences of Population Theories

GÖRAN P. OHLIN

The population of the world has more than doubled within the lifetime of most readers of this volume, and by the end of the century it will be almost four times as large as in 1900. It is obvious that this amounts to a momentous social transformation, which is one of the most important events of our time.

It is not surprising that great attention has been devoted to it. What is surprising is that there is still no agreed interpretation of this important phenomenon or of the demands that it might make on public policy. There is an abundance of data and much research on the proximate determinants of the classical demographic variables: fertility, mortality, and nuptiality. There is plenty of alarmist exhortation against the tidal wave of population, a few attempts to seek virtue in it, and some experiments in comprehensive modelling that would integrate demographic and economic assumptions. But, as Geoffrey McNicoll commented in a thoughtful overview a few years ago, these experiments seem thin and inadequate, partly because one must expect rapid population growth to have profound effects on social, political, and administrative institutions of all kinds, which are not easily modelled. As he noted, "The influence of population growth on social organization is that of an oceanic force for change, evident in distant perspective . . . but crowded out by a host of proximate determinants at close range."[1]

That distant perspective on world population growth is not contested. No one could possibly deny that the acceleration of this growth in the seventeenth century and that which is taking place in this century add up to a unique and sensational event in the history of mankind.

It is equally obvious that in this secular perspective the acceleration of the growth of world population has coincided with an outstanding outburst of economic progress and change. It is also clear that the present prospects of world population growth imply a sharp increase in the share of world population of the developing countries, the late entrants in the great industrial revolution of the last few centuries.

But the consensus on population and economics does not extend much beyond such general observations. There is, as McNicoll put it,

fundamental disagreement about the net impact of one of the most profound changes in social circumstances in the modern world—a disagreement founded, moreover, not in variant political or philosophical premises but in economic modeling and in readings of the empirical record.[2]

There may be said to be an international establishment view to the effect that rapid population growth, especially in poor countries, is a bad thing for development and should be checked by public intervention, but few of the arguments on which it rests have been satisfactorily settled.

The fact that the populations in many developed countries now tend to shrink rather than grow is adding a new dimension to the situation, as the public and the political establishments in those countries react to this situation with considerable alarm. Almost certainly, policies will turn more pronatalist. It may seem a bit strange that profertility policies should be advocated in the very countries that tend to insist on the need for antifertility policies in other countries. But there is nothing intrinsically absurd about the idea that growth should be restricted where it is very high and sustained where it is low or negative; ideas about optimal population and optimal growth rates for population have been around for a long time. The problem is that they are neither convincing nor operational, and that they are linked to national populations. Although there is a good deal of abstract worrying about world population too, it is even less precise than the thinking about national populations. There is a strong case for basing population policies on perceived national needs rather than on general ideas about the economics of population growth.

In this chapter I shall first discuss the lack of a compelling conception of the relationship between population growth and other aspects of economic and social change in the context of developing countries. Their population problem has dominated the attention for some time now. I shall then make some very simple observations about the hazards and advantages of defining this subject in terms of the two separate questions of the *determinants* of population trends and the *consequences* of such trends. Finally, I shall make a few comments on the underlying influences behind population thought.

THE STATE OF CONFUSION

It was around 1960 that the acceleration of population growth in the developing countries was detected. The projections in the 1950s had not expected it—so much for early warning. But in the 1960s it produced a sharp response from the developed countries, which were also the donors of aid. They insisted on policies to check it and on research to explore its consequences for development prospects. That research can be typified by the study by Ansley J. Coale and Edgar M. Hoover, which was an important state-of-the-art document, incorporating then-current growth models, with heavy emphasis on capital formation. It suggested that population growth would give rise to demographic investments cutting into capital formation and produce lower rates of growth of per capita output.[3]

I shall not review the vast literature on these matters that has since emerged, partly because it has been done very ably by others, but above all because my concern is with the bottom line and the present situation. The view that population growth was harming development was championed with great fervor in many quarters. However, the demographic profession is reluctant to embrace generalizations, perhaps too much so, to the point where important insights into major relationships are thwarted by the great diversity of social experience. Even the concept of the fertility transition, which is probably the most important paradigm of economic demography, received more erosive scrutiny than attempts to elaborate it and build on it.

Those who contested the view that population growth had been a negative influence on economic growth had a strong case; Jean-Claude Chesnais noted that in many developing countries high rates of population growth had been compatible with rapid economic growth over a very long time.[4] Ester Boserup suggested that population pressure stirred people out of their natural torpor.[5] Julian Simon insisted on seeing virtue in population growth, as it would bring forth more talented people to produce the innovations that eventually fuel economic growth and development.[6]

In this confused situation, the publication of the World Bank's *World Development Report 1984*, which had as its special theme the problem of population and population policy in developing countries, was an important event. It was soon followed by another document in which these questions were examined when a working group of the U.S. National Academy of Sciences produced a report on *Population Growth and Economic Development: Policy Questions.*[7]

The World Bank report sought to bolster a Malthusian opposition to rapid population growth. It made a number of concessions to academic scruples and explicitly said that a reduction in the rate of population growth was not "a panacea" for development, but it argued that "within most countries, for any given amount of resources, a slower rate of population growth would help to promote economic and social development."[8] It did not question that policies to reduce fertility could be effective. The National Academy working group sought balance and reviewed a vast literature. Apparently, one of its purposes was to present a counterweight to the World Bank report and to highlight evidence that did not show any relationship between population growth and growth in per capita income. One reviewer called it "a watershed in the assessment of the impact of population on economic development."[9] It examined nine issues and found the negative impact of population growth on such things as resource exhaustion, savings, urbanization, and unemployment to have been exaggerated.

Nonetheless, the conclusion was that many development problems were exacerbated by rapid population growth and that "on balance . . . slower population growth would be beneficial to economic development for most developing countries. Thus there appears to be a legitimate role for population policy, providing its benefits exceed its costs."[10] The remarkable thing about the conclusion is really its hesitancy.

ASKING THE WRONG QUESTIONS?

One characteristic of these and most discussions of population change and development is the sharp distinction between determinants and consequences of population trends, a distinction that has come to be accepted as a natural separation. It makes a certain sense, for obvious reasons, and it is not a bad way to group research findings, especially those that examine fairly short-term changes. Much effort has been spent on ascertaining the influence of female education on fertility restraint, the economic significance of changing age distributions, and a host of other partial relationships. These are of interest. But they do not enhance our understanding of the long-term implications of population growth. In that area there has been a fixation on simplistic notions: Does economic development produce fertility decline and growth adjustment? Does population growth produce misery and would policies to check it contribute to development?

These seem, however, to be the wrong questions. First of all, they do no justice to the complexity and pervasiveness of economic and social change. We still know rather little about it, whether in the past or in the future. But one thing we can safely assume is that population growth did not bring on the industrial revolution. Nor did it arrest it later on. It makes very little sense to ask for the consequences of population growth without some idea of what brought it about in the first place, since that is likely to have been a very important social change.

This mutual and simultaneous causation, along with the obvious need to enlarge the perspective, is the chief reason why some questions about population cannot be expected to find simple answers or clear evidence one way or another.

An exceedingly simple argument may illustrate the point. To begin with, assume in Malthusian tradition that population growth *ceteris paribus* has a negative influence on per capita income because a larger generation will inherit an asset base that may not have been enlarged at the same rate. Add the Schumpeterian force of growth and innovation. In the end it will affect the social system and population growth as well. One can model such an idea schematically, writing y for per capita income growth and p for the rate of population growth:

$$y = f(p) + g(t)$$
$$p = h(y) + k(t)$$

Figure 2.1
Declining Per Capita Income Growth with Population Growth

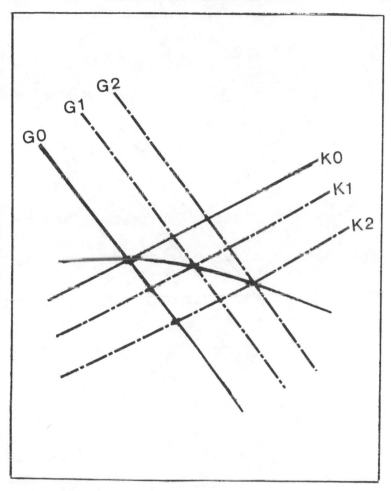

The functions g and k capture the role of technological and social change in a very schematic way.

Assume that y is basically negatively affected by population growth but raised by technological growth. The G0 curve in Figure 2.1 suggests an initial relationship between y and p. The shifts due to technological growth are illustrated by G1 and G2. Suppose that population growth is basically accelerated by growing prosperity and rising income; this makes for the rising K0 curve. Modernization and other social changes resulting from technical change shift it downward, producing K1 and K2.

Between y and p we could now expect to find any observed historical rela-

Figure 2.2
Increasing Per Capita Income Growth with Population Growth

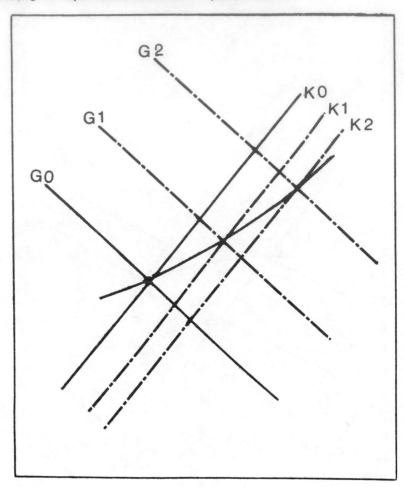

tionship, depending on the strength of their relationship to the other factors. In Figure 2.1, the impression would be that per capita income growth declines as population growth increases, but in Figure 2.2 the observed outcome is the opposite, and higher per capita income growth seems associated with fast population growth.

The approach is familiar from the Volterra equations, which produce a phase diagram to study the movement towards or away from the equilibrium. A similar pair of equations is presented by G. N. von Tunzelmann as a first approximation to Malthus' system. Ronald D. Lee has used it to reconcile what he terms the two grand themes in macro-demographic theory: ''The Malthusian one, that population equilibrates with resources at some level mediated by technology and a conventional standard of living; and the Boserupian one, that technological change is itself spurred by increases in population."[11] Both Malthus and Boserup engage in interesting discussions about the possible dynamic characteristics of different societies. Their discussions are far more ambitious—and speculative— than mine. I simply want to suggest that the entrenched approaches to determinants and consequences of population growth cry out for more and simultaneous attention to the differential impact of other factors on economic and demographic growth, respectively.

THE FAMILY

The consequences of population growth depend greatly on the determinants that called it forth, and on their simultaneous impact on the economy. Simon Kuznets was careful to describe this as a matter of "concurrence" among the many aspects of the complex process of economic and social change.[12]

Governments do not produce populations, but families and parents do. In the long run, their notions about the ideal family size are likely to be influenced by economic and social conditions, and there is a vast and fairly inconclusive literature on this, some of it assuming a high degree of economic rationality on the part of parents and some of it assuming a considerable time lag and a mediation through cultural and social change. J. C. Caldwell, in a series of papers, has outlined an approach to the role of the family and changing value systems, which particularly addresses the question of why the fertility transition in developing countries might be expected to be delayed.[13]

The argument is that traditional patterns of family formation and fertility in developing countries have been rudely shaken by the profound changes that development has brought in its wake. There may be dispute about the specific impact, but it has obviously implied both a rapid drop in infant mortality and the substitution of Western for traditional patterns of family morality and authority. Caldwell's interpretation of the links between traditional family-based organization of economic life and the characteristics generally shared by the many traditional family systems is illuminating, as is his suggestion that for some considerable time the traditional family could coexist with incipient modernization: "The situation in which the traditional family retained its ancient morality and produced obedient employees for a system not based on family production and not fundamentally in need of much of its morality, proved surprisingly stable."[14]

Caldwell's emphasis on the extraneous nature of the culture of modernization is also well taken:

The Western society, and above all the Western family pattern, is not for the Third World merely an external pattern. It is largely imposed. Western richness has been identified with the Western way of life. Missionaries, colonial administrators, imported legal systems, the media and schools have all taught it. International programmes, especially family planning programmes, both assume and, almost unconsciously, advocate the Western family. In United Nations statements about the 1975 International Women's Year and the 1979 International Year of the Child no concessions were made to family relationships that were not contemporary—even avant-garde—Western ones. The West has also exported a view of life and a secular scepticism of religion and traditional ways and ethics that has powerfully catalysed its direct teachings of family change.[15]

There is certainly reason to worry about the indifference to these cross-cultural issues and about the startlingly naive assumptions that still fuel many discussions about the fertility transition and about population policies for developing countries. There is a long tradition, going back at least to the Enlightenment, of seeing the root of social problems in the citizens' ignorance of their own interests, and in the efforts of both the priesthood and secular authorities to preserve it. In this particular context, parents tend to be considered ignorant of their own best interests. But this kind of analysis does not seem fully adequate to grasp the nature and role both of religion and of the family as a key social institution in traditional societies. The backlash of Islamic fundamentalism is a reminder of the seriousness of this clash between modern and traditional forces: It may well keep fertility high in strongly Muslim regions for a considerable time.

POPULATION THEORIES AND POPULATION POLICIES

In spite of the widespread attention that has been devoted to all aspects of population change, there is no hard theory of population any more than there is a theory of history. In particular, there are no two theories—one of its determinants, and another one of its consequences.

Having said this, it is still possible to believe that rapid population growth constitutes a very serious problem in developing countries. Even those who reject the economic or pseudo-economic arguments so often encountered tend to believe that this must be so. There are essentially two grounds for this, one derived from economic theory, the other from the study of institutions.

From economic theory comes the compelling suggestion that externalities drive a wedge between the fertility decisions of parents and the welfare consequences of these decisions for society as a whole. In developing countries, it can plausibly be argued that the benefits that parents derive from having children to help them and support them in their old age may be more than offset by the diminishing returns to labor, the social costs of a rapidly rising population, and so forth. (Externalities may also be thought of as playing the opposite role in postindustrial societies and thus to suggest that the fertility decline in those societies has become suboptimal.)

An even more compelling reason, however, may well be that the effects of rapid population growth on institutions of all kinds are stark and convincing. When a population doubles in one generation, and huge cities double in less than ten years, the strains on the political and administrative system can be debilitating. There is no theory of institutions and their role in economic growth, but there is a new awareness of their importance, and population growth has a strong claim for attention in this new line of analysis.

Much of population policy actually relates to family welfare considerations without much regard to overall consequences for growth. Family planning policies may be advocated simply because spacing births would improve maternal health. But fertility regimes are not easily changed by governments. Why not accept the fact that population growth is an aspect of development that will find a level and an answer in due time? Why the obsession with something that not much can be done about anyway?

There is a genuine concern about the future of an overcrowded world. There is a genuine concern about the ability of developing countries to cope with the task of improving the lot of populations which double in twenty-five years while they cannot cope with the needs of the present one.

But there is also reason to recall Max Weber's and Mannheim's "sociology of knowledge" in the social sciences, and the insidious and often unconscious ways in which deep concerns shape assumptions and approaches. Population is an especially vulnerable subject. It raises the eschatological issues of life and death, sex and sickness, love and reason, family and community. It is bound to evoke strong emotional responses. It is one of the achievements of formal demographic theory to have defused these issues by reducing them into sets and subsets of functions of cohort mortality, age-specific mortality, and the like.

But this makes it possible to raise the kind of questions put by Roger Schofield and David Coleman in their introduction to *The State of Population Theory*, in which they assert that "any subject which finds it necessary, or indeed possible, to consider its material divorced from an appropriate body of theory must be in trouble. This seems to be the case with demography at present."[16] As they go on to note, "demography abounds in ideas," but the whole of their volume only seems to confirm the lack of thrust and the difficulty of moving "forward from Malthus," to quote the subtitle.

Once one is aware of the heavy emotional charge surrounding the population issue, one is not very surprised to find that, except the community of scholarly demographers, most of those who are concerned about population growth really tend to worry about other populations growing too fast. Concerns about population growth tend to fasten on others. The rich worry about the growth of the poor, and rich countries worry about the growth of poor countries. Protestants worry about the growth of Catholics, and one state or province worries about the growth of another one with a different ethnic thrust. Worries about declining population, on the other hand, are expressed on behalf of one's own community or country.

There are exceptions. Certainly many governments in many developing countries find themselves in seriously unbalanced situations and would like to slow their population growth, if only they knew how. The same reasons that motivate families to opt for smaller size as more children survive and the cost of raising them increases commend themselves to governments seeing the nation as one big household.

However, the rivalry among populations is not a new phenomenon, and in a shrinking world it is becoming of ever greater importance. The claims on common resources represented by growing populations is becoming ever more contentious.

If it were agreed that the world had a limited carrying capacity, would governments be able to agree to share it according to some formula? It does not seem likely. Yet on a political level these considerations are already quite important. The growth of population in one country is no longer considered a purely domestic matter, except by countries themselves. Migration, legal and illegal, the depletion of nonrenewable resources, and the load on the ecosystem—these and other aspects combine to make the growth of world population into a far more sensitive issue than the simple Malthusian concern.

NOTES

1. Geoffrey McNicoll, "Consequences of Rapid Population Growth: An Overview and Assessment." Center for Policy Studies, The Population Council, Working Paper No. 105, May 1984, p. 69.

2. Ibid., p. 2.

3. Ansley J. Coale and Edgar M. Hoover, *Population Growth and Economic Development in Low-Income Countries* (Princeton: Princeton University Press, 1958).

4. J.-C. Chesnais, "Progrès economique et transition démographique dans les pays pauvres: trente ans d'expérience (1950–1980)," *Population* 40(1): (January-February 1985).

5. Ester Boserup, *The Conditions of Agricultural Growth* (London: Allen & Unwin, 1965); *Population and Technological Change* (Oxford: Blackwell, 1981).

6. Julian Simon, *The Ultimate Resource* (Princeton: Princeton University Press, 1981).

7. National Research Council, Working Group on Population Growth and Economic Development, Committee on Population, Washington, D.C., 1986.

8. Ibid., p. 81.

9. Allen C. Kelley, in a "Review Symposium," *Population and Development Review* 12, (3): 563 (September 1986).

10. Ibid., pp. 90–91.

11. G. N. von Tunzelmann, "Malthus's 'Total Population System': A Dynamic Reinterpretation"; and Ronald Demos Lee, "Malthus and Boserup: A Dynamic Synthesis," both in *The State of Population Theory: Forward from Malthus*, David Coleman and Roger Schofield, eds. (Oxford and New York: Blackwell, 1986).

12. Simon Kuznets, "Population and Economic Growth," *Proceedings of the American Philosophical Society*, June 1967, pp. 170–95.

13. J. C. Caldwell, "The Mechanism of Demographic Change in Historical Perspective," *Population Studies* 35(1): 5–27 (March 1981).

14. Ibid., p. 12.

15. Ibid., p. 21.

16. Coleman and Schofield, *The State of Population Theory: Forward from Malthus*, p. 1.

REFERENCES

Boserup, Ester (1965). *The Conditions of Agricultural Growth*. London: Allen & Unwin.
——— (1981). *Population and Technological Change*. Oxford and New York: Blackwell.
Caldwell, J. C. (1981). "The Mechanism of Demographic Change in Historical Perspective." *Population Studies* 35: 5–27.
Chesnais, J.-C. (1985). "Progres Economique et Transition Demographique dans les Pays Pauvres: Trente Ans d'Experience (1950–1980)." *Population* 40: 11–28.
Coale, Ansley J., and Edgar M. Hoover (1958). *Population Growth and Economic Development in Low-Income Countries*. Princeton: Princeton University Press.
Kelley, Allen C. (1986). In a "Review Symposium." *Population and Development Review* 12: 560–70.
Kuznets, Simon (1967). "Population and Economic Growth." *Proceedings of the American Philosophical Society* (June) pp. 170–95.
Lee, Ronald Demos (1986). "Malthus and Boserup: A Dynamic Synthesis." In *The State of Population Theory: Forward from Malthus*, David Coleman and Roger Schofield, eds. Oxford and New York: Blackwell.
McNicoll, Geoffrey (1984). "Consequences of Rapid Population Growth: An Overview and Assessment." Center for Policy Studies, The Population Council, Working Paper No. 105 (March).
National Research Council, Committee on Population (1986). *Report of the Working Group on Population Growth and Economic Development*. Washington, D.C.
Simon, Julian (1981). *The Ultimate Resource*. Princeton: Princeton University Press.
Von Tunzelmann, G. N. (1986). "Malthus's 'Total Population System': A Dynamic Reinterpretation." In *The State of Population Theory: Forward from Malthus*, David Coleman and Roger Schofield, eds. Oxford and New York: Blackwell.

3

Population Growth versus Economic Growth (?)

DAVID E. HORLACHER and F. LANDIS MACKELLAR

Three decades ago, Ansley Coale and Edgar Hoover (1958) wrote that "to postpone fertility reductions in low income countries is to shrink the potential growth in income per capita for the indefinite future." In the decades since, this view has been greatly expanded upon. Thus a recent statement signed by forty heads of state representing more than half of the world's population warned that "if this unprecedented population growth continues, future generations of children will not have adequate food, housing, medical care, education, earth resources and employment opportunities."[1]

Contrary to the preceding views, this chapter will advance the thesis that population growth has both beneficial and adverse effects and that we remain relatively uncertain concerning its net impact on development.* This position would seem to be consistent with the neutral character of the recommendation of the 1984 International Conference on Population—the only recommendation dealing with policies on population growth—which merely said: "Countries which consider that their population growth rates hinder the attainment of national goals are invited to consider pursuing relevant demographic policies."[2] Apparently, many policymakers have not been convinced that population growth really has important negative consequences for economic growth.

In its two editions of the *Determinants and Consequences of Population Trends* (United Nations, 1953 and 1974) and later studies, the United Nations provided carefully balanced assessments of the research findings available on the implications of population growth for socioeconomic development. Over the last decade, many institutions and individual researchers further illuminated the implications of population growth for socioeconomic development by giving em-

*The factual materials contained in this chapter are derived largely from the work of United Nations Population Division; however, the opinions expressed by the authors are their own and do not necessarily represent the views of the United Nations.

pirical content to arguments that heretofore were largely speculations.[3] Nevertheless, numerous unresolved issues remain, and the state of current knowledge does not provide planners and policymakers with unambiguous guidance.

The remainder of this chapter will review some of the evidence adduced thus far on the economic consequences of population growth. The first section assesses the results of international cross-sectional analyses of the aggregate relationship between the growth of per capita income and population growth. The second section is devoted to an examination of the effects of population growth on living standards, operating through changes in rates of capital formation, natural resource development, economies of scale, and technical advancement. Finally, findings on the implications of population growth for nutrition and the agricultural resource base will be considered.

INTER-COUNTRY RELATIONSHIPS

Reference is often made to the fact that in order to calculate the rate of growth of per capita gross domestic product (GDP), it is necessary to subtract the rate of growth of population from the rate of growth of GDP. It would be incorrect, however, to infer from this mathematical truism that had population not grown so rapidly in the developing countries, their per capita GDP would have grown more rapidly. To do so would be to ignore the contribution that population growth may have made to the growth of GDP. It may have resulted in a growth in the quantity and quality of the labor force, an augmentation of the pool of savings, a stimulus to new investment and technological improvement, besides hastening the discovery and exploitation of natural resources.

During the greater part of the modern era, overall historical trends suggested a broad positive association between population growth and economic growth, as population tended to grow faster in countries that also experienced more rapid economic progress. Nevertheless, in cross-country analyses, Simon Kuznets (1967), Richard Easterlin (1967), and others found that levels and growth of per capita income were negatively associated with population growth when the experience of the more developed countries was contrasted with that of the developing countries. However, no significant association was found when the samples were stratified; that is, when the more developed and less developed countries were considered separately. In particular, among the developing countries the growth of per capita income was apparently unrelated to population growth.

Using more recent data, P. Bairoch (1981) recalculated the relationship between population growth and the growth of gross national product (GNP) per capita for the periods 1950 to 1960 and 1960 to 1970. He also found no significant correlation in either period between population growth and the growth of per capita GNP. A. Rodgers (1984), using data for the period 1970 to 1977, found that when the growth of GNP per capita is the dependent variable, the coefficient of current population growth was not statistically significant.

Some recent cross-country analyses do, however, indicate that there may be a significant relationship between the growth of population and the growth of per capita income. Geoffrey McNicoll's (1984) scatter diagrams showing no significant association between the growth of total GNP and the growth of population for the years 1960 to 1980 imply that there was a significant negative relation between population growth and the growth rate of per capita income. He therefore concluded that rapid population growth hinders efforts to generate sustained increases in per capita product.

J.-C. Chesnais (1987) calculated correlations between rates of population growth and growth rates of per capita product for seventy-seven developing countries covering the periods 1960 to 1970 and 1970 to 1980. Though he found no significant correlation in the earlier period, he did observe a significant negative coefficient in the later period. He noted, however, that if four countries had been omitted from the study, the rate of population increase would not have had a statistically significant effect on living standards.

The United Nations (1987) subsequently undertook a comparable exercise in which the developed and developing countries were considered *in toto* and separately for the periods 1960 to 1983, 1960 to 1973, and 1973 to 1983. When the developed and developing were considered together for the period 1960 to 1983, the results of this study were consistent with those of McNicoll. When the developing countries were considered separately, the results were consistent with Chesnais's findings, namely that the regression coefficient was positive and not statistically significant in the period 1960 to 1973 and was negative and significant in the period 1973 to 1983.

Though these studies suggest that there may be an inverse relation between the growth of population and the improvement in living standards, particularly in developing countries since 1973, the absence of such a statistical association would not have ruled out the possibility of a strong inverse causal relationship. That absence could have been due to errors of measurement or to bias in the selection of countries. It may reflect the fact that population growth rates change slowly and their effect on economic growth may take many years to become apparent. The relationship between population growth and per capita income growth involves both current and lagged components, since current population growth, consisting primarily of additional children, will primarily add to the denominator of per capita income. Past population growth, however, would be reflected in increases in the current labor force and thus with more rapid output growth.

These studies implicitly assume a monotonic relationship between population growth and the growth of income. However, as development proceeds, the rate of population growth tends to rise and then fall in accordance with the successive stages of the demographic transition. Thus, for a given country, the correlation over time would be positive in the first phase of transition and negative in the last phase. If the whole transition period were measured, the correlation coefficients would tend toward zero. It is with this first stage in mind that McNicoll noted that strong economic performance will often increase the rate of population growth through natural increase or migration. Chesnais also observed that removing obstacles to economic growth should lead to reduced mortality and further population growth.

Finally, the relevance of international cross section analysis for drawing implications about relationships between demographic and economic trends is questionable. To interpret such results as equivalent to changes over time would imply that all countries, developed and developing, are moving along the same growth path.

POPULATION GROWTH AND LIVING STANDARDS

Capital Formation

Early economic-demographic models emphasized the competition for resources between maintaining the existing level of capital per worker and increasing the amount of capital per worker. This competition for capital underlies the neoclassical conclusion that, while an acceleration of population growth will not affect the rate at which per capita output expands, it will cause a once-and-for-all decline in the level of per capita output and, therefore, reduce the steady-state level of consumption per capita.[4]

As early as 1953, the United Nations questioned the significance of population for capital formation, stating: "If an increase in population exerts a negative influence on per capita output through reduced capital per worker, this influence may be counter-balanced by improvements in economic organization which a larger population makes possible."[5] Twenty years later, it reiterated that "significant economic growth has taken place in countries characterized by high population growth and low capital formation, suggesting that population growth and its implications for capital formation have not been dominant factors."[6] This position was confirmed by findings that indicated that the contribution of physical capital formation to long-term economic expansion was less than had been believed.[7]

On the other hand, the importance of capital accumulation for development may have increased in recent years. Countries wishing to expand exports or reduce imports often find that they must adopt capital-intensive production methods in order to meet international quality standards. Furthermore, if the capital requirements of population increase are satisfied, a faster-growing population will have a more modern capital stock. If technological progress is embodied in new capital, capital accumulation should increase productivity.

There is concern that the capital stock will not expand rapidly enough to absorb into the modern sector the increase in the labor force resulting from rapid population growth. Although the proportion of the labor force employed in the modern sector is increasing in many countries,[8] there is empirical evidence that rapid rates of population growth are associated with slow absorption of labor in the modern sector.[9]

Empirical research suggests that population growth rates and the rate of unemployment are uncorrelated.[10] In most developing countries, those who do not find employment in the modern sector will find work in other sectors rather than join the ranks of the unemployed. Furthermore, research findings indicate that informal sector employment is not only productive;[11] it also promotes the development of the skills that are a prerequisite for advancing into modern-sector employment.

Savings. In a closed economy, investment plans can be implemented only if the amount of income saved is sufficient to release an amount of product equal to the desired investment. In an open economy, domestic product released for investment purposes can be augmented by net imports of goods from abroad, but only if domestic savings are supplemented by capital inflows from abroad (foreign saving). Thus, even if population growth were to increase incentives to invest, actual capital formation would fall short of the desired level if a corresponding flow of savings were not forthcoming. The effect of increased incentives to invest would simply be to increase real interest rates, or to induce credit rationing.

It has been suggested that slowing population growth may increase the propensity of households to save by altering the dependency ratio. Specifically, households with fewer young dependents relative to producers may be able to save a larger portion of their incomes. However, empirical studies have generally found only weak statistical associations between dependency ratios and household savings.[12] Though a cross-national empirical study by Leff (1969) found a significant negative effect of dependency on the national saving rate, researchers have called into question Leff's method and results.[13]

In part, the weakness of the dependency effect could be explained by research findings that indicate that the consumption requirements of children are but a small fraction of adult requirements.[14] Furthermore, because of indivisibilities, especially in housing, consumption requirements vary inversely with birth order. In countries where high fertility is concentrated in poor households, which have inherently low propensities to save irrespective of the dependency ratio, the effect of changing fertility on the average household saving rate will be small.

A rapidly growing population is usually one in which there are many young households saving for retirement relative to the number of elderly households drawing down accumulated assets. Thus, rapid population growth should increase the average household propensity to save. However, a recent model of intergenerational transfers suggests the opposite, namely that a transition from high to low fertility would substantially increase the national saving rate.[15]

It has been argued that population growth in less developed countries (LDCs) represents, in part, the effect of parents' "investing in children" as a source of security and old-age support (Cain, 1981). According to this view, the high fertility associated with population growth reduces the level of monetary savings, because children are a substitute. There is, however, no consensus that the security motive is an important determinant of fertility behavior.[16]

Little is known of the effect of population growth on savings rates as it operates through the distribution of income. Neoclassical theory suggests that by increasing the supply of labor relative to that of capital, rapid demographic increase alters the distribution of income in favor of capitalists and rentiers, who are generally wealthier and thus save a higher portion of their income. However, if significant flight of financial capital is occurring, redistribution of income toward wealthy persons might not increase the supply of domestic savings.

The National Academy of Sciences (1986: 65) found that slowing population growth would reduce inequality in the distribution of income in the long run by increasing the rate of return of labor relative to other factors of production. Simulations with economic-demographic models have indicated, however, that the distribution of income is relatively insensitive to alterations in rates of population growth.[17]

It is important to bear in mind that the level of savings is a function both of the propensity to save and the level of income. Thus, it is difficult to determine the effect of additional children on savings, since they may contribute to household income as well as household consumption. The United Nations (1974: 442) asserted that a high dependency ratio may encourage earlier labor force entry. However, assertions that the net contribution of children to household production is positive and significant[18] have been countered by claims that, even in developing countries, children remain net consumers long after birth.[19] Parents and older siblings also respond to an increase in family size by increasing their work effort.[20] Standing (1978) found that high fertility is generally associated with an increase in agricultural and informal-sector labor force participation of mothers, but a decline in modern-sector labor force participation.

Some have argued that reductions in population growth could promote political stability by easing the strain on internal administrative and political systems or by lessening international conflict.[21] If so, slower population growth might reduce the risk premium levied by savers, especially foreign savers, and discourage capital flight.[22] Surveys of country-risk assessment procedures, however, do not mention population growth as a variable of interest.[23]

Investment. While early economic-demographic simulation models tended to emphasize the negative impact of population growth on the capital-labor ratio, recent models emphasize the role of population growth as an incentive for capital formation.[24] By making labor more plentiful, population growth can raise the return to capital relative to the return to the real wage rate, thus encouraging capital formation.[25] The increased rate of return on capital resulting from population growth might also be expected to encourage direct foreign investment.[26] However, the hypothesis that population growth raises the return on capital by increasing aggregate demand has not yet been verified empirically.[27]

Simon (1981) hypothesized that rapid population growth, by temporarily threatening to reduce living standards, may induce investment at both the national and household levels. However, this "challenge to development" thesis is not readily susceptible to empirical testing.

Recently there has been concern that population growth will reduce resources available for investments in human capital, particularly investments in improving levels of health and education. Some cross-household statistical analyses have found an inverse relationship between the number of offspring in a family and per-child educational expenditure.[28] In a related study, Rosenzweig and Wolpin (1980) found evidence that unwanted births, which are likely to be higher-parity births, are associated with lower school enrollment rates for all children in the family. However, it has not been shown that fertility (and by implication, family size) is negatively associated with children's educational attainment.

On the basis of cross-national analyses, T. P. Schultz (1987) found that educational expenditures per pupil were inversely related to the relative size of the school-age cohort. This did not, however, result in reduced enrollment rates, suggesting that rapid population growth may instead have resulted in reduced teacher salaries, increased pupil-teacher ratios, and fewer textbooks and other supplies per student. Thus, it appears to have been the quantity of educational resources rather than the number of students which was affected. However, there does not seem to be a strong linkage between quantitative inputs to education and measures of educational quality.[29] Furthermore, estimates of the rate of return to the quality of education are mixed.[30]

Rapid population growth is generally associated with short birth intervals, and closely spaced children are subject to significantly higher mortality.[31] A strong inverse empirical relationship was found between the number of children in the household and child nutrition.[32] Though empirical studies do not indicate that family size per se reduces the survival prospects of infants and children, [33] there are indications that large family size may adversely affect children's health.

The relationship between health and population growth has important implications for human capital formation, since low infant- and child-survival rates and poor health may discourage parents from investing in education and training.[34] Inadequate birth-spacing also adversely affects maternal health, and the demands of pregnancy, lactation, and child-care associated with high fertility reduce the return to the education of women, discouraging investment in this form of human capital.

Though there has been widespread concern that rapid population growth may strain public resources, leading to a dilution of health spending, the relationship between population growth and public spending on health appears to be weak.[35] Furthermore, aggregate levels of health in LDCs may be largely independent of government health expenditures.[36]

Natural Resource Development

It is not possible to reach a definitive conclusion on whether population growth has increased, or will increase, the scarcity of natural resources, in part, due to the lack of consensus on how resource scarcity should be measured. The use of relative prices to measure scarcity can be justified on the basis that, if resource markets were to function perfectly, prices would accurately reflect true economic scarcity. However, relative prices cannot be used to measure the scarcity of common-property resources, and market imperfections and price distortions, which are common in the case of private-property resources, may make it inappropriate to infer trends in scarcity from trends in resource prices. Unfortunately, quantity measures, such as per capita consumption, ratios of reserves-to-annual production, and unit extraction cost, are also potentially misleading.[37]

A widely accepted view on the long-run prospects for sufficiency of natural resources was based on the time-series analysis of Barnett and Morse (1963), which concluded that in all but a few cases, resource scarcity had diminished between the 1870s and the 1950s. However, attempts to update that study produced conflicting results.[38] While Slade (1982) concluded that scarcity began to increase in recent decades, surveys by Hall and Hall (1984) and MacKellar and Vining (1987) both reached mixed conclusions.

Though the debate concerning a generalized increase in the scarcity of resources remains inconclusive, there is considerable agreement that while some resources are becoming more scarce, at least in some places, others are becoming less so. Furthermore, possibilities for substitution are quite large. In the area of non-fuel minerals Leontief (1977) reached cautiously optimistic conclusions. The findings of a study by the United States Council on Environmental Quality (1980), which argued that in the absence of corrective actions much of the world's population would experience increasing resource scarcity, were challenged by Simon and Kahn (1984), who stressed the generally favorable long-term trends and the potential for technical progress.

The immediate effect of the increased resource demand resulting from population growth would be higher resource prices, which will, generally, encourage exploration for new deposits and stimulate research on extractive technology. There is also evidence that the development of renewable resources, such as commercial forests, responds to price signals in a similar fashion.[39] Furthermore, increasing natural resource prices and improving technology may lead to conversion of common-property resources to private-property resources, thus promoting conservation and improved management. As resource prices increase, consumers will attempt to substitute less resource-intensive goods, and producers will adopt less resource-intensive methods of production. Nevertheless, there may be significant dislocations due to lags in the adjustment process.

Economies of Scale

Among the positive effects of increasing population size may be a larger market, which should permit greater specialization and division of labor; economies of scale; reduced costs per head of public goods of various kinds; and reduced costs per head of transportation, communication networks, and other

forms of social infrastructure. The United Nations (1974) had noted that low
population density may impede efforts to increase the availability of infrastructure. This view has been supported by empirical studies, which confirmed that
regional population density can permit exploitation of scale economies in the
provision of some types of facilities such as roads and electric power.[40] However,
it is unlikely that further economies of scale can be gained from rapid demographic growth in those less developed countries which already have very high
rural population densities.

Demographic increase is one of the factors contributing to the growth of cities.
Initially there are economies of scale as cities grow but once some minimum
size has been reached, diseconomies of scale in the provision of public infrastructure are associated with further population increases. Unit transportation costs
may start to increase at very low city sizes because population density tends to
drive up land values.[41] And in the case of public housing, Montgomery (1987)
found no evidence of scale economies. So long as a nation has at least one city
of moderate size, national population growth does little to promote attainment
of localization economies, those which accrue to firms located in close proximity
to each other (Henderson, 1987).

Though the possibility of beneficial effects of population growth through
economies of scale is generally recognized, there is less agreement as to where
these economies are likely to be found. The United Nations (1974: 489) maintained, "Given the predominance of economies of scale in industry and diseconomies of scale in agriculture, it follows that diminishing returns is likely to
set in much earlier in predominantly agricultural developing countries." The
National Academy (1986: 52), however, found that "manufacturing economies
of scale exist principally at the urban level and are exhausted at a moderate level
of city size," while "economies of scale are . . . likely to occur in agriculture,
especially by spreading the fixed costs of infrastructure and research over a larger
number of people."

Insofar as population growth increases demand, it can contribute to the realization of economies of scale. However, the question of whether population
growth actually does increase total demand remains unresolved. Furthermore,
if the product can be sold in international markets, the rate of growth of the
national population may be irrelevant. Indeed, the possibility of scale economies
has long been cited as a justification for international specialization and trade.

Technical Change

Given the diminished importance of physical capital, it may be that the major
channel through which population growth affects productivity is its impact on
invention (development of new techniques) and innovation (application of new
techniques to production). In this regard, the more populous a nation, the more
likely that its market will be capable of supporting a domestic capital-goods
industry, and thus the more likely that indigenous technical change will take

place. However, modern research and development often depends less on market conditions than on government decisions.

In many LDCs, technical innovations are largely imported from abroad, with the result that the effect of population growth on the pace and direction of technical change is severely limited. If rates of innovation are influenced by relative factor prices, advances in response to rapid population growth would move in a labor-intensive direction. However, this adjustment may be thwarted by institutional rigidities. Many technologies developed in recent years are instead responses to high labor costs in developed countries and have little relevance for developing countries with rapidly growing labor forces.

Simon and Steinman (1981), hypothesizing that the number of gifted individuals varies directly with the size of the population, have argued that population growth may accelerate the pace of indigenous invention. According to this argument, the larger of two populations having equivalent standards of living will experience the higher rate of technical advancement. However, invention and, especially, innovation are often capital-intensive, so the effect of demographic increase will depend to a significant degree on whether it promotes or impedes the formation of physical and human capital. Simon's hypothesis implicitly assumes that population growth does not reduce rates of human capital formation. Even if that assumption were correct, the substantial emigration of gifted persons from countries experiencing rapid population growth renders it doubtful that developing countries would reap the major benefits from inventions produced as a result of rapid demographic expansion. Conversely, rapid rates of technical progress in countries with small populations suggest that many technical advances would be readily transferred to nations with slowly growing populations.

FOOD AND AGRICULTURE

The United Nations (1974: 427) was unduly pessimistic when it questioned the ability of the less developed countries to produce sufficient food to keep pace with population growth. According to the United Nations Food and Agriculture Organization (1985), between 1974 and 1983, per capita food production in the developing countries increased almost twice as rapidly as in the developed countries. However, this average conceals wide differences among countries (per capita production fell in fifty developing countries). Furthermore, for the developing countries as a whole, consumption increased more rapidly than production, necessitating sharply increased food imports. These imports in turn have hampered the growth of domestic food production and worsened already unfavorable trade balances.

Clark (1970) calculated that the earth could support between 35 and 47 billion people enjoying a North American diet. Since that time, various researchers have attempted to calculate the earth's ultimate carrying capacity. For example, Buringh, et. al. (1975), computed an absolute maximum, which was almost forty times the 1975 level of cereal production. But they were careful to point out that "the very high potentials of food production can never be attained because of economic, social or political limitations." Keyfitz (1984) observed that if as little as 1 percent of incident sunlight could be converted to usable biomass, the earth should be able to feed 10 times the present population. Gilland (1983) calculated that the global carrying capacity was only 7.5 billion people, assuming per capita consumption of 9,000 kilocalories per person per day. Though this is well below projected world population for the end of the next century,[42] the need to reach such upper limits had been questioned by Revelle (1975), who pointed out that attainment of the earth's maximum food production would require a large degree of agricultural modernization, and hence, social and economic development, which would in turn lead to a cessation of population growth long before the limits of carrying capacity were reached.

A study undertaken by the Food and Agriculture Organization and the International Institute for Applied Systems Analysis (1982) to determine the potential population-supporting capacities of developing countries evaluated production potentials under three assumed levels of input. Given low levels of inputs, sixty-four countries would have insufficient food production to support their projected populations for the year 2000. Under the high-input level, however, the number of critical countries fell to nineteen. Noting that such issues as comparative advantage and the gains from trade were ignored by the FAO study, T. N. Srinivasan (1987) pointed out that the methodology was such that the number of people counted as living in critical areas could be increased simply by dividing the world into smaller analytic units.

Population size and growth not only affect the availability of land and the amount of labor expended on it, but also its productivity. Although the expansion of agricultural land in developing countries remained a significant factor in the growth of agricultural output, higher yields had become the predominant factor. In this regard, Boserup's study (1965) indicated that population growth and the pressure it exerts are important stimuli for increasing agricultural yields. A more recent study by Boserup (1981) pointed out that population increase, which expands food requirements, also tends to produce increased food supplies by bringing about a shift toward more intensive land use.

The National Academy of Sciences (1986) study pointed out that some investments in land improvement may require a certain minimum population density before they become profitable. Pingali and Binswanger (1987) attributed the failure of some large-scale irrigation schemes in sub-Saharan Africa to sparseness of population and a corresponding lack of demand. Preston (1986) suggested, however, that in developing countries having high agrarian density, additional population should not be necessary to induce the adoption of technical improvements.

Mellor (1983) projected that the rate of growth of food production will continue to exceed the rate of growth of population. This belief is largely predicated on the assumption that in many developing countries the requirements for accelerated agricultural growth are now in place, while population growth rates are likely to decline. Mellor and Johnston (1984) suggest, however, the problem of expanding food supply has been made more complex and more dependent on technological progress by the encroachment of a burgeoning population on a limited land area.

In many developing countries the task of meeting the nutritional requirements of growing populations will require an increase in the population-supporting capacity of their agricultural lands. But unless carefully managed, such efforts could actually lead to a reduction in the productivity of these lands. In order to meet rapidly increasing food requirements, mankind has begun to cultivate marginal lands and has intensified cropping patterns, thereby increasing rates of soil erosion.[43] In large part this trend has been the result of cultivators moving up into hilly lands, reducing fallowed areas in dry-land farming regions, shortening the rotation cycles of shifting cultivators, and destroying field terraces and tree shelter belts.

The problems of desertification are largely the result of increasing population (and animal) densities in extremely fragile ecosystems, under conditions where the use of land is held in common. The National Academy (1986: 30) study observed, however, that this adverse short term effect of population pressure may foster the evolution of property rights that could promote conservation. Thus population growth could eventually result in better land use as institutions adapt.

Other forms of land degradation may occur as well. The FAO estimated that salinity and waterlogging have damaged about half of all the world's irrigated lands.[44] Although these problems appear to be the result of attempts to meet needs created in part by population growth, they can be resolved by improving, repairing, and maintaining existing irrigation works.

Allen and Barnes (1985) found that the rate of population growth is statistically associated with the rate of deforestation, which has reached serious proportions in some regions of the less developed countries. Recent findings on the extent of deforestation by the United Nations Food and Agricultural Organization and the United Nations Environmental Programme (1983), confirm that the destruction of forest resources is significant and widespread. Trends in the relative prices of forest products have long indicated increasing scarcity.[45] Furthermore, much of the current deforestation is taking place on lands that would better be devoted to watershed protection or similar purposes.

Although it has been claimed that the destruction of tropical moist forests is causing an unprecedentedly rapid extinction of species (Harrington and Fisher, 1982), research on the scope of this problem is still in its infancy. The number of species is not known even to an order of magnitude, and the economic costs of extinction are poorly understood. After assessing existing evidence, Eckholm (1982) took a pessimistic view, while Simon and Wildawsky (1984) were much more optimistic.

The United Nations (1974: 421) observed that sufficient food supplies and satisfactory levels of nutrition for a growing population can only be attained by raising the productivity of agricultural labor. To achieve this, considerable investments in land, material capital, and human resources, as well as technological progress and institutional change, would be necessary. If technological progress is not sufficiently rapid, the increase in labor demand will fail to keep up with the increase in labor supply arising from rapid population growth. The result could be increased income inequality in rural areas.

The rapid growth of the rural labor force in the developing countries could increase the problem of rural underemployment, particularly in the face of a diminishing scope for expanding land area. High rates of population growth add to a stock of agricultural labor which is already used at very low levels of average and marginal productivity, making labor absorption much more difficult.

It is, of course, impossible to absorb increases in the agricultural labor force indefinitely in the agricultural sector. Growth in rural incomes and returns to labor will require rapid growth in nonagricultural employment opportunities. The United Nations (1974: 421) observed that the transfer of agricultural labor to nonagricultural sectors is an essential prerequisite for, and a basic element of, the process of agricultural and overall development.

The assertion that rapid population growth will lead to surplus agricultural labor has been questioned by Reynolds (1983) who noted that multicropping typically requires large investments of labor time. Hayami and Ruttan (1987) found that since the 1960s, increases in labor productivity have become increasingly dependent on technological progress, which, when applied to smallholder agriculture, has generally resulted in increases in labor demand. Though capital-intensive agricultural development could accelerate the growth of food production, it could also lead to further concentration of land holdings, thereby increasing the number of landless people and aggravating other social and economic problems, including high rates of urbanization.

CONCLUSION

Though the findings concerning the existence of an inverse aggregate relationship between population growth and economic growth are mixed, there may still be reason to believe that population growth may be an important, though not decisive, barrier to the economic progress of developing countries. No consensus has been reached on the net effect of rapid population growth on either domestic or foreign savings. Similarly, it is not clear whether population growth on balance promotes or retards physical capital formation. Its impact on the formation of human capital, especially education and health, is equally open to question. To what extent population growth is associated with natural resource development, economies of scale, or technological advance is similarly unclear.

It is, however, clear that population growth has not prevented the growth of per capita food production in the developing countries as a whole. But in the last decade, some low-income countries have experienced increasing malnutrition, balance of trade deficits, a degradation of the agricultural resource base, and problems of landlessness and rural underemployment.

Taken as a whole, the evidence on the economic effects of population growth tends to support the position taken by the United Nations (1953: 233) more than two decades ago: "The net effect of population trends, whether it is favorable or otherwise, may be offset and indeed may be practically eclipsed by influences of a non-demographic nature." This view was reaffirmed by the National Academy (1986: 93), which concluded that, though "family planning programmes can play a role in improving the lives of people in developing countries," "family planning programmes by themselves cannot make a poor country rich or even move it many notches higher on the scale of development."

Paradoxically, this is a fundamentally optimistic view. It implies that because the rate of population growth does not play a decisive role, development is possible even in countries experiencing rapid demographic increase. Effective implementation of sound policies in the fields of agriculture, employment, education, health, urban development, and natural resource management can successfully surmount most of the economic challenges facing the developing countries. That is not to deny, however, that slowing population growth rates might contribute to the development process by giving planners and policymakers more time and a greater range of options in pursuing their goals.

NOTES

1. United Nations Fund for Population Activities, *Population* 11 (11): 1(1985).

2. United Nations, Recommendation 13 found in *Report of the International Conference on Population, 1984*, E/CONF.76/19 (New York: United Nations, 1984), p. 19.

3. Among such studies are the papers prepared for J. Simon and H. Kahn, eds., *The Resourceful Earth* (New York: Basil Blackwell, 1984); U.S. National Academy of Sciences, *Population Growth and Economic Development: Policy Options* (Washington, D.C.: National Academy Press, 1986); and World Bank, *World Development Report* (Washington, D.C.: World Bank, 1985).

4. R. Solow, *Growth Theory: An Exposition* (New York: Oxford University Press, 1971).

5. United Nations, *The Determinants and Consequences of Population Trends: A Summary of Findings of Studies on the Relationships between Population Changes and Economic and Social Conditions*, 53.XIII.2 (New York: United Nations, 1953), p. 233.

6. United Nations, *Determinants and Consequences of Population Trends*, E.71.XII.5 (New York: United Nations, 1974), p. 465.

7. E. Denison, *Accounting for United States Economic Growth, 1929–1969* (Washington, D.C.: Brookings Institution, 1974); and E. Dennison and Chung, *How Japan's Economy Grew So Fast: The Sources of Postwar Expansion* (Washington, D.C.: Brookings Institution, 1976).

8. D. Bloom and R. Freeman, "Population Growth, Labour Supply, and Employment in Developing Countries," in *Population Growth and Economic Development: Issues and Evidence*, D. G. Johnson and R. Lee, eds. (Madison, Wisc.: University of Wisconsin Press, 1987), pp. 105–47.

9. A. Oberai, *Changes in the Structure of Employment with Economic Development* (Geneva: International Labor Organization, 1978); L. Squire, *Employment Policy in Developing Countries* (New York: Oxford University Press, 1981).

10. P. Gregory, "An Assessment of Changes in Employment Conditions in Less Developed Countries," *Economic Development and Cultural Change* 28(4): 673–700.

11. S. Sinclair, *Urbanization and Labor Markets in Developing Countries* (London: Croom Helms, 1978).

12. J. Hammer, "Population Growth and Savings in Developing Countries," World Bank Staff Working Paper No. 687 (Washington, D.C.: World Bank, 1984).

13. R. Bilsborrow, "Age Distribution and Savings Rates in Less Developed Countries," *Economic Development and Cultural Change* 28 (October 1979): 23–45; and R. Ram, "Dependency Rates and Aggregate Savings: A New International Cross-Section Study," *American Economic Review* 72 (3): 537–44; see also Nathaniel Leff, "Dependency Rates and Savings" and R. Rau, "Dependency Rates and Savings: Another Look," *American Economic Review*, 74(1): 231–37.

14. A. Rodgers, *Poverty and Population* (Geneva: International Labor Organization, 1984), p. 31.

15. A. Mason, "National Saving Rates and Population Growth: A New Model and Evidence," *Population Growth and Economic Development: Issues and Evidence*, in D. G. Johnson and R. Lee, eds. (Madison, Wisc.: University of Wisconsin Press, 1987), pp. 523–60.

16. W. Robinson, "High Fertility as Risk Insurances," *Population Studies* 40(2): 289–98; M. Cain, "Risk and Fertility: Reply to Robinson," *Population Studies* 40(2): 299–304; M. Vlassoff, "Economic Utility and Fertility in Rural India," *Population Studies* 36(1): 45–60; and M. Vlassoff, and C. Vlassoff, "Old Age Security and the Utility of Children in Rural India," *Population Studies* 34(3): 487–99.

17. G. Rodgers, M. Hopkins, and R. Wery, *Population, Employment, and Inequality: BACHUE-Philippines* (Westmead, England: Saxon House, 1978); G. Rodgers, "Population Growth, Inequality and Poverty," in United Nations, *Population, Resources, Environment and Development: Report of an Expert Group on Population, Resources, Environment and Development*, E 84 XIII 12 (Geneva: United Nations, April 25–29 1983), p. 442.

18. F. Arnold, et al., *The Value of Children: A Cross National Study* (Honolulu: East West Institute, 1975).

19. R. H. Cassen, "Population and Development: A Survey," *World Development* 4: 785–830; and E. Mueller, "The Economic Value of Children in Peasant Agriculture," in *Population and Development*, R. Ridker, ed. (Baltimore: Johns Hopkins University Press, 1976).

20. J. Caldwell, et al., "The Control of Activity in Bangladesh." Paper presented to the Seminar on Individuals and Families and Income Distribution, 1981, sponsored by the IUSSP and East-West Institute, Honolulu; and A. Kelley, "Interactions of Economic and Demographic Household Behavior," in *Population and Economic Change in Developing Countries*, R. Easterlin, ed. (Chicago: University of Chicago Press, 1980), pp. 403–8; and P. Lindert, "Child Costs and Economic Development," in *Population and Economic Change in Developing Countries*, R. Easterlin, ed. (Chicago: University of Chicago Press, 1980).

21. R. McNamara, "Time Bomb or Myth: The Population Problem," *Foreign Affairs* 62 (5): 1107–31; G. McNicoll, "Consequences of Rapid Population Growth: An Overview

and Assessment," *Population and Development Review* 10(2): 177–240; and N. Choucri, *Population and Conflict: New Dimensions of Population Dynamics*, UNFPA Policy Development Studies, No. 8 (New York: United Nations Fund for Population Activities, 1983).

22. Y. Venieris, and D. Gupta, "Income Distribution and Socio-Political Instability as Determinants of Savings: A Cross-Sectional Model," *Journal of Political Economy* 94(4): 720–44.

23. T. Krazenbuehl, *Country Risk: Assessment and Monitoring* (Lexington, Mass.: Lexington Books, 1985); and E. Mayer, *International Lending: Country Risk Analysis* (Reston, Va.: Reston Financial Services, 1985).

24. A discussion of these models can be found in D. Ahlburg, "The Impact of Population Growth on Economic Growth in Developing Nations: The Evidence from Macroeconomic-Demographic Models," in *Population Growth and Economic Development: Issues and Evidence*, D. G. Johnson and R. Lee, eds. (Madison, Wisc.: University of Wisconsin Press, 1987), pp. 479–521; and W. Sanderson, *Economic-Demographic Simulation Models: A Review of Their Usefulness for Policy Analysis* (Laxenburg, Austria: International Institute for Applied Systems Analysis, 1980).

25. R. Lee, "An Historical Perspective on Economic Aspects of the Population Explosion: The Case of Pre-industrial England," in *Population and Economic Change in Developing Countries*, R. A. Easterlin, ed. (Chicago: University of Chicago Press, 1980), pp. 517–56.

26. A. Deardorff, "Trade and Capital Mobility in a World of Diverging Populations," in *Population Growth and Economic Development: Issues and Evidence*, D. G. Johnson and R. Lee, eds. (Madison, Wisc.: University of Wisconsin Press, 1987), pp. 561–88.

27. R. Lee, "Economic Consequences of Population Size, Structure, and Growth," *IUSSP Newsletter* 17: 43–59.

28. N. Birdsall, "A Cost of Siblings: Child Schooling in Urban Colombia," in *Research in Population Economics*, Vol. 2, J. Simon and J. DaVanzo, eds. (Greenwich, Conn.: JAI Press, 1980); J. Tan, and M. Haines, "Schooling and the Demand for Children: Historical Perspective," Background paper for 1984 World Development Report (Washington, D.C.: World Bank, 1983).

29. T. W. Schultz, "Investment in Population Quality in Low Income Countries," in *World Population and Development: Challenges and Prospects*, P. Hauser, ed. (Syracuse, N.Y.: Syracuse University Press, 1979), pp. 339–60.

30. J. Behrman, and N. Birdsall, *The Reward for Choosing Well the Timing of One's Birth: Cohort Effects and Earnings Functions for Brazilian Males* (Washington, D.C.: World Bank, 1985); S. Heyneman, and W. Loxley, "The Effect of Primary-School Quality on Academic Achievement across Twenty-Nine High- and Low-Income Countries," *American Journal of Sociology* 88(6): 1162–92; J. Simmons, and L. Alexander, "The Determinants of School Achievement in Developing Countries," *Economic Development and Cultural Change* 26(2): 341–58.

31. J. Cleland, and Z. Sathar, "The Effect of Birth Spacing on Childhood Mortality in Pakistan," *Population Studies* 38(3): 401–18; C. de Sweemer, "The Influence of Child Spacing on Child Survival," *Population Studies* 38(1): 47–72; D. Frenzen, and D. Hogan, "The Impact of Class, Education, and Health Care on Infant Mortality in a Developing Society: The Case of Thailand," *Demography* 19(3); J. Hobcraft, J. McDonald, and S. Rutstein, "Demographic Determinants of Infant and Early Child Mortality: A Comparative Analysis," *Population Studies* 39(3): 363–85.

32. R. Evenson, B. Popkin, and E. King-Quizon, *Nutrition, Work, and Demographic Behavior in Rural Philippine Households: A Synopsis of Several Laguna Household Studies*, Economic Growth Center Discussion Paper No. 308 (New Haven, Conn.: Yale University, 1979); P. Heller and W. Drake, "Malnutrition, Child Mortality and the Family Decision Process," *Journal of Development Economics* 6(2).

33. R. Anker, and J. Knowles, *Population Growth, Employment, and Economic-Demographic Interactions in Kenya* (New York: St. Martin's Press, 1983); A. Kelley and L. da Silva, "The Choice of Family Size and the Compatibility of Female Workforce Participation in the Low-Income Setting," *Revue Economique* 31(6); G. Simmons et al., "Post-Neonatal Mortality in Rural India: Implications of an Economic Model," *Demography* 19(3): 371–89.

34. S. Preston, "Causes and Consequences of Mortality Decline in Less Developed Countries During the Twentieth Century," in *Population and Economic Change in Developing Countries*, R. Easterlin, ed. (Chicago: University of Chicago Press, 1980).

35. F. Golladay, and B. Liese, *Health Issues and Policies in the Developing World*, World Bank Staff Working Paper No. 412 (Washington, D.C.: World Bank, 1980).

36. H. Mosley, "Will Primary Health Care Reduce Infant and Child Mortality? A Critique of Current Strategies, with Special Reference to Africa and Asia," paper prepared for IUSSP Seminar on Social Policy, Health Policy, and Mortality Prospects, Paris; United Nations, *Socio-Economic Differentials in Child Mortality in Developing Countries*, E.85.XIII.7 (New York: United Nations, 1985).

37. V. K. Smith, "Measuring Natural Resource Scarcity: Theory and Practice," *Journal of Environmental Economics and Management* 5(2): 150–71; G. Brown and B. Field, "The Adequacy of Measures for Signalling the Scarcity of Natural Resources," in *Scarcity and Growth Revisited*, V. K. Smith, ed. (Baltimore: Johns Hopkins University Press, 1979), pp. 218–48.

38. H. J. Barnett, "Scarcity and Growth Revisited," in *Scarcity and Growth Revisited*, V. K. Smith, ed. (Baltimore: Johns Hopkins University Press, 1979); M. Johnson, F. Bell, and J. Bennett, "Natural Resource Scarcity: Empirical Evidence and Public Policy," *Journal of Environmental Economics and Management* 7(3): 256–71; and V. Smith, "Measuring Natural Resource Scarcity: Elusive Quest or Frontier of Economic Analysis?" *Land Economics* 56(3): 257–98.

39. R. Haynes and D. Adams, "Changing Perceptions of the U.S. Forest Sector: Implications for the RPA Timber Assessment," *American Journal of Agricultural Economics* 65(5): 1002–9.

40. D. Glover and J. Simon, "The Effects of Population Density on Infrastructure: The Case of Road Building," *Economic Development and Cultural Change* 23(3): 453–68; P. Frederickson, "Further Evidence on the Relationship between Population Density and Infrastructure: The Philippines and Electrification," *Economic Development and Cultural Change* 29(4): 649–758.

41. J. Linn, *Cities in the Developing World: Policies for Their Efficient and Equitable Growth* (New York: Oxford University Press, 1983).

42. The United Nations has projected that at some time near the end of the 21st century, work population would stabilize at 10.2 billion. United Nations Secretariat, "Long-Range Global Population Projections as Assessed in 1980," *Population Bulletin of the United Nations*, 1984, No. 14, p. 21.

43. The annual net loss of topsoil is estimated to be 23 billion tons. L. Brown,

"Conserving Soils," in *State of the World* L. Brown, ed. (New York: W. W. Norton Co., 1984), p. 61.

44. Food and Agriculture Organization, *The State of Food and Agriculture, 1982* (Rome: Food and Agriculture Organization, 1983).

45. R. Sedjo and M. Clawson, "Global Forests," in *The Resourceful Earth*, J. Simon and H. Kahn, eds. (New York: Basil Blackwell, 1984), pp. 128–70.

REFERENCES

Allen, J., and D. Barnes (1985). "The Causes of Deforestation in Developing Countries." *Annals of the Association of American Geographers* 75(2): 163–84.

Bairoch, P. (1981). "Population Growth and Long-Term International Economic Growth." *International Population Congress*, IUSSP, Manila, pp. 141–63.

Barnett, H., and C. Morse (1963). *Scarcity and Growth*. Baltimore: Johns Hopkins University Press.

Boserup, E. (1965). *The Conditions of Agricultural Growth: The Economics of Agrarian Change Under Population Pressure*. London: Allen and Unwin.

———— (1981). *Population and Technical Change: A Study of Long-Term Trends*. Chicago: University of Chicago Press.

Buringh, P., H. van Heest, and G. Staring (1975). *Computation of the Absolute Maximum World Food Production of the World*. Waj ening en, The Netherlands.

Cain, M. (1981). "Risk and Insurance: Perspectives on Fertility and Agrarian Change in India and Bangladesh." *Population and Development Review* 7(3): 435–74.

Chesnais, Jean-Claude (1987). "Population Growth and Development: An Unexplained Boom," *Population Bulletin of the United Nations*.

Clark, C. (1970). *Starvation or Plenty*. London: Stoeker and Warburg.

Coale, A., and E. Hoover (1958). *Population Growth and Economic Development in Low-income Countries: A Case Study of India's Prospects*. Princeton, N.J.: Princeton University Press.

Easterlin, R. A. (1967). "The Effects of Population Growth on the Economic Development of Developing Countries," *The Annals of the American Academy of Political and Social Science* 369: 98–108.

Eckholm, E. (1982). *Down to Earth*. New York: W. W. Norton.

Gilland, B. (1983). "Considerations on World Population and Food Supply." *Population and Development Review* 9(2): 203–11.

Hall, D., and J. Hall (1984). "Concepts and Measures of Natural Resource Scarcity with a Summary of Recent Trends." *Journal of Environmental Economics and Management* 11(4): 363–79.

Harrington, W. and A. Fisher (1982). "Endangered Species." In *Current Issues in Natural Resource Policy*, P. Portney, ed. Washington, D.C.: Resources for the Future, pp. 117–48.

Hayami, Y., and V. Ruttan (1987). "Population and Agricultural Productivity." In *Population Growth and Economic Development: Issues and Evidence*, D. G. Johnson and R. Lee, eds. Madison, Wisc.: University of Wisconsin Press, pp. 57–101.

Henderson, V. J. (1987). "Industrialization and Urbanization: International Experience." In *Population Growth and Economic Development: Issues and Evidence*, D. G.

Johnson and R. Lee, eds. Madison, Wisc.: University of Wisconsin Press, pp. 189–224.

Keyfitz, N. (1984). "Impact of Trends in Resources, Environment, and Development on Demographic Prospects." In *Population, Resources, Environment, and Development: Proceedings of the Expert Group on Population, Resources, Environment, and Development, Geneva, 25–29 April, 1983*. E.84.XIII.12. New York: United Nations, pp. 97–124.

Kuznets, S. (1967). "Population and Economic Growth," *Proceedings of the American Philosophical Society* (June) pp. 170–195.

Leff, N. (1969). "Dependency Rates and Saving Rates." *American Economic Review* 59(5): 886–96.

Leontief, Wassily W., et al. (1977). *The Future of the World Economy: A United Nations Study*. New York: Oxford University Press.

MacKellar, L. and D. Vining, Jr. (1987). "Natural Resource Scarcity: A Global Survey." In *Population Growth and Economic Development: Issues and Evidence*, D. G. Johnson and R. Lee, eds. Madison, Wisc.: University of Wisconsin Press, pp. 259–329.

McNicoll, G. (1984). "Consequences of Rapid Population Growth: An Overview and Assessment." *Population and Development Review* 10(2): 177–240.

Mellor, J. (1983). "Food Prospects for Developing Countries." *American Economic Review* 73(2): 239–43.

Mellor, J. and B. Johnston (1984). "The World Food Equation: Interrelations among Development, Employment, and Food Consumption." *Journal of Economic Literature* 22: 531–74.

Montgomery, M. (1987). "The Impact of Urban Population Growth on Urban Labour Markets and the Cost of Urban Services Delivery: A Review." In *Population Growth and Economic Development: Issues and Evidence*, D. G. Johnson and R. Lee, eds. Madison, Wisc.: University of Wisconsin Press, pp. 149–88.

Pingali, P. and H. Binswanger (1987). "Population Density and Agricultural Intensification: A Study of the Evolution of Technologies in Tropical Agriculture." *Population Growth and Economic Development: Issues and Evidence*. D. G. Johnson and R. Lee, eds. Madison, Wisc.: University of Wisconsin Press, pp. 27–56.

Preston, S. (1980). "Causes and Consequences of Mortality Decline in Less Developed Countries During the Twentieth Century." In *Population and Economic Change in Developing Countries*, R. Easterlin, ed. Chicago: University of Chicago Press.

——— (1986). "Are the Economic Consequences of Population Growth a Sound Basis for Population Policy?" In *World Population and U.S. Policy*, J. Menken, ed. New York: W. W. Norton, p. 73.

Revelle, R. (1975). "Will the Earth's Food and Water Resources Be Sufficient for Future Populations? In *Population Debate: Dimensions and Perspectives*. 2, E-F-S.75.XIII.5. New York: United Nations, pp. 3–14.

Reynolds, L. (1983). "The Spread of Economic Growth to the Third World: 1850–1980." *Journal of Economic Literature* 21: 941–80.

Rodgers, G. (1984). "Population Growth, Inequality and Poverty." In *Population, Resources, Environment and Development: Report of an Expert Group on Population, Resources, Environment and Development*. E.84.XIII.12. Geneva: United Nations, p. 442.

Rosenzweig, M. and K. Wolpin (1980). "Testing the Quantity-Quality Fertility Model: The Use of Twins as a Natural Experiment." *Econometrica* 48(1): 227–40.

Schultz, T. P. (1987). "School Expenditures and Enrollment, 1960–80: The Effects of Income, Prices, and Population Growth." In *Population Growth and Economic Development: Issues and Evidence*, D. G. Johnson and R. Lee, eds. Madison, Wisc.: University of Wisconsin Press, pp. 413–76.

Simon, J. (1981). *The Ultimate Resource*. Princeton: Princeton University Press.

Simon, J. and H. Kahn, eds. (1984). *The Resourceful Earth*. New York: Basil Blackwell.

Simon, J. and G. Steinman (1981). "Population Growth and Phelps' Technical Progress Model: Interpretation and Generalization." In *Research in Population Economics*, J. Simon and P. Lindert, eds. Greenwich, Conn.: JAI Press, pp. 239–54.

Simon, J., and A. Wildawsky (1984). "On Species Loss, the Absence of Data, and Risks to Humanity." In *The Resourceful Earth*, J. Simon and H. Kahn, eds. New York: Basil Blackwell, pp. 171–83.

Slade, M. (1982). "Trends in Natural-Resource Commodity Prices: An Analysis of the Time Domain." *Journal of Environmental Economics and Management* 9(2): 122–37.

Srinivasan, T. (1984). "Population and Food." In *Population Growth and Economic Development: Issues and Evidence*, D. G. Johnson and R. Lee, eds. Madison, Wisc.: University of Wisconsin Press, pp. 3–26.

Standing, G. (1978). *Labor Force Participation and Development*. Geneva: International Labor Organization.

United Nations (1953). *The Determinants and Consequences of Population Trends: A Summary of Findings of Studies on the Relationships between Population Changes and Economic and Social Conditions*. 53.XIII.2. New York: United Nations.

——— (1974). *Determinants and Consequences of Population Trends*. 1, E.71.XII.5. New York: United Nations.

——— (1987). *World Population Trends and Policies: 1987 Monitoring Report*. ESA/P/WP.97 New York: United Nations, pp. 534–36.

United Nations Food and Agriculture Organization (1982). *Potential Population Supporting Capacities of Lands in the Developing World*. FPA-INT–513. Rome: Food and Agriculture Organization.

——— (1985). *The State of Food and Agriculture, 1984*. Rome: Food and Agriculture Organization.

United Nations Food and Agriculture Organization and U.N.E.P. (1981). *Tropical Forest Resources Assessment Project: Tropical Africa, Tropical Asia, and Latin America*. 3 vols. Rome: Food and Agriculture Organization.

United States Department of State and Council on Environmental Quality (1980). *The Global 2000 Report to the President*. Washington, D.C.: Government Printing Office.

United States National Academy of Sciences (1986). *Population Growth and Economic Development: Policy Options*. Washington, D.C.: National Academy Press.

World Bank (1984). *World Development Report*. Washington, D.C.: World Bank.

4

Population Growth, Aggregate Saving, and Economic Development

ANDREW MASON

The dependence of economic development on population growth has been examined from a variety of angles over the years.* This chapter focuses on a key aspect: the impact of declining population growth or declining fertility, to be more specific, on aggregate saving. The notion that a decline in childbearing will lead to increased saving has considerable intuitive appeal. The average household in a low fertility population must support fewer children and, hence, fewer members who consume yet fail to contribute to household income. It only stands to reason that such households are in a better position to save. The view is frequently restated at the macro level, as well. Countries with low population growth rates can achieve higher saving ratios because they have a low dependency ratio (the ratio of members of nonworking age to members of working age).

Attention to the so-called dependency effect underlies most studies of population growth and saving, and this study is no exception. But the model developed here goes further than other efforts in two important respects. First, more attention is devoted to a critical issue: the link between the number of children and expenditure on childrearing. In many circumstances, a decline in the number of children being reared results in reduced expenditure on children and, given the level of expenditures on adults, increased saving. But other plausible circumstances may lead to an increase in expenditure on childrearing with declining fertility. Indeed, the very desire to spend more per child may underlie the desire to bear fewer children. Thus, it is possible for reduced fertility to be accompanied by higher expenditure on childrearing and, given expenditures on adults, decreased saving by childrearing households.

The second distinctive feature of the model described here is its attention to showing the relationship between aggregate saving and expenditures on childrearing at the household level. Using a variant of the life-cycle model, the impact

*I would like to acknowledge the help of Norma Uejo in preparing this chapter.

of changes in saving at the household level are shown to depend on the rate of economic growth.

The distinctive aspects of the model proposed here are important for two reasons. First, the model explains why empirical evidence about the importance of the dependency effect varies so much, depending on the characteristics of the sample. The dependency effect will have its greatest impact in robust economies, such as those of several East and Southeast Asian countries. But in countries with stagnant or slowly growing economies, a decline in fertility may have a negligible effect on aggregate saving. Second, the model implies that the impact on saving of declining fertility depends upon the factors accounting for fertility decline. Thus, some antinatalist policies will encourage saving, but some antinatalist policies may even discourage saving and capital accumulation.

THE LINK BETWEEN CHILDREARING AND CONSUMPTION

The central idea behind economic models of fertility is that parents face a fundamental decision about resource allocation between themselves (or perhaps other adults, including their parents) and their children, if any. Bearing an additional child of given quality or raising higher "quality" children entails devoting more resources to childrearing and less to other purposes. Over the development process, a variety of forces affects the number of children that parents choose to bear, the resources devoted to each child, and, in combination, the share of household resources devoted to childrearing. Thus, decisions about childrearing and about consumption are inextricably linked.

Outside the determinants-of-fertility literature, the simplest and most widely used approach to modeling the link between childrearing and expenditures employs the equivalent adult consumer unit, which assumes that the price of providing for a child relative to the price of providing for an adult is constant. Using this approach, the share of the household's resources devoted to childrearing declines in an easily defined way with the number of children parents choose to rear. Despite its simplicity, the approach is not altogether without appeal. In very poor societies, if consumption is dominated by physiological need, then expenditures on members may be tied to caloric requirements or other similiar measures that have been used frequently to estimate the equivalent adult consumer unit. And even in rich societies, the notion that the claim of children on household resources increases in step with the claims of adult members has a certain attractive appeal.

On the other hand, the equivalent adult model is clearly at odds with some of the most important explanations of why childbearing declines as societies develop. Suppose parents opt for higher "quality" children spending more, for example, on their education. Because the price of children is thereby higher, parents choose to have fewer children. But the change in household resources devoted to childrearing depends on the sensitivity of fertility to the increase in price. If the demand for children is elastic, the share of resources devoted to childrearing declines in similar fashion to the equivalent adult consumer unit model. But if the demand for children is inelastic, the share of resources devoted to childrearing actually increases as fertility declines.

Thus, the relationship between resources devoted to childrearing and the level of childbearing should vary depending on what factors are responsible for declines in fertility and on empirical characteristics of the fertility function, such as the elasticity of demand.

The use to which a household puts its resources, that is, its decision about the allocation between childrearing and other activities, need not affect total expenditures at all. If the household is spending a fixed amount of resources in any period and only the choice about to whom the resources are devoted is at issue, then neither total consumption nor saving are influenced by household composition.

This is a plausible point of view if households engage in no life-cycle planning. But because childrearing is concentrated at a particular point in the household's life cycle, changes in the share of resources devoted to childrearing have clear implications for the life-cycle profile of consumption and saving. To be specific, a decline in resources devoted to childrearing implies a decline in consumption and a corresponding increase in saving during early stages of the household life cycle. With given lifetime household resources, lower consumption during childrearing years is balanced by higher consumption (and lower saving) during post-childrearing years.

As in any life-cycle saving model, the impact of changes in the life-cycle profile on national saving depends on the number and economic resources of households at each stage of the life cycle. In a growing economy, where young, childrearing households are relatively numerous and have relatively high lifetime resources, decisions to delay consumption generate reduced aggregate consumption and higher aggregate saving. And the greater the growth of the economy, the greater the impact of any given change in the life-cycle profile of consumption (Modigliani and Brumberg, 1954; Modigliani, 1986; Mason, 1987).

THE MODEL

Resources Devoted to Childrearing

The household engages in two utility yielding activities, childrearing (Q_1) and supporting adults (Q_2), and chooses activity levels so as to maximize its utility function:

$$U = U(Q_1, Q_2) \tag{1}$$

subject to:

$$V \geq P_1 Q_1 + P_2 Q_2 \tag{2}$$

where V is the household's lifetime resources. Given a well-behaved utility function, the demand for each activity is given by:

$$Q_i = F_i(P_1, P_2, V) \tag{3}$$

The share of total lifetime resources devoted to childrearing or supporting adults, represented by s_i, is equal to:

$$s_i = P_i Q_i/V = P_i F_i(P_1, P_2, V)/V \tag{4}$$

If the utility function is homothetic, as assumed below, s_i is independent of lifetime resources and is uniquely determined by either the price of childrearing relative to supporting adults or by the quantity of childrearing relative to the quantity of adult support, that is,

$$s_i = f(p) = g(q) \tag{5}$$

where $p = P_1/P_2$ and $q = Q_1/Q_2$.

The equivalent adult consumer unit model is, in a sense, a special case of the homothetic utility function where prices are held constant and exogenous factors account for fertility change. Measuring the quantity of childrearing and adult support in person-years, resource shares vary with the number of children relative to the number of adults, depending on the fixed equivalent adult consumer unit. Childrearing's share of lifetime resources is:

$$s_1 = p'q/(1+p'q) \tag{6}$$

and the adults' share is:

$$s_2 = 1/(1+p'q) \tag{7}$$

where p', the equivalent adult consumer unit, is given.

A somewhat more flexible but quite tractable approach allows for variation in price and response in the demand for children using the direct homogeneous translog utility function (Christensen, Jorgenson, and Lau, 1975). The budget shares are given by:

$$s_1 = a_1 + b_1 \ln q \quad \text{and} \quad s_2 = (1-a_1) - b_1 \ln q \tag{8}$$

Of course, other specifications of the share devoted to childrearing are available depending upon one's assumption about the form of the household's utility function. In addition, the impact of exogenous factors that lead to shifts in the demand for children can be incorporated easily into the share equations.

Life-Cycle Consumption Pattern

The life-cycle consumption pattern depends on the share of resources devoted to each activity because the intensity with which activities are pursued varies over the household's life cycle. The household is assumed to have a known lifetime, commencing at age 0 and ending at age L. Households engage in activities at one or more ages, and the proportion of Q_i "consumed" at each age is determined by the density function $d_i(a)$, where $d_i(a) \geq 0$ and $\int d_i(a)da = 1$. The proportion is assumed to be independent of prices, income, and the total level of each activity. The amount "consumed" at age a is equal to $d_i(a)Q_i$, and the value of expenditures on activity i at age a is given by:

$$C_i(a) = P_i Q_i d_i(a) \tag{9}$$

Total expenditure, in the two activity case, by households aged a is equal to:

$$C(a) = P_1 Q_1 d_1(a) + P_2 Q_2 d_2(a) \tag{10}$$

and the fraction of lifetime resources expended at age a, $c(a)$, is equal to:

$$c(a) = C(a)/V = s_1 d_1(a) + s_2 d_2(a) \tag{11}$$

Thus, the life-cycle profile of consumption is determined by the share of lifetime resources devoted to each activity and the life-cycle density function for each activity.

As discussed in more detail below, the aggregate saving function can be approximated as a function of the life-cycle pattern of consumption using the average age of consumption. The average age of consumption, A_c, is defined by:

$$A_c = \int a\, c(a)\, da \tag{12}$$

The average age of consumption is a weighted average of the average age of each activity, where the weights are the share of lifetime resources devoted to each activity.

$$A_c = s_1 A_1 + s_2 A_2 \tag{13}$$

where the average age of each activity is calculated by:

$$A_i = \int a d_i(a)\, da \tag{14}$$

Equation 13 formalizes the observation made in the introduction to this section that a shift in resources away from childrearing delays consumption (raises the average age of consumption) to the extent childrearing activities are localized at early stages of the life cycle ($A_1 < A_2$).

Characterization of the household's life cycle is completed by describing the age earning profile. The fraction of lifetime earnings accruing at age a is given by:

$$y(a) = Y(a)/V \qquad (15)$$

where $Y(a)$ is the age a earnings by the household. The average age of earning is given by:

$$A_y = \int ay(a)\, da \qquad (16)$$

Aggregate Consumption

Aggregate consumption depends on the relative importance of households that are at different stages of the life cycle, where relative importance is determined by two factors: the number of households and the average lifetime resources of households. In countries experiencing rapid population growth, "young" households are relatively numerous, and their lifecycle behavior plays a dominant role. In countries experiencing rapid economic growth, "young" households have relatively high lifetime resources, and, again, their life-cycle behavior plays a dominant role.

The age distribution of household resources is easily characterized for steady-state economies where per capita income and population growth are both constant. Lifetime resources of all households of the cohort currently aged a is given by:

$$H(a)V(a) = e^{-ga}H(0)V(0) \qquad (17)$$

where $H(a)$ is the number of households aged a, $V(a)$ is the lifetime resources per age a household, g is the rate of growth of GNP, and $H(0)V(0)$ is the lifetime resources of all newly formed households combined.

Current consumption by the age a cohort is equal to the average consumption rate, $c(a)$, times the total lifetime resources of the cohort, $H(a)V(a)$. Aggregate consumption, C, is found by "summing" across all cohorts, that is:

$$C = \int c(a)H(a)V(a)\, da = H(0)V(0) \int e^{-ga}c(a)\, da \qquad (18)$$

Likewise, current income of the age a cohort is equal to the earning rate, $y(a)$, times the lifetime resources of the cohort. Total national income, Y, is found by integrating across all household ages:

$$Y = \int y(a)H(a)V(a)\, da = H(0)V(0) \int e^{-ga}y(a)\, da \qquad (19)$$

The aggregate consumption ratio is simply total consumption divided by total national income. Dividing equation 18 by equation 19 yields the consumption ratio, c:

$$c = \int e^{-ga}c(a)\, da \Big/ \int e^{-gu}y(a)\, da \qquad (20)$$

Finally, taking the logarithm of both sides and approximating the integral terms using a Taylor series expansion:

$$\ln c - u_0 + (A_y - A_c)g \qquad (21)$$

This representation of the aggregate consumption function captures the observation in the introduction and a central feature of the life-cycle saving model that delayed consumption at the household level translates into lower consumption and higher saving at the national level to the extent that younger household cohorts have relatively high lifetime resources. In terms of equation 21, a delay in consumption is captured via an increase in the average age of consumption, A_c. The magnitude of the decline in consumption and the increase in saving depends on the rate of growth of aggregate income, which captures the relative wealth of young cohorts.

The model of life-cycle saving, as employed here, is essentially complete, consisting of the aggregate consumption function, equation 21; the timing of consumption function, equation 12; and the demand-for-children equation and its corresponding expenditure share, equation 5. Because one of the expenditure share equations is redundant, the timing of consumption function can be modified to depend only on the share devoted to childrearing:

$$A_c = A_2 + s_1(A_1 - A_2) \qquad (22)$$

and the model is then completed by the demand-for-children equation and its corresponding childrearing share equation:

$$q = q(p,x) \qquad (23)$$

$$s_1 = f(p,x) = g(q,x) \qquad (24)$$

where x has been included to represent exogenous variables that influence childbearing.

Figure 4.1
Impact of Change in Price of Children

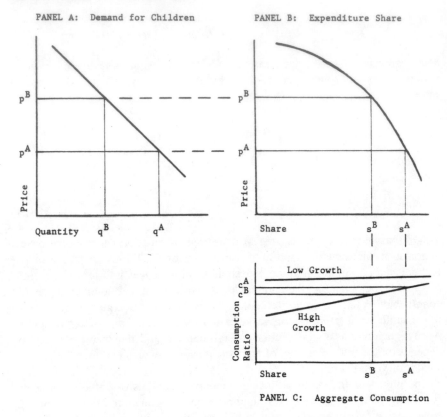

PANEL A: Demand for Children

PANEL B: Expenditure Share

PANEL C: Aggregate Consumption

A Graphical Presentation

A simple graphical presentation of the model is provided in Figures 4.1 and 4.2, which illustrate the impact of price changes and shifts in the demand for children. In Figure 4.1, panel A shows the decline in the number of children corresponding to a increase in relative price from P^A to P^B. Panel B shows the share function which corresponds with the demand function in Panel A. The share function is downward sloping because the demand function is inelastic. Thus, the price increase induces a decline in the share of resources devoted to childrearing. The impact on aggregate consumption and saving is shown in Panel C, which includes a family of aggregate consumption curves corresponding to alternative rates of economic growth. For the high growth of income case, the decline in childrearing expenditure leads to substantially lower consumption, a shift from C^A to C^B and correspondingly higher saving. The magnitude of the effect would be reduced were the rate of growth of income lower.

Figure 4.2
Impact of Shift in Demand for Children

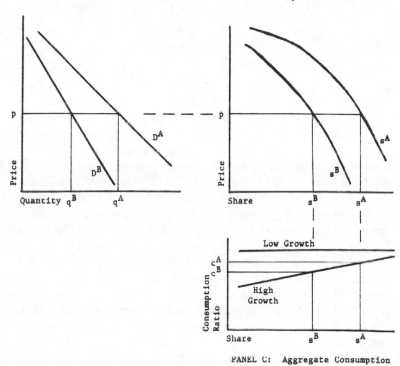

PANEL A: Demand for Children   PANEL B: Expenditure Share

PANEL C: Aggregate Consumption

The demand curve in Figure 4.1 is drawn to yield the traditional result, that is, a rise in saving with reduced fertility. There is no a priori reason, however, why price increases cannot yield the opposite finding. If the demand curve is inelastic, the share curve will be upward sloping and price increases will result in fewer children, but more expenditure on childrearing and lower aggregate saving.

No such ambiguity attaches to shifts in the demand function. Figure 4.2 shows a decline in fertility resulting from a leftward shift in the demand function from D^A to D^B. A leftward shift in the share function accompanies the shift in demand because, at a given price, reduced childrearing unambiguously reduces childrearing expenditure. As shown in Panel C, aggregate consumption is thereby reduced and aggregate saving increased.

To summarize the implications of this model of fertility and saving:

1. Reductions in childrearing, given relative price, unambiguously increase aggregate saving (in growing economies).

2. Reductions in childbearing due to increased price have an impact on aggregate saving that depends on the elasticity of demand for children.

3. The magnitude of the impact of any reduction in childrearing, irrespective of its source, varies in direct proportion with the rate of growth of aggregate income.

Evidence

Empirical research on the link between fertility decline and saving has come to decidedly mixed conclusions depending on the level of analysis (aggregate data versus household level data) and the country or group of countries examined. A more extensive review of this literature is reported in Mason (1987). An overview is provided here that emphasizes the relationship of empirical evidence to the theoretical model presented in the preceding sections.

Studies of household data from industrialized countries (Eizenga, 1961; Sommermeyer and Bannink, 1973; Espenshade, 1975; Mason, 1975; and David and Menchik, 1985) generally support the view that the current consumption ratio is directly related to current family size or the current number of children. For developing countries, on the other hand, there is very little reliable evidence that the number of children affects household consumption. It is impossible to say whether the absence of evidence should be attributed to the great difficulty of collecting survey data on consumption and earning particularly in countries with only partly monetized economies; the small sample sizes of surveys that have been made available to researchers; or, the absence, in fact, of any underlying relationship between consumption and household membership in developing countries.

A clearer picture of the relationship between household consumption and demographic characteristics of the household in developing countries may emerge as the quality and availability of survey data improves. Many developing countries now conduct extensive surveys on consumer expenditure and, in a few instances, these data are being made available to researchers. Deaton and Muellbauer (1986), for example, analyze data from Indonesia and Sri Lanka to estimate a relative price of children of 0.3 to 0.4 of adult consumption.

The only direct analysis of the model described above is a study of international cross-section data based on aggregate saving in sixty-nine countries during the 1960s and 1970s (Mason, 1987). These results are discussed in somewhat more detail later, but, in general, support the view that expenditure by households in low-fertility industrialized countries is delayed in comparison to households in high-fertility developing countries. And that as a result, aggregate saving is higher in low-fertility than in high-fertility countries. Furthermore, the impact of fertility varies directly with the rate of growth of national income.

But results from other analyses of national income account data reach varying conclusions. Leff's studies of national saving rates (1969, 1980) have concluded that a reduction in the youth dependency ratio leads to a higher saving ratio. And analyses of international cross-section data by Mason (1981) and time series data by Fry and Mason (1982) and Fry (1984) yield similiar results, while confirming that the impact of the dependency ratio depends on the rate of growth income.

However, aggregate results are not robust with respect to sample composition and specification. Ram (1982, 1984), in particular, has shown that empirical results differ depending on which countries are analyzed, which period considered, and which control variables introduced. And recent analysis by Kelley (1986) shows that the saving-fertility relationship varies depending upon the continent of the country analyzed. These analyses suggest that:

1. Differences between the developing and industrialized countries are generally supportive of the view that high fertility depresses saving;

2. Variation in saving among industrialized countries may support a modest inverse relationship, whereas variation in saving among developing countries does not;

3. Variation in national saving rates in the 1970s is less consistent with the fertility-saving link than variation during the 1960s.

The sensitivity of results to sample selection is not very surprising, given the complexity of the saving-fertility relationship. A significant inverse relationship should not be discernible in countries with stagnant or slowly growing economies. Thus, A. Kelley's (1986) finding of a negative population effect in South America and no effect in Africa is entirely consistent with the relative strengths of their economies. At the same time, a very strong inverse relationship should be apparent among the robust economies of East and Southeast Asia, an observation confirmed by Fry and Mason (1982) and Fry (1984).

The sensitivity of empirical results to the level of development of the countries included in the sample is also consistent with the model described above. Recent results from Mason (1987) are characterized by Figure 4.3. Roughly speaking, the analysis shows that the industrialized and the developing countries can be characterized by two distinct demand curves. The relative price of children is not all that different between the two groups and, surprisingly close to the Deaton and Muellbauer estimates mentioned above, is estimated to be about one third. Thus, the high fertility of developing countries apparently depresses saving as compared with the lower fertility of industrialized countries. But to the extent that there is variation in fertility within the two groups, price variation is an important determinant. Furthermore, evidence suggests an elasticity of demand near unity so that variation in childbearing is not accompanied by variation in expenditures on childrearing. Under these circumstances, aggregate saving should not be systematically related to variation in fertility.

To the extent that achieving a higher rate of saving is a legitimate policy objective, the policy implications of this characterization of the fertility-saving link are quite interesting. This research suggests that one vehicle for achieving higher saving is to implement policies that, directly or indirectly, discourage expenditure on childrearing. Policies that shift the demand for children downward

Figure 4.3
Demand for Children in Industrialized versus Developing Countries

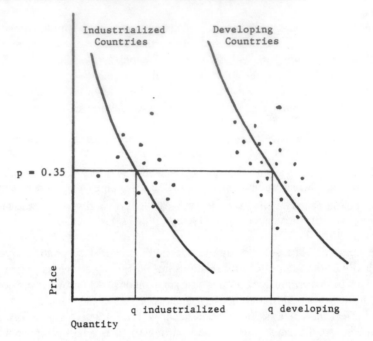

accomplish this without adversely affecting expenditures per child (as contrasted with the claims of all of the children combined) relative to those per adult because the relative price of children is unaffected.

A family planning communication program that encourages small family norms seems like a plausible example of a policy that primarily shifts the demand for children, but this would clearly depend upon the nature of the family planning message. If the possibility of devoting more resources to fewer children is stressed as an advantage of smaller family size, the impact on saving might be negligible or even perverse. But, at the same time, programs that discourage expenditure per child may encourage saving and greater accumulation of physical capital by sacrificing the accumulation of human capital.

Many incentive and disincentive programs are essentially pricing policies that seek to raise the relative price of childrearing. But the impact on aggregate consumption is not easily discerned. If the relative price is increased and demand is inelastic, expenditure on childrearing (including the tax) and current household expenditure (including the tax) will rise. But because the demand for children is downward sloping, consumption—expenditure less taxes paid—will decline. But disposable income will decline, as well. The impact on the household con-sumption ratio (consumption divided by disposable income) is ambiguous and the impact on the national consumption ratio will depend on the use to which additional tax revenues are put.

REFERENCES

Christensen, L. R., D. W. Jorgenson, and L. J. Lau (1975). "Transcendental Logarithmic Utility Functions." *American Economic Review* (March): 367–83.

David, Martin, and Paul L. Menchik (1985). "The Effect of Social Security on Lifetime Wealth Accumulation and Bequests." *Econometrica* 52 (November): 421–34.

Deaton, Angus S., and John Muellbauer (1986). "On Measuring Child Costs: With Applications to Poor Countries." *Journal of Political Economy* 94 (August): 722–44.

Eizenga, W. (1961). *Demographic Factors and Savings*. Amsterdam: North-Holland.

Espenshade, Thomas J. (1975). "The Impact of Children on Household Saving: Age Effects Versus Family Size." *Population Studies* 29 (January): 123–25.

Fry, Maxwell J. (1984). "Terms of Trade and National Saving Rates in Asia." *Journal of Development Economics* (September 1).

Fry, Maxwell, and Andrew Mason (1982). "The Variable Rate of Growth Effect in the Life-Cycle Saving Model." *Economic Inquiry* 20 (July): 426–42.

Gupta, Kanhaya L. (1975). "Foreign Capital Inflows, Dependency Burden, and Saving Rates in Developing Countries: A Simultaneous Equation Model." *KYKLOS* 28: 358–74.

Kelley, Allen C. (1986). "Review Symposium." *Population and Development Review* 12: 563.

Leff, Nathaniel H. (1969). "Dependency Rates and Savings Rates." *American Economic Review* 59 (December): 886–95.

———— (1980). "Dependency Rates and Savings Rates: A New Look." In *Population Economics*, Julian Simon, ed., vol. 2. Greenwich, Conn.: JAI Press, pp. 205–14.

Mason, Andrew (1975). "An Empirical Analysis of Life Cycle Saving, Income and Household Size." PhD. diss., University of Michigan.

———— (1981). "An Extension of the Life-Cycle Model and Its Application to Population Growth and Aggregate Saving." *East-West Population Institute Working Papers* 4 (January).

———— (1987). "National Saving Rates and Population: A New Model and New Evidence." In *Population Growth and Economy Development: Issues and Evidence*, D. Gale Johnson and Ronald D. Lee, eds. Madison, Wisc.: University of Wisconsin Press and The National Academy of Sciences.

Modigliani, Franco (1986). "Life Cycle, Individual Thrift, and the Wealth of Nations." *American Economic Review* 76 (June): 297–313.

Modigliani, Franco and Richard Brumberg (1954). "Utility Analysis and the Consumption Function: An Interpretation of Cross-Section Data." In *Post-Keynesian Economics*, K. Kurihara, ed. Princeton, N.J.: Princeton University Press.

Ram, Rati (1982). "Dependency Rates and Aggregate Savings: A New International Cross-Section Study." *American Economic Review* 72 (June): 537–44.

———— (1984). "Dependency Rates and Savings: Reply." *American Economic Review* 74 (March): 234–37.

Sommermeyer, W. H. and R. Bannink (1973). *Consumption-Savings Model and Its Applications*. Amsterdam: North Holland Publishing Co.

5

Population Growth and Human Carrying Capacity in Sub-Saharan Africa

DENNIS J. MAHAR

Concern about the earth's ability to support growing populations on a sustainable basis has been widely expressed at least since the publication of Thomas Malthus' *Essay on Population* in 1798.* Dire Malthusian predictions still appear from time to time in books with provocative titles like *The Limits to Growth* and *The Population Bomb,* but there is a growing consensus that the global resource base is sufficient to support much larger populations than the 5 billion people who exist today (see, e.g., National Research Council, 1986; IBRD, 1986b). Bernard Gilland, for example, has estimated that even at a relatively high average daily per capita allowance of 9,000 calories of "plant energy" (including plants consumed indirectly through meat consumption), the earth has the capacity to support about 7.5 billion people (Gilland, 1983). By applying Gilland's parameters regarding average crop yields and land area appropriate for food production to a more modest daily energy allowance of 6,000 calories per capita—about the present world average—one arrives at a sustainable maximum world population of some 11.4 billion. This latter number is higher than what is currently projected to be the world stationary population.

The rosy picture of the future painted above and in such publications as Julian Simon's *The Ultimate Resource* (1981), although reassuring, must provide precious little comfort to the estimated 730 million persons in the developing countries who do not consume enough calories each day to lead an active working life (IBRD, 1986b). Although it may seem so at first glance, there is no inconsistency between the apparent abundance of food in the world and the widespread incidence of malnutrition. A recent World Bank study has concluded that a lack of purchasing power on the part of individuals, rather than an insufficient food supply, is the root cause of chronic malnutrition (IBRD, 1986b). There are

*The author wishes to thank Neeta Sirur for her assistance with the preparation of this chapter. The views expressed are solely the author's and do not necessarily represent those of the World Bank.

countries, however, that are so poor that even if the total food supply (local production plus imports) were to be distributed evenly, per capita caloric requirements would still not be met. Such countries would include Burkina Faso, Ethiopia, Mali, Nepal, Tanzania, and Uganda.

The continued existence of extreme poverty on a national scale, coupled with rapid population growth, suggests that the Malthusian predictions may still be valid in some parts of the world. It is the purpose of this chapter to investigate this hypothesis in greater detail, with special emphasis on the situation in Sub-Saharan Africa. In doing so, the concept of "carrying capacity" will be discussed and its operational usefulness assessed through several case studies.

THE CONCEPT OF CARRYING CAPACITY

"Carrying capacity" is a concept commonly used by biologists and wildlife managers to refer to the maximum number of animals that can be sustained indefinitely in a specified ecosystem. In this traditional sense the concept is rather straightforward: the sustainability of a given animal population is dependent on the availability of food; if this animal population for some reason exceeds food availability, the excess population dies off from starvation; this process continues until an equilibrium between the animal population and its food supply is once again reached. With some modifications, this basic definition of carrying capacity has in recent years been increasingly applied to human populations by development economists, planners, and others.

Though many variations of the human carrying capacity concept have been put forward, the working definition adopted for purposes of this discussion is taken from W. Allan's early work on Zambia (then Northern Rhodesia): "the maximum number of persons that can be supported in perpetuity on an area, with a given technology and consumptive habits, without causing environmental degradation" (Fearnside, 1986: 73). As implied in this definition, the role of technology is critical. Indeed, it is mainly this remarkable ability of humans to radically alter our natural environment that separates us from other members of the animal kingdom.

It is clear that changes in technology can have major effects on an ecosystem's capacity to support human life. Improvements in technology—agricultural or otherwise—can immensely increase the productivity of the natural resource base and thus expand the carrying capacity of a given geographical area. In fact, advances in agricultural technology have in many parts of the world largely invalidated Malthus' prediction that population growth would inevitably outpace food production and thus lead to generalized misery. Over the past thirty years, for example, world food production per capita has increased by some 10 percent. The developing countries, taken as a whole, have experienced a similar growth in per capita food production, albeit with considerable regional variations in evidence (U.S. Dept. of Agriculture, 1986).

Though technology plays a key role, there are limits to the extent to which it can increase a region's carrying capacity. As Kirchner et al. (1985: 48–49) point out, all technological advances eventually run into the law of diminishing returns. They cite the case of fertilizers, which at high levels of application can actually lead to nutrient "poisoning" and declines in crop yields. These authors also point out that technology can neither increase the total supply of resources ultimately available nor increase the Earth's natural waste elimination capacity. There are, moreover, numerous examples in which the application of inappropriate technology has resulted in a reduction of a region's carrying capacity. In the Brazilian Amazon, for example, a combination of widespread cultivation of annual crops, extensive cattle ranching, and predatory timbering practices has greatly reduced the productivity—perhaps permanently—of large areas of tropical rain forest (Fearnside, 1986). A similar phenomenon can be observed in Africa, where inappropriate plowing techniques and deforestation are causing widespread soil erosion (Harrison, 1987).

Another complicating factor in seeking to apply the concept of carrying capacity to human populations is interregional trade. Today, except for those of a few primitive societies, all economies are linked by exchange relationships to a greater or lesser extent. Through trade, societies are frequently able to overcome limitations imposed by their particular resource endowments by exchanging locally abundant resources (including human skills) for locally scarce resources. In this manner, densely populated city-states like Singapore and Hong Kong can expand their local carrying capacities and maintain relatively high standards of living by trading manufactured goods, financial services, and so forth for food items and other necessities. For many poor, food-deficit countries, however, the size of the surplus of nonfood resources—minerals, timber, manufactures and so forth—is insufficient to finance the purchase of necessary foodstuffs from abroad. In such cases, the country must somehow secure international resource transfers—for example, foreign exchange grants or loans, direct food aid—or face a rising incidence of malnutrition.

As stated in the working definition of human carrying capacity presented previously, the concept assumes not only a given level of technology but also a given level of consumption. Thus, a final complication associated with practical applications of the carrying capacity concept stems from the vast differences of opinion as to what constitutes a minimum acceptable level of consumption. As has been shown by the experiences of prisoners of war, concentration camp internees, and victims of natural calamities, human beings can survive for extended periods of time on very little. However, such conditions could hardly be referred to as an acceptable standard of living. At the other extreme, in the United States, the poverty threshold is calculated by multiplying the cost of a minimum nutritious diet by three, under the assumption that poor Americans spend on the average about one-third of their incomes on food. By this measure, in 1984, any American with an income of less than $5,278 ($10,609 for a family of four) was considered to be in absolute poverty. Such an income would no doubt be considered a king's ransom by a vast majority of the citizens of the low-income developing countries where 1984 GNP per capita averaged a scant $260 (IBRD 1986c: World Development Indicators, Table 1).

In order to avoid problems emanating from cultural and societal differences in what are to be considered "normal" consumptive habits, most calculations of human carrying capacity are based exclusively on some notion of an adequate food intake. The most common of these yardsticks is the Food and Agriculture Organization/World Health Organization (FAO/WHO) daily calorie requirement per capita, which refers to the minimum energy intake necessary to sustain a person at adequate levels of activity and health. For a "moderately active" adult man with a 65 kilogram body weight, for example, the standard is estimated to be 3,000 calories (FAO, 1974). Although one may argue that a reasonable level of personal consumption must go beyond minimum caloric requirements to include some allowance for other "basic needs" such as clean water, decent shelter, health and education services, the FAO/WHO standard (or its monetary equivalent) would seem to be a reasonable surrogate for the absolute poverty threshold in developing countries.

POPULATION AND AGRICULTURAL DEVELOPMENT

Various studies show that complex interactive relationships exist between demographic factors and agricultural development. In a recent survey article, R. E. Bilsborrow (1987) points out that population pressures in rural areas can result in purely demographic responses (changes in nuptiality and declines in marital fertility), purely economic responses (including changes in farming intensity and technology), or a combination of the two (exemplified by various types of migration). He further argues that the probability of any given response occurring depends on a number of factors intrinsic to a locality, including the availability of untapped, potentially cultivable land, the availability of non-farm employment opportunities, the prevailing institutional structure, and so forth. While recognizing the complexity of the subject and the important role of demographic responses to population pressures on the natural resource base, the present discussion is focused on the economic responses and, in particular, on the relationship between population growth and changes in farming systems and technology. The latter issue is of prime importance to the carrying capacity debate, since if population growth can, by itself, ensure technological change, then there is much less risk that carrying capacities can be exceeded.

Perhaps the most prominent school of thought regarding the economic responses to population growth in rural areas—most commonly associated with the work of Ester Boserup—holds that increasing population pressures tend to induce farmers to adopt more intensive farming methods in order to maintain their average crop yields and standards of living. This process is often described in terms of stages in the evolution of farming systems, relating each of these stages to prevailing population densities (Boserup, 1981). At very low average densities, the prevailing farming system tends to be forest-fallow, a type of shifting cultivation. Under this system, an area of forest is cleared, cultivated for one or two years, and then left to rest for twenty to twenty-five years. Over time, as population pressures mount, fallow periods continue to decline, and bush savannah and, eventually, grasses invade the previously forested area. The latter usually occurs when population densities reach the range of sixteen to sixty-four persons per square kilometer (Pingali and Binswanger, 1983: 2a). Further increases in population densities eliminate fallows altogether, causing a transition to annual cultivation and multicropping, the most intensive forms of cultivation.

In the absence of technological change, the movement from lower to higher intensity farming systems is normally associated with greater agricultural employment. H. Ruthenberg has shown that—holding technology constant—the movement of cultivating rice under forest-fallow to cultivating it under annual cropping results in an increase in labor input per hectare from 770 hours in Liberia to 3,300 hours in Cameroon (Pingali, Bigot and Binswanger, 1987: 29). This additional demand for labor rises from both the number of field operations and the intensity with which these operations are performed. Under forest- and bush-fallow systems, for example, land is generally cleared by fire, a method that requires relatively little labor. The fire also restores fertility to the soil and reduces weed growth, thus further reducing labor requirements between planting and harvesting for weeding and manuring. Annual and multicropping systems, in contrast, call for much larger labor inputs in order to maintain soil fertility, eliminate weeds and protect plants.

The increases in the use of labor observed during the agricultural transition can lead to higher crop yields. One regression analysis, based on data for fifty-three locations in Africa, Asia, and Latin America, found that yields per hectare increased by 4.4 percent for each 10 percent increase in farming intensity (Pingali and Binswanger, 1983: 10). Rising crop yields, however, are not guaranteed by agricultural intensification. Under certain agroclimatic conditions, the shorter fallows associated with more intensive farming systems lead to dramatic declines in yields unless chemical inputs are employed. In the humid forest zone of eastern Nigeria, for example, cassava yields fall from over 10 tons per hectare to only 2 tons per hectare if the fallow period is reduced from three to five years to one to four years (FAO, 1986: Annex III, p. 5). Similar results have been observed in Brazil and Indonesia when tropical forests have been converted to farmland or pasture.

In land-abundant countries, farm populations faced with exhausted soils, declining crop yields, and falling living standards have the option to migrate to frontier areas. When this option is not open, the introduction of modern inputs may be the only means of restoring the land's productivity. However, even in more robust environments, where intensification is associated with constant or rising yields, improvements in technology (such as the introduction of animal traction or tractors) will probably be required to prevent declines in labor productivity. The development of policies and programs to promote agricultural modernization is therefore a major challenge to the governments of developing countries.

Historically, technological innovations leading to large gains in labor productivity have been induced when the greater demand for labor associated with the transition to more intensive farming systems could not be met with the available labor supply, that is, the point when labor started to become scarce relative to land and capital. In Great Britain, for example, increases in labor productivity in agriculture began only in the mid-nineteenth century when the rapid absorption of labor into the industrial sector created labor shortages in the rural areas (Birdsall, 1985: 43–44). Similar relative shortages of agricultural labor also stimulated technological change in the rural areas of the United States and Japan during the past century. Government policies that favored the agricultural sector—for example, the development of transport systems and rural extension services—also played a critical role in this transformation. It is argued below that the absence of some of these historically important factors, as well as the existence of certain region-specific factors, help explain the economic stagnation of Sub-Saharan Africa's rural areas.

THE RECENT EVOLUTION OF AFRICAN AGRICULTURE

The performance of Sub-Saharan Africa in food production has been deteriorating over the past two decades. Total food output, which increased by an average rate of 2.5 percent during the 1960s, grew at only 1.7 percent annually between 1970 and 1982.[1] The deceleration in the rate of growth of food production, moreover, was accompanied by an increase in the population growth rate from 2.4 percent per annum in 1960 to 1970, to 2.8 percent per annum in 1970 to 1982, to about 3.1 percent per annum in 1987. As a result, per capita food production in Sub-Saharan Africa as a whole has declined by about 1 percent per year since 1970. During this period, only six Sub-Saharan countries—Chad, Burkina Faso, Niger, Rwanda, Swaziland, and Cote d'Ivoire—have managed to increase food production faster than population growth. As shown in Table 5.1, not one of their ten largest countries, accounting for around 70 percent of the region's population, has succeeded in doing so.

Today, Sub-Saharan Africa finds itself in the unenviable position of having the highest population growth rate and lowest rate of growth of food production of any major region in the developing world. This predicament has clearly frustrated attempts on the part of African governments to achieve self-sufficiency in food production. As of 1976–1980, self-sufficient countries accounted for only 7 percent of the region's population and 9 percent of its food production (Paulino, 1987: 25). The widening gap between local production and consumption has led to massive commercial imports and emergency food aid. This has completely reversed the region's position in world food trade: Sub-Saharan Africa, which as late as 1966–1970 averaged 1.3 million tons of net food exports per year, was a net importer of some 10 million tons by the mid–1980s (Paulino,

Table 5.1
Food Production and Population Growth in the Ten Most Populous Countries of Sub-Saharan Africa, 1970–1982

Region or Country	Average annual percentage change		
	Food Production	Population	Food Production per Capita
Sub-Saharan Africa	1.7	2.8	-0.9
Nigeria	2.5	2.6	-0.2
Ethiopia	1.7	2.0	-0.3
Zaire	1.3	3.0	-1.7
Sudan	2.9	3.2	-0.3
Tanzania	2.1	3.4	-1.3
Kenya	2.0	4.0	-1.9
Uganda	1.7	2.7	-1.0
Mozambique	-1.0	4.3	-5.1
Ghana	-0.2	3.0	-3.1
Cameroon	2.1	3.0	-0.9

Source: IBRD (1984)

1987: 31). Despite these imports, the number of people in Sub-Saharan Africa with energy-deficient diets totalled an estimated 150 million in 1980, up by 30 percent over the 1970 level (IBRD, 1986b: 18).

The summary statistics presented in Table 5.1 clearly suggest that population growth has not yet led to a generalized intensification of agriculture. Indeed, among food crops, expansion of the harvested area has accounted for about two-thirds of the recent growth in cereals output, and for all of the growth in noncereals output. World Bank data show that yields per hectare of such staples of the Sub-Saharan diet as millet and maize actually fell in the decade between 1969 and 1979, while yields of rice, sorghum, and roots and tubers remained about the same (Meerman and Cochrane, 1982). The lack of progress in agriculture is also indicated by FAO calculations which show that average labor productivity in the staple foods sector declined at a rate of 0.7 percent annually during the 1970s (FAO, 1986: Annex V, p. 13).

The stagnation of Sub-Saharan Africa's agricultural sector over the past two decades is largely attributable to a lack of technological change. The use of modern inputs is minimal, even by developing country standards. Fertilizer consumption, for example, averages only 6 kilograms per hectare; a third of the countries use 1 kilogram or less per hectare. In India and Brazil, by comparison, consumption averages 26 kilograms per hectare and 59 kilograms per hectare, respectively. Mechanization of agriculture is also in its very early stages. Presently, there is, on average, less than one tractor for each 1,000 hectares of cropland; this is about half the level of tractor use in India. Finally, the development of irrigation, which has been instrumental in the growth of agricultural production in Asia, has been extremely limited. Only about 1 percent of the cropland is now under irrigation, versus 22 percent in India and 28 percent in Indonesia (Paulino, 1987: 36).

The reasons for the slow pace of change in Sub-Saharan agriculture are varied. Some are intrinsic to the region's natural environment and demography, while others are related to poor macroeconomic and sectoral policies. In the first category, one would include the widespread incidence of trypanosomiasis, which not only prevents the use of animal traction in many areas, but also reduces the supply of manure for agricultural use. An additional environmental factor is the generally flat topography (outside of East Africa), which, combined with a relative scarcity of dependable water resources, greatly limits opportunities for irrigation. In addition, the low average population densities over most of Sub-Saharan Africa remove a major incentive for intensification of agriculture. In the second category, government policies in developing countries often have an urban bias. Typically, overvalued exchange rates and price controls, intended to keep down the cost of living in the cities, reduce the incentives for farmers to produce and modernize. The same urban-based mentality is also frequently manifested in large public investments in showcase industrial projects and new government facilities, while urgent needs in such areas as rural transport, research and extension, storage, and marketing go unmet.

Even though average population densities in much of the region still have not reached levels where intensification is inevitable, it should not be concluded that population growth and rising densities will eventually solve the problem of rural stagnation. On the contrary, as Paul Harrison has pointed out: "If we wait for this process to take its course, a great deal of Africa's land will have been damaged irreparably, and holdings will be so small that they will still afford no more than a subsistence" (Harrison, 1987: 78–79). As will be discussed in the following section, severe environmental damage and falling incomes are already in evidence in many parts of Sub-Saharan Africa, partially as a result of population pressures. In order to reduce the further spread of this damage and to raise rural living standards, African governments will have to make a special effort to accelerate the rate of technological change in agriculture. This process will involve improvements in producer incentives, rural infrastructure, and rural services. The provision of family planning can also help by reducing some of the immediate pressures on the land while new technologies are being designed and implemented.[2]

CARRYING CAPACITY IN THE AFRICAN CONTEXT

The combination of rapid population growth and slow technological change suggests that in some parts of Sub-Saharan Africa the land's carrying capacity is currently being reached or even exceeded. The evidence of this is not only the declining per capita production of food and worsening standards of living, but also the extensive environmental degradation observed throughout the region.

It is therefore useful to consider some of the recent attempts to measure carrying capacity in Sub-Saharan Africa.

The "Land Resources for Populations of the Future" Project

The most ambitious attempt ever made to measure carrying capacity was carried out by the Food and Agriculture Organization (FAO) with funding from the United Nations Fund for Population Activities (UNFPA). The scope of this undertaking, known as the "Land Resources for Populations of the Future" (LRPF) Project, included 117 developing countries divided into six regions (Higgins et al., 1982). The methodology employed was extremely complex, but essentially involved combining detailed data on soils, topography, and other physical characteristics of land with data on climate in order to arrive at potential yields for each of the major food crops by geographical area. Separate calculations of yields were made under three different assumptions regarding the level of agricultural technology: low (no fertilizers or chemicals, traditional seeds and farming practices, no conservation measures); intermediate (basic package of fertilizers and chemicals, some improved varieties, some conservation measures, and the most productive crop mix on half the land); high (extensive application of fertilizers and chemicals, improved varieties and conservation measures, and the ideal crop mix on all the land). Human carrying capacity was calculated by converting into calories the potential food production in each region or country and then dividing that figure by the FAO/WHO minimum calorie requirement per capita.

The results of the LRPF Project, published in 1982, confirm the general consensus that there is no problem of food supply at the global level.

As shown in Table 5.2, even under the "low technology" assumption (approximately the level at which most of Africa is today), the earth is capable of producing sufficient food for twice the actual population of the world in 1975, and 1.6 times the expected world population in the year 2000. Under the "intermediate" (the level of farming currently found among small and medium farmers in development areas of Asia) and "high" (roughly corresponding to farm practices in North America) assumptions, it was calculated that the earth could produce enough food to support 4.2 and 9.3 times, respectively, the world population projected for the year 2000.

The finding that there is excess carrying capacity at the global level was also found to be true for Africa taken as a whole. Calculations show that under the "low" assumption, the continent could support 3 times its 1975 population, and 1.6 times its year 2000 population. This does not, however, mean that Sub-Saharan African governments have nothing to be concerned about. The LRPF Project regional carrying capacities were calculated under the assumption of a free movement of food and labor across national borders and an equal distribution of that food among the population. These are clearly heroic assumptions that do

Table 5.2
Potential Population Carrying Capacity Ratios in Developing Regions

Alternative levels of agricultural inputs	Africa[a]	South-west Asia	South America	Central America	South-east Asia	Average
Multiples of 1975 population that could be supported						
Low	3.0	0.8	5.9	1.6	1.1	2.0
Intermediate	11.6	1.3	23.9	4.2	3.0	6.9
High	33.9	2.0	57.2	11.2	5.1	16.6
Multiples of projected year 2000 population that could be supported						
Low	1.6	0.7	3.5	1.4	1.1	1.6
Intermediate	5.8	0.9	13.3	2.6	2.3	4.2
High	16.5	1.2	31.5	6.0	3.3	9.3

a/ Excludes South Africa.
Source: Higgins et al (1982).

not conform to the real situation in Africa today. When one considers the country-level calculations, it is obvious that there is some cause for alarm.

The findings of the LRPF Project clearly indicate a major mismatch in Sub-Saharan Africa between the distribution of good farmland and the distribution of population. LRPF calculations indicate that much of Africa's food-producing potential is concentrated in the humid tropical countries of central Africa: Gabon, for example, would not even at low input levels reach the limits of its carrying capacity until the year 2202 (Ho, 1985: 116). On the other hand, there is a group of fourteen countries, largely located in the Sahel, the highlands of East Africa, and the drier areas of southern Africa, which had by 1982 already surpassed their potential population-supporting capacities. This group of countries, which includes Niger, Kenya, Nigeria, Uganda, Senegal, and Burkina Faso, had a 1985 population of 220 million, or about half of the total in Sub-Saharan Africa. It was projected by the LRPF Project that seven additional countries, including Zimbabwe, Ghana, and Mali, would enter this "critical list" by the year 2000.

Although the LRPF Project may be criticized on methodological grounds—for example, it made no allowance for land devoted to nonfood crops, did not assess countries' foreign exchange-earning potential with which they could import food items, and assumed that the world's tropical rain forests could be fully utilized for food production—it does offer some useful benchmark data and a call to action for the very poor and densely populated countries of the world. It also clearly shows the value of assessing human carrying capacity at the subregional, national, or even local levels. In order to further illustrate the latter point, some case studies of human carrying capacity in Sub-Saharan Africa at the subregional (Sahelian and Sudanian zones), national, and local (Kenya) levels are discussed below.

Case Study I: The Sahelian and Sudanian Zones

A World Bank team led by J. Gorse has recently completed a study of the carrying capacity, under traditional production systems, of the Sahelian and Sudanian Zones (SSZ) of northern Africa (Gorse et al., 1985). Although this subregion comprises all or part of thirteen countries, the study focused on the seven—Burkina Faso, Chad, Gambia, Mali, Mauritania, Niger, and Senegal—that are totally included. Together these countries cover 5.3 million square kilometers, and in 1985 had a combined population of about 36 million. Population is growing at the rapid rate of about 3 percent per annum and is projected to reach 55 million by the end of this century. The climate and physical features of the SSZ make cultivation and animal husbandry risky undertakings. Rainfall is low and variable and droughts are a constant threat; soils are generally of low fertility and structurally fragile. The result of this combination of negative natural factors is that only 12 percent of the land area is suitable for cultivation and 28 percent for pasture.

Historically, several traditional production systems had evolved in the SSZ that allowed the then-sparse populations to sustain output over the centuries under extremely harsh natural conditions. However, with the consolidation of colonial rule in 1920, a number of factors were introduced that upset the traditional equilibrium between humans and the natural environment. Perhaps most important, improvements in medical and veterinary services led to major increases in both the human and animal populations of the SSZ, thus dramatically increasing pressures on the land. Other factors had essentially the same effect: increasing monetarization of the economy and the transfer of political authority to a central government both broke down the authority of the extended family and with it the traditional rules governing land use, and the implementation of economic policies favoring the urban populations through subsidized prices for food and fuelwood essentially eliminated incentives to intensify agricultural production and to conserve on the use of wood.

The joint effect of these factors has been to substantially reduce the carrying capacity of the subregion. The most palpable evidence of this is the accelerated onset of desertification, a condition characterized by ecological degradation and ultimately desert-like conditions. United Nations estimates suggest that this process as of the early 1980s had substantially reduced the productivity of 4.2 million square kilometers of land in the SSZ—an area larger than India and Pakistan combined—potentially suitable for agriculture or grazing (World Resources Institute, 1986: 278).[3] Another indication of a declining carrying capacity is the growing scarcity of fuelwood, the major energy source for most poor African families. In 1980, the area being deforested annually in Africa (3.7 million hectares) exceeded that being planted in new trees by a factor of approximately 30 to 1. This phenomenon is clearly reflected in real prices for fuelwood, which in Ouagadougou, Burkina Faso, rose from $2.50 a solid cubic meter to $5.14 between 1970 and 1978, an average increase of about 9 percent per year (IBRD, 1986a: 27).

The calculations of carrying capacity contained in the Gorse et al. study, summarized in Table 5.3, indicate that in 1980 the rural population that could be sustained through traditional agricultural and livestock production systems (36 million) was substantially higher than the actual population (27 million). However, the data when broken down by subzones (defined by average annual rainfall) show that in three areas—Saharan, Sahelo-Saharan and Sahelo-Sudanian—potential carrying capacity had already been surpassed by 1980. The calculations with respect to sustainable fuelwood production indicate an even more critical situation: in 1980, carrying capacity of the SSZ as a whole had been exceeded by some 10 million people.

With continued population growth, and in the absence of major technological breakthroughs, it is clear that the bad situation described above will only get worse. Even if rural populations increase by only 2 percent annually in the coming decades, the carrying capacities of traditional agricultural and livestock production systems will be exceeded by some 4 million persons by the year 2000. In order to ameliorate this situation, Gorse et al. recommend that a series

Table 5.3
Sahelian and Sudanian Zones of West Africa: Actual and Sustainable Numbers of People, 1980

Zone[a]/	Crop/Livestock Sustainable Population (1)	Actual Rural Population (2)	(1 - 2)	Fuelwood Sustainable Population (3)	Actual Total Population (4)	(3 - 4)
			(million)			
Saharan	1.0	0.8)	-0.8	0.1	0.8)	-1.7
Sahelo-Saharan		1.0)			1.0)	
Sahelian	3.9	3.9	—	0.3	4.0	-3.7
Sahelo-Sudanian	8.7	11.1	-2.4	6.0	13.1	-7.1
Sudanian	8.9	6.6	2.3	7.4	8.1	-0.7
Sudano-Guinean	13.8	3.6	10.2	7.1	4.0	3.1
Total	36.3	27.0	9.3	20.9	31.0	-10.1

a/ Defined according to average annual rainfall, increasing from top to bottom.
Source: Gorse et al. (1985).

of actions be taken on the basis of ratios of actual populations to potential carrying capacities. Such actions, they emphasize, should take the form of a holistic approach to the development of the SSZ, which includes, inter alia, family planning, encouragement of spontaneous migration from low- to high-potential areas, focused agronomic research, and an improved policy environment.

Case Study II: Southern Kenya

Kenya's current population is approximately 20 million and could reach 36 million by the year 2000. It has among the most technologically advanced agricultural sectors in Sub-Saharan Africa, and since the early 1970s production has increased at an average annual rate of 3.5 percent. Though an impressive performance by Sub-Saharan standards, it did not keep up with population growth. As a result, per capita food production and average nutritional standards have deteriorated. In 1983, for example, the daily calorie supply per capita stood at only 83 percent of the minimum requirement, versus 98 percent two decades earlier.

The average population density in Kenya is now around thirty-two persons per square kilometer, well above the Sub-Saharan average of seventeen, but well below the levels reached in countries like Rwanda and Burundi, where densities are in the range of 175 to 225 persons per square kilometer. The relatively low average population of Kenya is, however, deceptive since it masks the country's highly unequal population distribution. By and large, population is concentrated in the regions of greatest agricultural potential, which constitute perhaps 20 percent of the national territory. At the time of the 1979 census, Central, Western, and Nyanza provinces—mostly comprised of high- to medium-potential lands— had a combined population density of 200 persons per square kilometer. Calculations by a World Bank team in the early 1970s indicated that the carrying capacities of these provinces, as well as Eastern province, had already been reached or surpassed (IBRD, 1980: 45). Since there would appear to be no additional unoccupied agricultural land in these provinces and, with population expected to continue to grow at around 4 percent per annum until the end of this century, pressures on the local resource base are likely to become intolerable, if they have not already become so.

Two recent studies illustrate vividly the impact of rapid population growth and other disruptive factors on indigenous societies and their natural environment in southern Kenya. One of these studies, by F. E. Bernard and D. J. Thom (1981), concerns the Wakamba people of the Machakos and Kitui districts of Eastern province. The other, by L. M. Talbot (1986), concerns the Maasai of extreme southern Kenya and adjacent Tanzania. Like the inhabitants of the Sahelo-Sudanian zone, both the Wakamba and the Maasai had over the centuries developed economic systems that enabled them to sustain their population without unduly taxing the local resource base. From their base in the hilly area, the Wakamba practiced a mixed economy combining pastoral activities with shifting cultivation. Long fallow periods were made possible by the continued availability of open lands and a flexible social structure that permitted the formation of new households in frontier areas. The traditional Maasai society was semi-nomadic and based on cattle-raising. Villages were moved seasonally in accordance with the grazing needs of the livestock: during the rainy season the population migrated to the open plains and in the dry season to the hilly areas to take advantage of permanent water sources.

The traditional production systems of these were severely destabilized by the onset of colonial rule: high-potential areas in the highlands were reserved for the European population, access to the lowland grazing areas was limited, and improved medical and veterinary services led to major increases in both human and animal populations. The Maasai, for example, suffered a reduction of their habitat from 200,000 square kilometers at the start of colonial rule to 93,000 square kilometers in 1961. During the same period, their population increased from 45,000 to 117,000, a five-fold increase in average density (Talbot, 1986: 445).

In just a short time these new demographic and political realities led to severe environmental degradation through reductions in fallow periods and overgrazing. The colonial authorities did take some measures to ameliorate the situation through various soil conservation and range management programs starting as early as the late 1920s. Though some isolated successes were achieved in repairing the environmental damage, the situation prevailing some 50 years later in Ukambani (the home of the Wakamba) has been described as "an advanced state of decay" (Bernard and Thom, 1981: 386). Talbot argues that the results of pre- and post-Independence development assistance efforts in Maasai have been the opposite of what was intended: by removing many of the factors that had traditionally limited herd size—control of animal diseases and predators, improvement of water supply, and so forth—overgrazing problems have become even more severe.

In order to measure the present extent of demographic pressures in the Machakos and Kutui districts, Bernard and Thom calculated carrying capacities for forty-one locations employing a methodology virtually identical to that used in the LRPF Project. The results of this exercise offer no major surprises: they clearly indicate that the populations of the better agricultural lands in the districts are currently in excess of carrying capacity, in some cases by a factor of two. Although no carrying capacity calculations were made for Maasailand, it is clear that the region is under substantial ecological stress. Moreover, pressures on the fragile resource base are building rapidly as agriculturalists pushed from densely populated areas of Kenya flow into the area. The authors of both studies suggest that while the diffusion of new technologies, the vigorous implementation of soil and water conservation practices, and the development of nonfarm sources of income have the potential to increase the carrying capacity of Maasailand and Ukambani, they must be combined with family planning if they are to have a chance for success.

CONCLUSIONS

With 20 percent of the world's arable land, but only 7 percent of its population, Sub-Saharan Africa would seem to be in a good position to provide for the future sustenance of its growing population. Indeed, there are still vast tracts of land, chiefly in humid central Africa, that have not yet been brought under cultivation. But the regional statistics on per capita output, crop yields, labor productivity, and environmental damage clearly indicate that the situation in many rural areas— particularly the ecologically fragile Sahelo-Sudanian Zones of West Africa and the highlands of East Africa—have reached crisis proportions. Rapidly growing populations in these subregions, coupled with inappropriate macroeconomic and sectoral policies, have caused reductions in fallow periods and soil depletion while at the same time removing the material incentives for farmers to modernize their production systems.

Several recent studies argue persuasively that human carrying capacity has already been exceeded in certain parts of Sub-Saharan Africa. In other words, the agricultural production systems currently practiced in these areas cannot be sustained without irreparably damaging the natural resource base. Though the concept of human carrying capacity was found to be flawed in several respects— for example, it sheds little light on the factors leading to technological change in agriculture, the possibilities for nonfarm employment, and declines in marital fertility—such calculations are useful in that they provide a warning to governments that urgent action must be taken if economic, social, environmental, and political disasters are to be avoided.

The available evidence of the relationships between population growth, farming intensity and technological change in Sub-Saharan Africa suggests that improvements in the living standards of the vast majority of the population will require concerted efforts to hasten the adoption of new agricultural technologies. Unfortunately, the region's overall performance in this area has until now been relatively poor. Initiatives made to extend the "Green Revolution"—the use of high-yielding seeds, fertilizers, and new modes of production to increase agricultural output—to Sub-Saharan Africa have achieved only mixed results to date. Part of the problem has been an over-reliance on the import of Asian technologies, with their implicit assumptions about soil and water conditions and farm management methods, to the African context, where geographic and social conditions are entirely different. According to recent reports, however, this initial misconception is now changing. The major agricultural research centers in Sub-Saharan Africa have already developed varieties of several African staple crops—for example, sorghum and cassava—that have the potential to increase yields dramatically under conditions found in peasant societies (Harrison, 1987).

Though a promising start, it is doubtful that the recent breakthroughs in agricultural research will, by themselves, lead to a redynamization of African agriculture. In order for these and other innovations to be successfully diffused among the farm population, African governments will need to take steps to improve producer incentives, extension and marketing services, and rural infrastructure. The introduction of family planning services must also be accorded a high priority in the overall strategy. Although it is difficult to characterize rapid population growth as the major cause of the region's agricultural problems, it has greatly aggravated the situation. Quite aside from its deleterious effects on agricultural development and the natural environment, rapid population growth has, in a broader sense, placed tremendous strains on African societies as a whole, as burgeoning demands for schooling, health services, and housing have reduced the availability of public resources for new investments in agriculture and the other productive sectors.

NOTES

1. The slow growth of food production in Sub-Saharan Africa is frequently attributed to an alleged government bias in favor of export crops. This argument is not supported by regional production statistics, which show total agricultural output increasing at even a slower rate (i.e., 1.4 percent p.a.) than that of food crops.

2. It is worth bearing in mind that the current rate of population growth in Sub-Saharan Africa is nearly six times as high as the growth rates experienced in Europe and Asia when these regions were undergoing their agricultural transformations. In other words, what took the Europeans and Asians centuries to accomplish is expected by the Africans in one generation.

3. Desertification affects an additional 2.5 million square kilometers of drylands in southern Africa.

REFERENCES

Bernard, F. E., and D. J. Thom (1981). "Population Pressure and Human Carrying Capacity in Selected Locations of Machakos and Kutui Districts." *Journal of Developing Areas* 15: 381–406.

Bilsborrow, R. E. (1987) "Population Pressures and Agricultural Development in Developing Countries: A Conceptual Framework and Recent Evidence." *World Development* 15. 183–203.

Birdsall, N. (1985). "A Population Perspective on Agricultural Development." In T. J. Davis, ed. *Proceedings of the Fifth Agriculture Sector Symposium*. Washington, D.C.: World Bank.

Boserup, E. (1981). *Population and Technological Change*. Chicago: University of Chicago Press.

Fearnside, P. M. (1986). *Human Carrying Capacity of the Brazilian Rain Forest*. New York: Columbia University Press.

Food and Agriculture Organization-FAO (1974). *Handbook on Human Nutritional Requirements*. Rome: FAO.

——— (1986). *African Agriculture: The Next 25 Years*. Rome: FAO.

Gilland, B. (1983). "Considerations on World Population and Food Supply." *Population and Development Review* 9: 203–11.

Gorse, J., et al. (1985). *Desertification in the Sahelian and Sudanian Zones of West Africa*. Washington, D.C.: The World Bank.

Harrison, P. (1987). *The Greening of Africa*. New York: Penguin Books.

Higgins, G. M., et al. (1982). *Potential Population Supporting Capacities of Lands in the Developing World*. Rome: FAO.

Ho, T. J. (1985). "Population Growth and Agricultural Productivity." In *Proceedings of the Fifth Agriculture Sector Symposium*, T. J. Davis, ed. World Bank: Washington, D.C.

International Bank for Reconstruction and Development-IBRD (1980). *Kenya: Population and Development*. Washington, D.C.: IBRD.

———— (1981). *Accelerated Development in Sub-Saharan Africa*. Washington, D.C.: IBRD.

———— (1984). *Toward Sustained Development in Sub-Saharan Africa*. Washington, D.C.: IBRD.

———— (1986a). *Population Growth and Policies in Sub-Saharan Africa*. Washington, D.C.: IBRD.

———— (1986b). *Poverty and Hunger*. Washington, D.C.: IBRD.

———— (1986c). *World Development Report—1986*. Washington, D.C.: IBRD.

Kirchner, J. W., et al. (1985). "Carrying Capacity, Population Growth and Sustainable Development." In *Rapid Population Growth and Human Carrying Capacity*, D. J. Mahar, ed. World Bank: Washington, D.C.

Meerman, J., and S. Cochrane (1982). "Population Growth and Food Supply in Sub-Saharan Africa." *Finance and Development* 19: 12–17.

National Research Council (1986). *Population Growth and Economic Development: Policy Questions*. Washington, D.C.: National Academy Press.

Paulino, L. A. (1987). "The Evolving Food Situation." In *Accelerating Food Production in Sub-Saharan Africa*, J. W. Mellor et al., eds. Baltimore: Johns Hopkins Press.

Pingali, P., Y. Bigot, and H. Binswanger (1987). *Agricultural Mechanization and the Evolution of Farming Systems in Sub-Saharan Africa*. Baltimore: Johns Hopkins University Press.

Pingali, P., and H. Binswanger (1983). *Population Density, Farming Intensity, Patterns of Labor Use and Mechanization*. Agriculture and Rural Development Department Report No. 11. World Bank: Washington, D.C.

Simon, J. L. (1981). *The Ultimate Resource*. Princeton, N.J.: Princeton University Press.

Talbot, L. M. (1986). "Demographic Factors in Resource Depletion and Environmental Degradation in East African Rangeland." *Population and Development Review* 12: 441–51.

U.S. Department of Agriculture (1986). *World Indices of Agricultural and Food Production, 1975–1985*. Washington, D.C.

World Resources Institute (1986). *World Resources—1986*. New York: Basic Books.

PART TWO

Migration, Population Growth, and Economic Development

6

Internal Migration, Urbanization, and Economic Development

DOMINICK SALVATORE

Two of the most serious problems facing developing nations today are the large and growing urban unemployment and underemployment. These resulted from rapid population growth and rural-urban migration, in the face of grossly inadequate growth in new modern-sector jobs in urban centers. Rapid urban population growth also created overwhelming needs to provide basic services and increased congestion and pollution.

During the 1950s, rural-urban migration, far from being viewed as contributing to the serious urban unemployment and underemployment problems in developing countries, was regarded as necessary to eliminate surplus labor in agriculture and to satisfy the staffing needs of newly established industries in urban centers. This intersectoral labor transfer was also expected to increase real agricultural and industrial incomes and be the main vehicle for economic development. In view of the realization that surplus labor hardly existed in agriculture at planting and harvest seasons, and in the face of large amounts of unutilized labor in urban centers of developing nations, these early analyses seem to be almost completely irrelevant today except, perhaps, for focusing attention on dualistic development and for pointing out the need for sectoral shifts in resources in order to eliminate or at least reduce dualism.

This chapter first presents some data on population growth, rural-urban migration, and urban unemployment in developing countries in order to provide an overall view of the dimension of the problem that these nations face. Subsequently, various models of rural-urban migration are presented, evaluated, and reformulated. Finally, various policies are advanced and evaluated for dealing with the serious urban unemployment and underemployment problem facing most developing countries today.*

---

*This chapter was presented as a paper at the Annual Meetings of the Canadian Economics and Regional Science Associations, June 3–4, 1988, Windsor, Canada.

Table 6.1

Estimates of Average Annual Growth Rates of Total, Urban, and Rural Population in Various Regions, 1950–2000 (percentages)

Regions	1950–1960	1960–1970	1970–1980	1980–1990	1990–2000
World Total					
Urban	3.4	2.9	2.5	2.4	2.4
Rural	1.1	1.6	1.5	1.2	0.8
More Developed Regions					
Urban	2.4	2.0	1.3	0.9	0.8
Rural	-0.3	-0.7	-0.3	-0.2	-0.4
Less Developed Regions					
Urban	4.7	3.8	3.6	3.4	3.4
Rural	1.4	2.0	1.7	1.3	0.9

Source: United Nations, Population Division, Urban and Rural Population Projections - 1984 Assessment (New York: U.N., 1987), Tables A-4, A-6.

URBAN POPULATION GROWTH, RURAL-URBAN MIGRATION, AND THE UNEMPLOYMENT PROBLEM IN LESS DEVELOPED COUNTRIES

Table 6.1 shows that the urban population growth in less developed countries is expected to be almost four times larger than the growth of the urban population in more developed countries during the 1980s, and even larger in the 1990s. In an absolute sense, an urban population growth of 3.4 percent per year is an extremely rapid growth and implies a doubling of the urban population of less developed countries every 21 years.

Urban population growth can result from three factors: the natural increase in urban population, rural-urban migration, and the reclassification of some rural areas into urban centers as their population grows over time. Abstracting from the reclassification cause (which does not seem to be very large), the United Nations (1980) estimated that about 60 percent of urban population growth in less developed countries was attributable to natural increase and the remaining 40 percent to rural-urban migration.[1]

The large contribution of the natural increase to urban population growth in developing areas is due to the combination of sharply declined death rates with still very high birth rates. On the other hand, rural-urban migration results primarily from the desire on the part of people in rural areas to improve their socioeconomic conditions, even though the probability of quickly finding a high-paying urban job is rather small.

The sharp increase in urban population growth over the past three decades has been accompanied by an equally sharp increase in the rate of urban unemployment and underemployment throughout the developing world. Data on the rate of urban unemployment in developing nations are hard to come by, and whatever data are available are subject to large degrees of error. For example, an individual who cannot find a job in the modern urban sector may be so discouraged that he or she will stop looking for one, opting instead for a meager living in the informal urban service sector (as a porter, self-appointed parking attendant, shoe shiner, and so on). Since this individual is not actively seeking a job, he or she would not be included in the number of unemployed. While the difficulty with this unreported hidden unemployment also occurs in developed nations, the dimension of the problem is overwhelming in developing nations.

Be that as it may, less developed countries certainly have a very serious urban unemployment problem, but face an even greater urban underemployment problem. Underemployment results when a worker is overqualified for his or her occupation or works fewer days or hours than he or she is willing to work. Turnham (1971) estimated that during the late 1960s the rate of urban unemployment in developing countries was in the range of 15 percent (or about twice the average rate of open unemployment in developed countries in the early 1980s) and the rate of urban underemployment was another 20 or 30 percent. The problem was certainly more serious in the 1970s and is expected to worsen during the next decade.

Looking back, it now seems entirely unrealistic to have expected industrial expansion to create enough new jobs to absorb the entire growth of the urban labor force. A simple example can confirm this. Modern industry typically employs less than one-quarter of the urban labor force in developing countries, so that industrial output would have had to increase by over 16 percent per year to absorb the entire increase of four percent per year in the urban labor force. Since more than one-half of any increase in industrial output typically results from productivity increases, industrial output would, in fact, have to rise by well over 30 percent per year. With any capital bias in production (i.e., with capital substituted for labor in production), industrial output would have to rise even faster to absorb the entire increase in the urban labor force into modern industry. These, of course, are unheard-of growth rates. In fact, modern industry was barely able to absorb about 1 percent, or one-quarter of the growth of the urban labor force. The result was a sharp increase in the rate of urban unemployment and underemployment throughout the developing world. And conditions are bound to worsen, at least in the immediate future.

Since the creation of industrial jobs was insufficient to absorb even the natural increase in the urban labor force in developing nations, rural-urban migration magnified the urban unemployment and underemployment problem. Thus, less developed countries can be said to have a migration problem. This is clearly brought out by a United Nations (1978) survey, which indicated that 90 out of the 116 nations responding regarded rural-urban migration as a serious problem that required policies to slow it down.

The rapid urban population growth in developing countries is also the primary cause of the squalid living conditions, congestion, and pollution in the largest urban centers of these nations. One can only imagine living conditions in a city such as Mexico City, which had 3 million inhabitants in 1950, 12 million in

1975, 17.3 million in 1985, and is expected to grow to more than 27 million by the year 2000. The population of Sao Paulo in Brazil grew from 2.5 million in 1950, to 10.7 million in 1975, 15.9 million in 1985, and is expected to be more than 25 million by the end of the century. While other cities in the developing world are not expected to end up with such spectacular populations, many of them are nevertheless growing extremely rapidly, some even more rapidly than Mexico City and Sao Paulo.

Since rural-urban migration contributes so importantly to urban population growth and unemployment, we now turn to models that seek to explain the causes and effects of rural-urban migration in the hope of arriving at policies that would lead to a better sectoral labor utilization and more rapid growth and development. The main point is that the social costs of rural-urban migration exceed the private costs, thus leading to excessive urban population growth.

At this point, it is useful to distinguish between urban population growth from urbanization. The latter refers to the growth in the proportion of the population living in urban areas. Since the natural increase in rural population exceeds that of urban areas, urbanization throughout the world is occurring primarily because of rural-urban migration (with reclassification of rural into urban areas being of much less importance). This, once again, points to the need and importance of studying rural-urban migration.

MODELS OF RURAL-URBAN MIGRATION AND DEVELOPMENT

During the 1950s and early 1960s, most analyses of economic development centered on the celebrated two-sector model of W. A. Lewis (1954) and its extension by J.C.H. Fei and G. Ranis (1961). The W. A. Lewis model postulated the existence of a traditional subsistence agricultural sector characterized by zero marginal productivity of labor and a high-productivity modern urban industrial sector. The subsistence of surplus labor in agriculture was ensured by the extended family system. Development was postulated to occur by the transfer of labor from agriculture to industry. This would result in a rise in industrial output without any decline in agricultural output. The incentive for labor to move to industry was provided by industrial wages being higher (by about 30 percent, according to Lewis) than the average agricultural income that surplus labor received (shared) on the farm. The growth of industrial jobs occurred as capitalists reinvested profits in industry. The process would continue until all agricultural surplus labor was absorbed into industry, at which point industrial wages and rural incomes would begin to rise, thus slowing down the process of industrialization.

While the W. A. Lewis model is elegant and may have captured the essence of potential development in the past, it does not work well under present conditions. First, it is now clear that surplus labor does not exist in agriculture during planting and harvesting seasons, so that a transfer of labor from agriculture to industry cannot usually be accomplished without a reduction in agricultural output (in the absence of a concomitant improvement in agricultural productivity). Secondly, there is no need to transfer labor from agriculture to satisfy growing industrial labor requirements. Indeed, as we have seen, the problem is just the opposite: Industry is unable to provide jobs for more than a minority of the expansion of the urban labor force. Furthermore, capitalists might not reinvest their profits in domestic industrial projects or might reinvest them in labor-saving equipment that expands output but not jobs.

Starting from the early 1960s, attention shifted from the W. A. Lewis model to the determinants of rural-urban migration. Migration was then viewed as an investment in human capital (see Schultz, 1961; Becker, 1962; Sjaastad, 1962), resulting in a return or economic benefit to the migrants (the higher lifetime earnings associated with migration than without migration) and involving an economic cost (for transportation and job search), as well as psychic costs (the breaking away from friends, familiar surroundings, and so on). This human capital approach to migration seemed to explain well the direction of the migratory labor flow (from low-income rural areas to high-income urban areas) as well as the pattern of migration (for example, that the young are more likely to migrate since they have a longer remaining working life over which to capitalize the higher earnings associated with migration). However, the human capital approach predicted that rural-urban labor migration would lead to the elimination or reduction in urban-rural earnings differentials. It could thus not explain the observed increase in urban-rural earnings differentials, nor could it explain the large-scale rural-urban migration in the face of persistent and increasing urban unemployment.

It remained for M. P. Todaro (1969) and J. R. Harris and M. P. Todaro (1970) to fill in the gap by extending the theory so that it would more nearly conform to the facts. According to Todaro and Harris, migration proceeds in response to the positive urban-rural difference in expected earnings. Expected earnings refer to real earnings weighted by the probability of finding employment. Thus, higher urban real earnings can attract workers from the countryside even in the face of a great deal of urban unemployment, as long as expected urban real earnings exceed rural real earnings. Thus, actual urban-rural earnings differentials could persist and even increase, urban unemployment could rise, and still there could be large-scale rural-urban migration. If rural-urban labor migration proceeds faster than jobs are created in the modern urban sector, the probability of finding modern urban employment declines. This reduces expected urban real earnings, until they are equal to real rural earnings (or the positive difference reduced to the threshold required for migration to occur). There would then be an equilibrium rural-urban migratory flow equal to the rate at which modern sector jobs are created in urban areas—unless urban-rural real income differentials continue to grow. Urban-rural earnings differentials could continue to grow, even in the face of large and rising urban unemployment, because of trade union pressure with the government's tacit approval.

Figure 6.1
The Effect of Rural-Urban Migration on Real Wages and Productivity

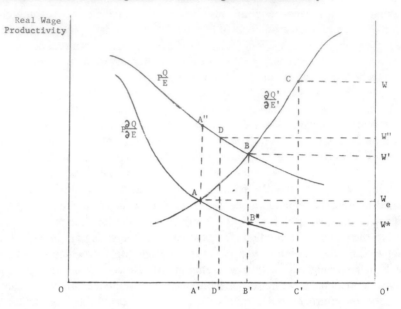

Graphic Presentation

The essence of the rural-urban migration models presented above can conveniently and profitably be shown graphically. In Figure 6.1, the horizontal axis measures the size of the total (urban and rural) labor force, while the vertical axes measure real wages or productivity (W). The left-hand origin (O) refers to the traditional rural agricultural sector and the right-hand origin (O') refers to the modern urban industrial sector. We assume that this is a small open economy so that the commodity terms of trade (P) are given exogenously. The marginal revenue product curve of the traditional rural sector is given by $P(\partial Q/\partial E)$, while the average product curve is given by PQ/E, where Q refers to physical output and E to employment in the traditional rural sector. On the other hand, the marginal product curve of the modern urban sector is given by $\partial Q'/\partial E'$, where Q' is output and E' is employment in the modern urban sector.

If the market mechanism operated unhampered in the rural as well as in the urban sector, equilibrium would occur at point A, where the marginal revenue product curves of the rural and urban sectors cross. Real wages would be equalized at W_e in the rural and urban sectors. OA' of labor would be employed in the rural sector, $O'A'$ would be employed in the urban sector, and there would be no unemployment. With the extended family system in the rural sector, equilibrium would instead occur at point B where the rural average product curve crosses the urban marginal product curve. Real wages in the two sectors are equalized at W', with OB' of labor employed in the rural sector and $O'B'$ in the urban sector, and there would be no open unemployment. However, because of the distortion introduced by the existence of the extended family system in the rural sector, $\partial Q'/\partial E' = PQ/E > P(\partial Q/\partial E)$ by $BB*$ in the figure. Too much labor is employed in agriculture and too little in the urban sector for national output to be maximized. Had $P(\partial Q/\partial E) = 0$ at point B', we would have the W. A. Lewis model. As it is, $P(\partial Q/\partial E) > 0$ at B' to reflect the fact that there is no surplus labor in agriculture at planting and harvest seasons, so that the transfer of labor from the rural to the urban sector would reduce agricultural output.

Suppose now that unions succeed in raising wages to $\overline{W}$ in the modern urban sector. Employment in the modern urban sector falls by $B'C'$, from $O'B'$ to $O'C'$. The high modern urban wage also attracts some labor from rural areas, say $B'D'$. This leaves OD' employed in the rural sector at a real wage of W'' with no open unemployment (real earnings in the traditional rural sector would remain unchanged only if the average product curve were horizontal). $D'C'$ ($B'C' \mid B'D'$) are now openly unemployed in urban areas and must find some precarious employment in the traditional urban service sector while awaiting a chance for high paying modern urban employment. $W'' = O'C'\overline{W}/O'D'$, where $O'C'/O'D'$ is the probability of employment in the modern urban sector. This is a representation of the Harris-Todaro model (1970). If wages in the modern urban sector were raised higher than $\overline{W}$, there would be more labor migration from rural areas. Urban open unemployment would grow until expected earnings in the modern urban sector once again equal real rural wages, or the positive difference is reduced to the threshold required for migration. However, if positive modern-urban to rural real income differentials continue to grow, rural-urban migration will increase and urban open unemployment is likely to rise. Thus, excessive and "politically" determined minimum modern-urban-sector wages result in urban unemployment and may cause a reduction in the output of both sectors.

The Todaro Migration Model—Mathematical Presentation

The Todaro migration model can be presented mathematically as follows:

$$\frac{M}{L}(t) = F\left[\frac{V'(t) - V(t)}{V(t)}\right], \quad F' > 0 \tag{1}$$

where,

M = net rural-urban labor migration in period t

L = existing size of the total rural labor force in period t

$V'(t)$ = discounted present value of the expected urban real income stream over an unskilled worker's planning horizon

$V(t)$ = discounted present value of the rural income stream over the same planning horizon

$$V(0) = \int_{t=o}^{n} Y(t)e^{-rt}dt \qquad (2)$$

$$V'(0) = \int_{t=o}^{n} P'(t)Y'(t)e^{-rt}dt - C(0) \qquad (3)$$

where,

$Y(t)$ = net rural real income in period t

r = discount factor reflecting the degree of consumption time preference of the typical unskilled worker

$P'(t)$ = probability of having a modern-sector urban job in year t

$Y'(t)$ = net urban real income in period t

$C(0)$ = initial fixed cost of rural-urban migration and urban relocation

$$P'(t) = \frac{E'}{L'}(t) \qquad (4)$$

where,

E' = existing employed urban labor force

L' = existing total urban labor force

Note that the extended family system is assumed to ensure the absence of open unemployment in the traditional rural or agricultural sector.

Assuming with Todaro (1969: 143–44) and others (see Harris and Todaro, 1970: 129; Laber and Chase, 1971: 798; and Yap, 1976: 126) that urban-rural real income differentials remain constant over time, the empirical estimation of the model can be greatly simplified by dealing with one period time horizon, as indicated in equation 5.

$$\frac{M}{L}(t) = F\left[Y^*(t)\right], \quad F' > 0 \qquad (5)$$

where,

$$Y^*(t) = \left[\frac{E'}{L'}(t)Y'(t) - Y(t)\right]\Big/ Y(t)$$

EVALUATION, REFORMULATION AND EXTENSIONS OF THE RURAL-URBAN MIGRATION MODEL

By combining the income and probability-of-employment variable into the composite expected-real-income variable, the Todaro migration model given by equation 5 is collapsing two separate and independent variables into a single composite variable. In the process, some information is necessarily lost. This problem can be avoided by keeping the income and the probability-of-employment variable separate as indicated in equation 6:

$$\frac{M}{L}(t) = G\left[Y''(t), \dot{E}''(t)\right], \quad G'_{Y''} > 0 \text{ and } G'_{E''} > 0 \tag{6}$$

where,

$$Y''(t) = \frac{Y'(t) - Y(t)}{Y(t)} > 0$$

$$E''(t) = \frac{(E'/L')(t) - (E/L)(t)}{(E/L)(t)} = (E'/L')(t) < 1$$

since $E/L = 1$ in the traditional rural or agricultural sector because of the extended family system.

Since the urban unemployment rate, $u' = 1 - E'/L'$, testing equation 6 empirically is equivalent to testing equation 7:

$$M(t) = H\left[Y''(t), u'(t)\right], \quad H'_{Y''} > 0 \text{ and } H'_{u'} < 0 \tag{7}$$

This author (Salvatore, 1981a) tested empirically a slight variation of equation 5 and equation 7, utilizing Italian data and strongly confirmed the superiority of equation 7 over equation 5. Another advantage of equation 7 over equation 5 is that the short-run as opposed to the long-run components of the migration decision can be separated (i.e., the long-run contribution of the higher urban income as opposed to the short-run effect of urban unemployment).

Reformulation and Extension of the Rural-Urban Migration Model

If we assume that migrants respond to the ratio of urban-to-rural income rather than to urban-rural income differentials so as to avoid nonlinearity problems (see Salvatore, 1977b; Hart, 1975; Lowry, 1966; Rogers, 1968; and Sahota, 1968), we can test a variant of the Todaro migration model rather directly:

$$M/L = F\left[(E'/L')(Y'/Y)\right], \quad F' > 0 \tag{8}$$

If the regression is run in double-log form, we get:

$$\ln(M/L) = \beta_0 + \beta_1\ln(E'/L') + \beta_2\ln(Y'/Y) \tag{9}$$

which is a variant of the Todaro migration model corresponding to the imposition of the $\beta_1 = \beta_2$ constraint. One can test whether the relaxation of that constraint yields a significant improvement in the fit.

There is a theoretical rationale for $\beta_1 \neq \beta_2$ and it is of some interest. Assume for simplicity that:

$$U(Y') = (Y'/Z)^a \tag{10}$$

where Z is the precarious consumption of the urban unemployed from hustling or transfers from the country, etc. This is equivalent to letting $U(Z) = 1$, and the unit is arbitrary for a Neumann-Morgenstern utility function. Note that if migrants are risk averse, $a<1$.

Assume rural utility is k. Then migration is positive when expected urban utility exceeds k, that is, when:

$$(E'/L')(Y'/Z)^a > k \tag{11}$$

For convenience, suppose that migration is a function of the ratio of urban-to-rural expected utility (this, once again, to avoid nonlinearity problems). Then:

$$M/L = F\left[\frac{(E'/L')(Y'/Z)^a}{k}\right] \tag{12}$$

Specifically:

$$M/L = \gamma\left[\frac{(E'/L')(Y'/Z)^a}{k}\right] \tag{13}$$

Then in the logarithms:

$$\ln(M/L) = \ln(\gamma/kZ^a) + a \ln Y' + \ln(E'/L') \tag{14}$$

but, actually β_2 need not be one. We may plausibly bound M/L at zero and assume in place of equation 13:

$$M/L = \gamma\left[\frac{(E'/L')(Y'/Z)^a}{k}\right]^b \tag{15}$$

where $b>0$. Then in the logs:

$$\ln(M/L) = (\ln \gamma - b \ln k - ab \ln Z) + ab \ln Y' + b \ln(E'/L') \tag{16}$$

so that $\beta_1/\beta_2<1$ is the elasticity of the utility-of-income function, and β_2 is the elasticity of migration to the urban-rural utility ratio.

Other Extensions of the Rural-Urban Migration Model

As pointed out in Salvatore (1981a), there are several theoretically justifiable ways to improve the fit of the rural-urban migration model as expressed by equation 7. One of these is to include the lagged dependent as an additional explanatory variable. This would result if migration in a given year is regarded as a function of the expected value of the explanatory variables, with expectations generally formed on the basis of a distributed lag of current and past values of the explanatory variables. The inclusion of the lagged dependent as an additional explanatory variable can lead to a significant improvement of the fit (see Salvatore, 1977a and 1977b) but also leads to some econometric problems, which, however, can be surmounted by the appropriate estimating technique (see Salvatore, 1981a: 504–505).

A second way to extend the model and improve its empirical performance is to separate the "push" from the "pull" forces of migration (see Salvatore, 1977a). The model could be further refined by stratifying migrants into various classes, depending on the level of training and education, age, sex, and sector of the economy and by utilizing sector-specific real wages and rates of unemployment. However, this type of detailed time series data are hard to come by.

The above extensions are hardly sufficient, however, since migration, real earnings, and the rate of employment (and unemployment) are simultaneously determined. But even on this account, the single-equation rural-urban migration model given by equation 7 can be made part of a simultaneous equations model in a more natural and straightforward manner than the original Todaro model (see Salvatore 1980, 1981b, 1982). This will also allow for the objective evaluation of the socioeconomic effects, as well as the causes of migration in both rural and urban areas.

Another possible extension is to formally introduce the traditional urban sector as the third sector (besides the traditional rural or agricultural sector and the modern urban or industrial sector) into the rural-urban migration model. This is a potentially important extension, in recognition of the fact that rural-urban migrants will have to scratch a living in the traditional urban sector while awaiting a high-paying modern urban job rather than remaining completely unemployed. Similarly, as a fourth sector, a modern agricultural sector could be included whenever appropriate. The addition of a third and possibly of a fourth sector may significantly alter the two-sector model results.

Finally, the rural-urban migration model must be extended to consider some natural limits to urban growth in general, and to rural-urban migration in particular. The most important of these is perhaps given by rising urban housing costs. The greater urban housing requirements may also absorb most household savings, thus limiting the growth of the modern sector and the expansion of modern-sector urban jobs. Rising urban housing costs and the reduction in the expansion of new modern urban jobs thus operate as natural limits to rural-urban migration and urban growth (see Kelley and Williamson, 1982).

It must be pointed out, however, that most developing nations at present do not even have the data to test the basic Todaro migration model. Nevertheless, and in view of the very influential nature of the Todaro model in the theoretical analysis of rural-urban migration, it is important to recognize the theoretical shortcomings of such a model and the need for reformulating and extending it as indicated in preceding sections. It is also very important that developing nations begin to collect adequate data to permit the empirical application of the reformulated and extended migration model presented previously.

POLICIES TO DEAL WITH URBAN UNEMPLOYMENT IN LESS DEVELOPED COUNTRIES

The choice of policies to deal with the urban unemployment problem in less developed countries can be evaluated with the help of Figure 6.1. Urban unemployment can be eliminated if the government kept the urban minimum wage at W' instead of $\overline{W}$. Equilibrium in the labor market would then be at point B, with OB' of labor employed in the rural or agricultural sector and $O'B'$ in the modern urban sector. While the urban unemployment problem would be solved, keeping the minimum wage at W' does not represent the optimal solution because at point B, $\partial Q'/\partial E' = PQ/E > P(\partial Q/\partial E)$. Too much labor is used in the traditional rural agricultural sector and too little in the modern urban sector for the total output of the nation to be maximized.

A better solution would be to set the urban minimum wage at W_e and at the same time impose a tax of AA^* (see Figure 6.1) per worker in agriculture. Equilibrium in the labor market would then be at point A, with OA' of labor employed in agriculture and $O'A'$ in urban areas (and no unemployment). This solution would be superior to the previous one because the reduction in agricultural output of $A'AB^*B'$ would be smaller than the increase in urban or industrial output of $B'BAA'$ by BAB^*. However, this optimal solution may be impossible or difficult to achieve because the government may be unwilling or unable to keep the urban minimum wage at W_e, and it may be unwilling or unable to impose the AA^* tax per worker in agriculture.

If a low-productivity traditional urban sector were included as a third sector into the analysis, the policies to deal with the urban unemployment problem would, of course, have to be modified. Policies would also be different in the unlikely event that agricultural income depends on the marginal, not the average, productivity of labor in agriculture (see Corden and Findlay, 1975).

The government may want or be forced to keep the urban minimum wage at $\overline{W}$ and attempt to solve the urban unemployment problem by wage subsidies to urban employers and by encouraging and subsidizing industrial investments to expand urban employment. However, these policies may lead to difficulties that conceivably could even increase urban unemployment. This is the case because any attempt to stimulate urban employment will reduce the rate of urban unemployment and attract more labor from rural areas, so that in the end urban unemployment may in fact be greater.

Todaro (1976) has indicated that the elasticity of migration with respect to job probability in urban areas is so small that most developing nations face the paradox that the more urban jobs they create, the larger, rather than smaller, the rate of urban unemployment is likely to be. This is indeed what occurred as a result of the so-called Tripartite Agreement in Kenya in 1964, where labor unions agreed to hold the line on urban wages while the government and the private sector agreed to take on, respectively, 15 and 10 percent more workers in 1964 and 1965 in the hope of solving the serious urban unemployment problem in the greater Nairobi area. The result was instead the opposite, as more labor migrated from rural areas so that there was a net increase in the rate of urban unemployment (see Todaro, 1971).

In short, there seems to be no strictly urban solution to the urban unemployment problem in developing nations. Rural development must be an essential part of any solution (in the absence of an equilibrium urban minimum wage). An alternative might be to restrict rural-urban migration or to establish government-run urban labor exchanges. The latter system would control migration; only when jobs opened up in urban centers would an equal number of workers be allowed to migrate to cities to fill those jobs. However, this system not only restricts personal freedom but may be very difficult or even impossible to enforce.

Rural development refers not only to the usual measures advocated to increase agricultural productivity, but also to all those steps that would improve the well-being of the rural population. These include better educational, health, housing, and recreational facilities (such as movie theaters so as to bring "city lights" to the countryside) and other amenities (such as electricity, water supply systems, roads, etc.) that will induce people to remain in rural areas even in the face of falling urban unemployment. It would, however, be self-defeating if urban wages continued to rise relative to average real rural incomes. Therefore, it is essential that urban wages be restrained. This is as much a political as an economic problem that the governments of less developed countries must face.

In the long run, a population policy may also be required to solve the urban unemployment problem in developing countries. Such a policy is very important, but only in the long run, because the potential labor force of a nation is already determined for the next fifteen years or so by past birth and death rates. A slight reduction in population growth may already be occurring in developing nations as the process of urbanization proceeds and because of the general improvement in living standards. Nevertheless, the process may be too slow. Investments in population control (family planning programs) may bring much higher future benefits per dollar spent on such an effort than the alternative of having to create many more modern-sector jobs in the long run.

CONCLUDING REMARKS

During the past two decades, urban unemployment and underemployment have become two of the most serious problems facing developing nations the world over. Since these problems are inextricably connected to the huge rural-urban migration taking place in developing nations, there is great need to study the causes as well as the effects of this migration on urban as well as on rural areas.

The Todaro-Harris migration model provides the most useful framework for the study of rural-urban migration in developing nations. That model, however, has a number of shortcomings, and it views rural-urban labor migration in a framework far too restrictive to permit adequate analysis of the migration process and urbanization in developing nations.

This chapter attempts to overcome both difficulties by reformulating and extending the basic migration model so as to better serve as a tool of analysis. This more general model is then utilized to determine the policy options at the disposal of the government of developing nations to overcome or at least to prevent the urban unemployment and underemployment problem from worsening in the future.

The best short-run policy seems to be the elimination of factor-price distortions. These are the primary cause of the huge rural-urban migration taking place in developing nations today and are an important contributor to their serious urban unemployment and underemployment problem. Agricultural development, broadly defined, must necessarily be an integral part of the proposed solution. In the long run, a population policy may also be required to speed up the rate of development and slow down the process of urbanization in developing nations.

NOTES

1. A more recent publication of the United Nations (1985) points out, however, that if the indirect effect (through natural increase) of migration to urban population growth is considered, the contribution of migration to urban population growth in developing countries would be even greater.

REFERENCES

Becker, G. S. (1962). "Investment in Human Capital: A Theoretical Analysis." *Journal of Political Economy*, Supplement, part 2 (October): 9–49.

Bloom, David E., and Richard B. Freeman (1986). "Population Growth, Labor Supply and Employment in Developing Countries." NBER, *Working Paper No. 1837*, February.

Corden, W. M., and R. Findlay (1975). "Urban Unemployment, Intersectoral Capital Mobility and Development Policy." *Economica* (February): 59–78.

Fei, J. C. H., and G. Ranis (1961). "A Theory of Economic Development." *American Economic Review* (September): 533–65.

Gosh, P. K., ed. (1984). *Urban Development in the Third World*. Westport, Conn.: Greenwood.

Greenwood, M. J. (1985). "Human Migration: Theory, Models, and Empirical Studies." *Journal of Regional Science* (November): 521–44.

Harris, J. R., and M. P. Todaro (1970). "Migration, Unemployment and Development: A Two-Sector Analysis." *American Economic Review* (March): 126–42.

Hart, R. A. (1975). "Interregional Economic Migration: Some Theoretical Considerations." *Journal of Regional Science* (August): 127–38.

Henderson, V. J. (1985). "Industrialization and Urbanization: International Experience." Background Paper prepared for the Working Group on Population Growth and Economic Development, Committee on Population, National Research Council.

Kelley, A., and J. Williamson (1985). *What Drives Third World City Growth?* Princeton, N. J.: Princeton University Press.

Laber, G., and R. X. Chase (1971). "Interprovinical Migration in Canada as a Human Capital Decision." *Journal of Political Economy* (October): 795–804.

Lewis, W. A. (1954). "Economic Development with Unlimited Supplies of Labor." *Manchester School of Economic and Social Studies* (May): 139–91.

Linn, J. (1983). *Cities in the Developing World.* New York: Oxford University Press.

Lowry, I. (1966). *Migration and Metropolitan Growth: Two Analytical Models.* San Francisco: Chandler.

National Research Council (1986). *Population Growth and Economic Development: Policy Questions.* Washington, D. C.: National Academy Press.

Richardson, H. W. (1981). "National Urban Development Strategies in Developing Countries." *Urban Studies* (March).

Rogers, A. (1968). *Matrix Analysis and Interregional Population Growth and Distribution.* Berkeley: University of California Press.

Sahota, G. S. (1968). "An Economic Analysis of Internal Migration in Brazil." *Journal of Political Economy* (February): 218–45.

Salvatore, D. (1980). "A Simultaneous Equations Model of Internal Migration with Dynamic Policy Simulations and Forecasting." *Journal of Development Economics* (June): 231–46.

——— (1972). "The Operation of the Market Mechanism and Regional Inequality." *Kyklos* (September): 518–636.

——— (1973). "Regional Inequality and the Market Mechanism." *Kyklos* (September): 627–33.

——— (1976). "Interregional Capital Flows and Economic Development." *Economia Internazionale* (May): 66–88.

——— (1977). "Testing Various Econometric Models of Internal Migration." *Review of Regional Studies* (Spring): 31–41.

——— (1977b). "An Econometric Analysis of Internal Migration in Italy." *Journal of Regional Science* (December): 395–408.

——— (1981a). "A Theoretical and Empirical Evaluation and Extension of the Todaro Migration Model." *Regional Science and Urban Economics* (November): 499–508.

——— (1981b). *Internal Migration and Economic Development.* Washington, D.C.: University Press of America.

——— (1982). "Migrazioni Interne e Sviluppo Economico in Italia." *Rivista di Politica Economica* (December): 1–30.

——— (1984). "An Econometric Model of Internal Migration and Development: Extensions and Tests." *Regional Science and Urban Economics* (February): 77–87.

——— ed. (1988a). *African Development Prospects: A Policy Modeling Approach.* New York: Taylor and Francis.

——— ed. (1988b). *Population Growth and Economic Development.* Special Issue of *The Journal of Policy Modeling* (Spring).

Salvatore, D., and Fred Campano (1988). "Kuznet's U-Shaped Hypothesis, Income Inequality, and Economic Development. *Journal of Policy Modeling* (July):1–20.

Schultz, T. (1961). "Investment in Human Capital." *American Economic Review* 51: 1–14.

Sjaastad, L. A. (1962). "The Costs and Returns of Human Migration." *Journal of Political Economy*, Supplement (October): 80–93.

Stark, Oded, ed. (1985). "Symposium on Advances in Migration Theory." *Journal of Development Economics* (Jan.-Feb.).

Todaro, M. P. (1969). "A Model of Labor Migration and Urban Unemployment in Less Developed Countries." *American Economic Review* (March): 138–48.

——— (1971). "Income Expectations, Rural-Urban Migration and Employment in Africa." *International Labor Review* (September/December): 387–413.

——— (1976). "Urban Job Expansion, Induced Migration and Rising Unemployment." *Journal of Development Economics* (September): 211–25.

Turnham, D. (1971). *The Employment Problem in Less Developed Countries*. Paris: Development Centre of O.E.C.D., pp. 47–63.

United Nations (1987). *The State of the World Population 1987*. New York: United Nations.

United Nations, Department of International Economic and Social Affairs (1987). *World Population Policies: 1987 Monitoring Report*. New York: United Nations.

United Nations, Population Division (1980). *Patterns of Urban and Rural Growth*. New York: United Nations, pp. 11–14.

——— (1985). *Migration, Population Growth and Employment in Metropolitan Areas of Selected Developing Countries*. New York: United Nations.

Vanderkamp, J. (1971). "Migration Flows and Their Determinants and the Effects of Return Migration." *Journal of Political Economy* (Sept.–Oct.): 1012–31.

World Bank (1984). *World Development Report*. Washington, D.C., pp. 51–186.

Yap, L. (1976). "Internal Migration and Economic Development in Brazil." *Quarterly Journal of Economics* (February): 119–37.

7

National Urban Policies and the Costs and Benefits of Urbanization

HARRY W. RICHARDSON

Many countries, most of them developing countries, have attempted to implement national urban policies in the past two decades. These policies may involve at least four types of actions: measures to slow down rural-urban migration by intervening in both origin and destination areas; policies to slow down or better manage the growth of the primate city and, occasionally, other large metropolitan areas; steps to promote the expansion of other urban centers, usually in the medium or small size ranges; and macro and sectoral policies (e.g., tariff measures, pricing strategies, transport investments) that have both direct and indirect urban impacts. A national urban policy may include intervention on all these four fronts, and in general there has been some shift in emphasis in recent years from controls on migration and city sizes to priority-city boosting strategies and, most recently of all, to sectoral as opposed to spatial policies (Richardson, 1981, 1983, 1987a). Whatever its focus, the existence of a national urban policy implies a position on the costs and benefits of urbanization that is sometimes explicit but often implicit. The aim of this chapter is to review what we know and do not know about urbanization costs and benefits in the context of population distribution patterns and the debate about how much these are amenable to policy influence.

An obvious but important point is that it is impossible to estimate a measure of net social benefits of urbanization. This was the one clear result of the optimal city size literature of the early 1970s (Alonso, 1971; Cameron and Wingo, 1973; Richardson, 1973). This research showed that first, there are benefits to city size that have to be considered alongside the costs; and second, there are so many intangibles on both the benefit and the cost sides that it is not feasible to derive aggregate benefit and cost functions. If there is no method of obtaining a net benefit function for the size of a single city, it is clearly impossible to say anything very specific about the net benefits of a particular distribution of city sizes. The concept of an optimal settlement pattern remains elusive.

INCOME AND PRODUCTIVITY

Some analysts (e.g., Mera, 1973) have suggested that urban income per capita might be used as a proxy for the net benefits of a particular city. The essential idea, superficially supported by the positive association between income per capita and city size, is that bigger cities are more productive because of superior agglomeration economies and that this higher productivity is reflected in higher wages and incomes. Unfortunately, there is a competing explanation for the positive correlation between income and city size. This is that bigger cities generate negative net externalities (such as congestion and environmental damage), and workers require "compensating payments" for the disamenities associated with living there. In one of the latest researches into this idea (based on U.S. cities), Kahn and Ofek (1987) find that there is a nonlinear (either quadratic or cubic) relationship between wages and city size, after standardizing for human capital characteristics (such as education, work experience, nonlabor income, and occupation) and natural amenities (such as climate and a coastal location). For a small city (say, about 100,000 population) wages increase by between 6.6 percent and 9.5 percent per million increase in population. However, wages peak in the 3.7 to 4.9 million range of city sizes, suggesting a "worst" city in terms of size-related disamenities. Moreover, the particular distribution of city sizes existing in the United States currently generates city-size disamenities equivalent to 6.7 percent of gross national product (GNP) (1984 data), a deflator that has been climbing steadily over recent decades at a rate of about 0.5 percent per decade. The only research on these lines in a developing country was undertaken as a minor aspect of the National Urban Policy Study (NUPS) project in Egypt (PADCO, 1982). Using a function borrowed from developed country contexts, the conclusion was that a concentrated settlement pattern emphasizing Cairo reduced net benefits by about 3 percent if size-related disamenities were taken into account.

It is very plausible that the two city-size-related influences on urban income per capita—the productivity effect and the environmental disamenities effect (including compensating payments)—operate simultaneously. An attempt to unscramble these two components has been made by Garofalo and Fogarty (1979). Comparing a representative U.S. city of 1 million and another of 2 million, they show that a productivity gain of $672 million is partially offset by a social cost of $186 million ($105 million in compensating payments and $81 million in uncompensated environmental disamenities), implying a reduction in the real productivity differential of about 28 percent. These results are derived from a static model of the urban economy and are specific to conditions in the United States. No one has attempted to operationalize this approach in a developing country context.

On a much narrower interpretation of costs and benefits, namely the capital investment costs of urban population absorption and the economic efficiency benefits of city sizes and urban settlement systems, there has been some research. In a frequently quoted paper, Sveikauskas (1975) found that a doubling of city size in the United States was associated with a 6 percent increase in productivity. Wheaton and Shishido (1981) undertook a cross-sectional analysis of thirty-eight countries, both developed and developing, in which they hypothesized that the efficient level of production for an urban area was an S-shaped function of the level of GNP per capita. Dividing the optimum output by nonagricultural GNP per capita yields the optimum size for a metropolitan area. Their data suggested that this optimum population size is very high, slightly above 20 million, and occurred around a level of development near $2,000 per capita.

Both these studies focus on the economic efficiency benefits of individual cities. Although their results could be the raw material for a study of the relative economic efficiencies of alternative urban settlement patterns, taking this step requires the assumption that these productivity advantages are a strict function of city size. Qutub and Richardson (1986) showed that this assumption was incorrect, at least in the case of Pakistan. Productive and unproductive cities were found in each city size class. Many of the more productive cities were in the medium size classes, approximately between 50,000 and 200,000 people, and were either manufacturing towns or service-oriented towns located in fertile agricultural regions, but there were low-productivity towns in this size range too. If this result could be generalized to other countries, it makes the task for national urban policymakers very difficult because policy measures would have to be city-specific rather than size-class specific. High-productivity cities would have to be identified individually, and policy instruments would have to be very discriminatory both within city size classes and among locations (regions). Even if the data base were available to permit identification, political acceptability constraints and balancing regional interests could make implementation almost impossible.

Qutub and Richardson (1986) did attempt to measure the relative efficiencies of alternative urban population distributions, using the level of nonagricultural value added per urban employee as a proxy for urban productivity. The "high-efficiency" population distribution generated 22.1 percent more value added than the "least-cost" distribution (i.e., the distribution of urban population that minimized the sum of intraurban infrastructure and job creation investment costs), 18.0 percent more than the most decentralized settlement pattern (i.e., maximizing the growth rates of small towns), 9.4 percent more than the most centralized pattern, and 14.2 percent more than the "most likely" future trend pattern of urban development. However, there were major limits on the promotion of high-efficiency urban population distributions because these tended to be high-cost in terms of absorbing investment resources. Also, the evidence on the environmental disamenity costs of a spatially concentrated settlement pattern cited above suggests that the efficiency benefits might have to be reduced by a quarter, a third, or even more.

URBAN INVESTMENT COSTS

This finding leads to the consideration of the cost side of the picture, where there has been much more research. The capital costs of urban absorption involve several components: housing and intraurban infrastructure costs; job creation costs; growth management costs (reflecting supply inelasticities and implementation capacity constraints); interurban infrastructure costs (e.g., transportation and communication networks); depreciation and maintenance expenses for urban capital stocks; and the elimination of existing service and infrastructure deficits. UNDP (1985) and Richardson (1987c) present some data on how the first component, housing and intraurban infrastructure costs, varies with city size for Indonesia and Pakistan respectively. In Indonesia, the per capita cost in the urban size classes below 100,000 is less than one-half of that in Jakarta; in Pakistan, per capita costs in the size class below 50,000 are 32.5 percent and in the size class between 50,000 and 250,000 within the range of 37.5 percent to 48.3 percent of those in Karachi. However, regional differentials are often wider than city size differentials: For example, in Egypt per capital shelter and service costs were estimated to be 10.8 times higher in the remote areas than in Cairo and up to 2.4 times higher in Upper Egypt (PADCO, 1982). In Pakistan, on the other hand, costs in Karachi were more than double those among cities of the Punjab, excluding Lahore (Richardson, 1987c), while in Indonesia, costs in Jakarta were 50 percent higher than in the rest of Java but 37.2 percent lower than in Irian Jaya (PADCO-DACREA, 1985). In general, with the exception of primate cities and other very large metropolitan areas, peripheral regions are more costly than core regions and big cities are more costly than small. But because the incidence of small cities is greater in peripheral regions, the city-size effect and the regional differential effect tend to cancel each other, reducing the infrastructure cost savings from alternative, such as decentralized, urban population distributions.

Nevertheless, there have been some attempts to compare the investment costs of alternative settlement patterns. In Indonesia, the cost of a highly centralized, but gradually decentralizing, urban population distribution in terms of both intraurban and interurban infrastructure (plus transmigration) was only 5.3 percent more costly than a rapidly decentralizing alternative (UNDP, 1985). In Pakistan, shelter and service costs per capita were 24.6 percent higher in a centralized scenario (emphasizing the very rapid growth of the largest cities, such as Karachi and Lahore) than in the least-cost population distribution allocation, but they were only 9.7 percent more costly in the more plausible "no trend" scenario (Richardson, 1987c). In Egypt, these costs were almost 50 percent higher in the strategy emphasizing remote areas and multiple growth centers than in the least-cost scenario, but the high-cost remote areas are not typical of most developing countries, and the Egyptian data are distorted by underestimation of the capital costs of population growth in Cairo (PADCO, 1982). Leaving aside the exceptional Egyptian case, the cost savings of a decentralized settlement pattern compared with the trend pattern are very small, within the range of 4.3 percent to 6.4 percent for the three countries, Bangladesh, Indonesia, and Pakistan.

Although the cost savings of alternative urban population distributions appear both small and very similar in percentage terms across countries, this should not be taken to imply that the absolute values of per capita urban absorption costs are more or less the same in each country. Housing and intraurban infrastructure costs may vary widely, largely because of differences in standards of provision, but also because of differences in technology and in construction costs; as a result, per capita costs in Egypt are five times higher than in Bangladesh, more than double the level in Indonesia, and sixty times higher than in Pakistan. Job creation costs depend heavily on the industry mix and the degree of capital intensity; once again, Egypt is very expensive with per capita costs 13.5 times higher than in Bangladesh, more than three times higher than in Pakistan, and more than double the level in Indonesia (Richardson, 1987a). The other components of urban absorption costs tend to be smaller: interurban infrastructure costs may be sizeable, but much depends on the level of development of the national transportation system (in a less developed country such as Bangladesh, they may account for one-third of national urban investment requirements but 15–20 percent is a more typical share); growth management costs tend to be small (2–3 percent of the total) because they become substantial only when a large number of cities in the settlement system grow very rapidly; maintenance costs are very small, perhaps about 2 percent of the urban capital stock; slum upgrading and deficit elimination depend on the level of past urban investments and urban growth rates, but may require heavy investments in countries with major urban service lags.

If housing and intraurban infrastructure costs and job creation costs are the two major items in national urban investment, and if cost savings from alternative urban population distributions are modest, the implication is that sectoral policy decisions, such as a nationwide reduction in urban service standards or the design of a labor-intensive employment strategy, may be more important in economizing on investment than strategies to change the urban settlement pattern. This finding suggests that a successful national urban policy may need to give much more attention to sectoral policies with urban impacts than to the more traditional emphasis on spatial strategies (Richardson, 1987b, elaborates this argument in more detail). Moreover, the goal of easing the pressures of urban absorption per se may be much more important than measures to influence the distribution of urban population. Two policy inferences stand out. Because urban absorption costs per capita are 2.5 to 4 times higher than rural per capita costs, policies to slow down rural-urban migration and promote rural population retention result in major investment economies. The problem is that policies to improve labor absorption in rural areas often focus on areas showing little promise, such as promoting on-farm employment (usually difficult to reconcile with measures to improve agricultural productivity) or rural industrialization rather than on rural public works programs (such as small- or medium-scale irrigation projects or farm-to-market road systems). The other policy inference is the capital-saving potential of policies to reduce fertility. Existing programs suggest that the cost of a birth averted is a tiny fraction, between 0.5 percent and 3.0 percent depending on the local situation, of the average per capita urban absorption cost.

GENERATING THE RESOURCES

Although investment costs and economic growth benefits represent a very narrow evaluation of the costs and benefits of urbanization, they refer to critical elements because the marginal increase in the flow of output associated with each new urban resident may generate enough investment resources to pay for that individual's marginal urban absorption cost. However, analysis of plausible numbers suggests how difficult this is. If marginal urban absorption costs per capita were U.S. $3,750 and rural absorption costs per capita were U.S. $1,250, the net increase in marginal product per worker associated with rural-urban migration would have to generate enough investment resources to bridge the gap of $6,250, assuming a labor participation rate of 40 percent. Assuming that the urban capital stock lasts forever without depreciation and maintenance, a discount rate of 10 percent, and a 25 percent gross domestic investment-GDP ratio, this implies an urban-rural marginal product differential of $2,500 ($6,250 × 0.10/ 0.25). This is impossibly high at current output and income levels in almost all developing countries. It is not surprising, therefore, that a substantial proportion of the urban population will continue to suffer from inadequate housing and urban services even in the long run. This is not necessarily a damning indictment of urbanization, however. Urban absorption costs may be reduced substantially below current levels via reductions in service standards and changes in employment strategy. Deprivation of services in urban areas may nevertheless be much less acute than in rural areas, unless it is argued that the concentration of population at high densities within urban areas severely aggravates the problems resulting from inadequate water supply, poor sanitation, and deficiencies in other urban services. Urban residents may consider that they have enough compensation for urban service deficiencies in higher incomes, even if the income differential is not large enough to finance the investment costs of urban absorption.

If urbanization generates wider economic growth benefits to society as a whole, a more appropriate comparison than the urban-rural marginal product differential with the urban-rural absorption cost may be between the aggregate investment resource pool and the overall capital costs of urbanization. This comparison is a little more optimistic. With appropriate policy adjustments, three out of four countries for which data exist (Egypt, Indonesia, and Bangladesh, but not Pakistan) could generate an urban investment resource pool (i.e., the total resource pool minus allocations for agriculture and rural development, natural resources exploitation, and defense) large enough to cover the burden of urban investment costs (Richardson, 1987a). However, even if this is the case, another problem is the institutional question of whether or not urban-oriented ministries and agencies can muster the budgeting resources to pay for the public sector component of urban development costs. The difficulty is that resolution of this problem usually involves a quantum leap in the share of national development budgetary resources allocated to agencies involved in housing, urban services, and urban job creation. Unfortunately, there are major rigidities inhibiting substantial resource transfers among central government departments and agencies. Because at least one-half of urban investment requirements have to be met by the public sector, this institutional obstacle may be even more severe than the resource generation obstacle.

QUALITATIVE BENEFITS AND COSTS

The focus on the output benefits of alternative urban population distributions is clearly too narrow. Unfortunately, many of the other potential benefits of the spatial distribution component of a national urban policy are very difficult to quantify, especially once the income-per-capita differential measure is discarded because of its mixing of economic benefits with compensation payments. Because of the modest variation among urban (and regional) settlement pattern scenarios in their capital costs in Indonesia, the NUDS report selected a preferred regional population allocation scenario in terms of expected benefits. The preferred scenario was a "balanced" scenario, both sectorally and spatially, emphasizing both industrialization and agriculture, and implying an intermediate pace of decentralization out of Java to the other islands and out of Jakarta to smaller cities. The idea was that desirable policies (selected on macroeconomic and sectoral grounds) would tend to promote an appropriate degree of spatial decentralization, and would aim for consistency between spatial strategies and sectoral policies. These policies included: promotion of diversification in both agriculture and industry, especially with an emphasis on labor-intensive subsectors with high export potential and low import intensity (these are more likely to be located outside Java); reduction of protection for Jakarta-oriented import-substitution industries; elimination of implicit subsidies and policies favoring Jakarta and other large cities; and measures to strengthen the economic base of small urban centers and their rural hinterlands. If these criteria determined the selection of a preferred population distribution strategy rather than its capital costs, and successful implementation of these policies was considered easier with the preferred strategy rather than with some alternative, the expected economic policy gains become in effect the benefits of the strategy. However, in practice, this is not very different from choosing a strategy in terms of economic efficiency or maximizing economic growth benefits. The only differences are a looser, and not rigidly quantified, definition of economic efficiency, the inclusion of economic policy output impacts alongside direct economic growth effects (highly appropriate in a mixed economy), and possibly a longer time horizon over which future benefits are discounted.

In addition to their attempts to measure the nonagricultural output benefits of alternative urbanization patterns, both NUPS (Egypt) and NHSPS (Pakistan) included a broader-based assessment of benefits, using scaling techniques to discriminate among scenarios for a relatively long list of criteria. For example, NHSPS ranked seven alternative urban population distribution scenarios on each of ten criteria (nineteen were used in NUPS), and then summed ranks to obtain a simple benefits score for each scenario. The benefits criteria were: improvement in interregional equity; improvement in interpersonal equity; delivery of services to the urban population; efficiency-cost performance; GNP maximization; availability of financial resources to create jobs; balance of payments impact; ability to achieve target urban growth rates; implementation capacity within cities; and minimizing the risks of exceeding resource constraints. Somewhat surprisingly, the relatively spatially decentralized scenarios tended to score better than the more centralized scenarios. The approach clearly had weaknesses. First, the benefits criteria include more economic factors than alternatives such as political, social, or environmental benefits. Second, assigning equal weights to each criterion is inappropriate (the use of a Delphi panel without feedback resulted in too much variance in the weight distributions chosen by "experts"). Third, in the case of qualitative or ordinal assessments, the question of who does the scoring is critical (researchers, policymakers, or citizens); the NHSPS benefits ranking was carried out by the research project staff and the policymakers, but without citizen participation. Finally, even in cases where monetary quantification is impossible, there are more satisfactory measurement techniques than ranks or simple n-point scale methods. The use of improved qualitative measures is becoming more important with the development of new econometric methods for handling soft data (Bloomestein and Nijkamp, 1983; Nijkamp, 1983).

A broader assessment of costs beyond the capital costs of housing, infrastructure, and job creation is as appropriate as a broader interpretation of benefits beyond output effects. However, estimating these costs is just as difficult. The problem is that alternative urban settlement patterns generate different social costs, but there is little agreement among researchers about how large these costs are or on their incidence. There are at least four dimensions to this problem: first, the identification of the cost items; second, the distribution of these costs between rural and urban areas; third, the distribution of these costs within rural and urban areas among different segments of the population; and fourth, the question of quantification. There is little consensus on any of these issues. Much of the discussion has focused on the effects of rural-urban migration. There is a wide measure of, but not universal, agreement that the private benefits to migrants are positive. Then the agreement stops (Sabot, 1982; Brown and Neuberger, 1977). Consider the two extreme positions. The optimist might argue that any social costs of urbanization are outweighed by higher marginal products in urban areas, urban-induced declines in fertility, continuing urban agglomeration effects, and labor supply impacts dampening inflationary tendencies. Similarly, in the rural areas any social costs associated with out-migration are overwhelmed by the reduction in the agricultural labor surplus, higher agricultural output per capita, and the multiplier effects of urban-rural remittances. Such an optimist rarely attempts to itemize the social costs (e.g., congestion effects in the city, disruption of rural life, and settlement instability in the rural areas), let alone measure them. The economic benefits are considered so dominant that any compensation criteria could be met. The pessimist, on the other hand, tells a different story. In the rural areas, out-migration is so selective in age and skill that rural human resources are severely depleted, capital flows out of the rural areas along with labor, the rural income distribution becomes more unequal, and public service provision declines because of rising costs associated with reductions in scale economies. In the urban areas, in-migration leads to higher unemployment, increasing congestion and pollution, higher marginal costs of housing and public service provision, the risks of political instability, and lower wages (or, at least, smaller increments in income growth).

These perspectives are extremes. The truth probably lies somewhere in between, but not necessarily in the middle. The net effects may differ from case to case. In any event, there are two insuperable obstacles to a determinate outcome, resulting in net assessments based on value judgments more than on the sifting of evidence. The first is that so many identifiable social costs (or benefits) cannot be measured in ways that permit aggregation. The second, a familiar problem in all cost-benefit assessments of public policy intervention, is that all changes in the national settlement pattern, whether spontaneous or policy-induced, involve distributional impacts that are difficult to evaluate even in cases where the policymaker adopts an equity-based preference function. For instance, even focusing on the narrow variable of direct income effects, in-migration may result not only in higher income for the migrants but in income losses for some current urban residents, because of labor supply effects, and income gains for others, especially landowners, because of increasing pressure on land and housing markets. In these circumstances, it may be advisable for policymakers to limit their evaluations to factors that are to some degree under their control, such as the capital cost requirements and the investment resource pool from which these requirements must be drawn.

THE STREAM PROBLEM

A recurrent problem in cost-benefit assessments stems from the fact that costs and benefits are not synchronous. The usual situation is that the cost stream is heavily skewed to the present and the early future, while the benefits stream is skewed towards the medium- or long-term future. This explains why the choice of the discount rate can be so critical. The problem is particularly acute with respect to urbanization, because the phase of rapid urbanization usually precedes the phase of rapid increases in per capita income (usually associated with the direct and indirect effects of industrialization). At GNP per capita levels between U.S. $100 and U.S. $2,000 per annum, the urbanization curve is very steep; above U.S. $2,000, the curve becomes very flat. The kink occurs when the urban population share is about 55 percent, when the urbanization curve is derived from cross-sectional data (Mills and Hamilton, 1984: 383). The policy implications of this finding are very strong. If urban policy goals aim at creating jobs and providing housing and public services for urban residents, the capital costs of urbanization will be required before countries have generated the GNP levels and investment streams needed to pay for these costs. Urban investments will lag, often dramatically, behind needs unless countries are willing to borrow from abroad (from both international and bilateral lenders) to finance urbanization. Unfortunately, easy access to international credit is often treated as a cost-free supplement to domestic investment resources rather than a garnishment of future income streams. As a result, policymakers have not been sensitive enough to the importance of reducing service standards, developing cost-recovery mechanisms, and other policy innovations to hold down urban investment requirements.

CONCLUSIONS

This brief review of the costs and benefits of urbanization in the context of national urban policy, or more generally population distribution policy, discussions suggests several conclusions:

1. It is only feasible to measure these costs and benefits when they are defined very narrowly, such as the capital costs and the output benefits of urbanization.
2. Nevertheless, even this narrow evaluation is useful to policymakers, particularly in capital-constrained developing countries. Common, although not universal, findings are:
    i. The investment requirements of urbanization are substantial, placing a heavy burden on scarce capital resources.
   ii. Gains from changes in the urban settlement system are modest, because city-size effects (capital savings from absorption in small rather than large cities) tend to be offset by interregional effects (capital costs are higher in remote and peripheral regions). Promoting decentralized settlement systems usually implies investing in smaller urban centers located in peripheral regions.
  iii. High urban absorption costs per capita imply that there is a big payoff from successful rural absorption (at 25 to 40 percent of the urban costs) or fertility reduction strategies (0.5 to 3.0 of the urban per capita absorption cost).
   iv. Although the output and productivity increases associated with urbanization may be very substantial, the lags in economic growth benefits may make it difficult to generate the investment resources fast enough to pay for upfront urban investment costs. The results are the need to borrow abroad or major medium-term, or even long-term, urban service deficits.
    v. Even when the growth rate of GNP and the savings rate are high enough to provide an investment resource pool capable of covering urban investment requirements

and other claims on resources (e.g., rural development, defense), there may be institutional and budget allocation barriers in the way of marshalling the public investment component of urban investments.

3. There are other societal benefits associated with urbanization, some of them of a non-economic character. Progress in measuring these has been very slow. It should be possible in the future to achieve more with the development of more satisfactory analytical techniques for soft data and qualitative measures.

4. The analysis of the social costs of urbanization, both in the cities and in rural areas impacted by out-migration, is in a state of disarray because of the lack of consensus among researchers about whether or not these social costs are likely to be greater than social benefits. Once again, the lack of quantification and the impossibility of aggregating individual items are major obstacles to a resolution of the disagreement.

5. These observations suggest that it is difficult to develop a convincing rationale for population distribution policies aimed at changing the urban settlement pattern in favor of generating higher net social benefits. In these circumstances, the recent shift in emphasis in national urban policies away from spatial strategies towards macro and sectoral policies that impact upon urban development is probably appropriate.

REFERENCES

Alonso, W. (1971). "The Economics of Urban Size." *Papers, Regional Science Association* 26: 67–83.

Bloomestein, H., and P. Nijkamp (1983). "Multivariate Methods for Soft Data in Development Planning: A Case Study in Natural Resources." In *Spatial, Environmental and Resource Policy in the Developing Countries*, M. Chatterji, P. Nijkamp, T. R. Lakshmanan and C. R. Pathak, eds. Aldershot, Hampshire: Gower, pp. 343–60.

Brown, A. A., and E. Neuberger, eds. (1977). *Internal Migration: A Comparative Perspective*. New York: Academic Press.

Cameron, G. C., and L. Wingo (1973). *Cities, Regions and Public Policy*. Edinburgh: Oliver and Boyd.

Fogarty, M. S., and G. Garofalo (1980). "Urban Size and the Amenity Structure of Cities." *Journal of Urban Economics* 8: 350–61.

Garn, H. A. (1984). "The National Urban Policy Study for Egypt: An Approach to National Urban Settlement and Investment Strategies." Washington, D.C.: World Bank, mimeo.

Garofalo, G., and M. S. Fogarty (1979). "Estimating the Productivity of Cities: A Merger of the Net Agglomeration and Disamenities Views." Mimeo.

Gilbert, A. G. (1976). "The Arguments for Very Large Cities Reconsidered." *Urban Studies* 13: 27–34.

Kahn, J., and H. Ofek (1987). "City Size, Quality of Life and the Urbanization Deflator of GNP, 1910–84." *Southern Economic Journal*. Forthcoming.

Mera, K. (1973). "On the Urban Agglomeration and Economic Efficiency." *Economic Development and Cultural Change* 21: 309–24.

Mera, K., and H. Shishido (1983). "Cross-Sectional Analysis of Urbanization and Socioeconomic Development in the Developing World." Mimeo.

Mills, E. S., and B. W. Hamilton (1984). *Urban Economics*. Glenview: Scott, Foresman.

Nijkamp, P. (1983). "Qualitative Impact Assessments of Spatial Policies in Developing Countries." *Regional Development Dialogue* 4 (1): 44–62.

UNDP (1985). *National Urban Development Strategy Project: Final Report.* Jakarta.

PADCO (1982). *National Urban Policy Study—Egypt.* 2 vols. Washington, D.C.: PADCO, USAID Grant 263–0042.

PADCO-DACREA (1985). "Analysis of Urban Services, Standards, Technologies and Costs." Jakarta: National Urban Development Strategy Project.

Qutub, S. A., and H. W. Richardson (1986). "The Costs of Urbanization: A Case Study of Pakistan." *Environment and Planning A* 18: 1089–1113.

Richardson, H. W. (1973). *The Economics of Urban Size.* Lexington, Mass.: Lexington Books.

——— (1981). "National Urban Development Strategies in Developing Countries." *Urban Studies* 18: 267–83.

——— (1983). "Population Distribution Policies." *United Nations Population Bulletin* No. 15: 35–49.

——— (1987a). "The Costs of Urbanization: A Four-Country Comparison." *Economic Development and Cultural Change* 35: 561–80.

——— (1987b). "Whither National Urban Policy in Developing Countries?" *Urban Studies* 24: 227–44.

——— (1987c). "Spatial Strategies, the Settlement Pattern, and Shelter and Services Policies." In *Shelter, Settlements and Development,* L. Rodwin, ed. Boston: Allen and Unwin, pp. 207–35.

Sabot, R. H., ed. (1982). *Migration and the Labor Market in Developing Countries.* Boulder, Colo.: Westview Press.

Sveikauskas, L. (1975). "The Productivity of Cities." *Quarterly Journal of Economics* 89: 393–413.

Wheaton, W. C., and H. Shishido (1981). "Urban Concentration, Agglomeration Economies and the Level of Economic Development." *Economic Development and Cultural Change* 30: 17–30.

8

Population Growth and International Migration

GURUSHRI SWAMY

Continued rapid population growth in most developing countries will tend to exacerbate economic disparities between developed and developing countries. Between now and the year 2000, for example, the increase in the number of young adults (aged twenty to forty) in developed countries will be 19 million, less than one-third of what it was during the preceding twenty years. In developing countries the increase will be 600 million, almost one and a half times what it was in the preceding twenty years (Demeny, 1983). The economic implications of these demographic changes are pervasive. First, even with high rates of domestic savings, there are serious constraints on increasing the amount of capital per worker in most developing countries. If all investment in countries like Bangladesh, Ethiopia, Nepal, and Rwanda had been allocated to potential new workers in 1980, for example, each person would have had less than $1,700 invested on his or her behalf. In the United States, investment per worker would have been close to $200,000. Second, even if per capita income grows faster in developing than in industrialized countries, the absolute income gap will not decrease significantly because the initial difference in per capita income is so large for many developing countries. For example, the absolute gap in per capita income between Indonesia and the United States increased from about $8,000 in 1960 to more than $12,000 in 1981, although per capita income in Indonesia grew at a rate almost double that in the United States.

The links that bind developing and industrialized economies could help narrow these disparities and increase income and employment in developing countries in three main ways: through trade, capital flows, and migration. This chapter makes an assessment of one of these links: international migration. It provides an analysis of the dimensions of past and present-day migration, the nature of constraints on free movement of people, and the effects on and costs and benefits to sending and receiving countries.

Table 8.1
Gross Permanent Immigration as a Percentage of Total Population Growth

Period	United States	Canada	Australia and New Zealand	Latin America
1851–1880	29.3	42.4	20.0	9.3
1881–1910	43.1	106.3 a/	80.7	22.1
1911–1940	23.4	59.6	52.4	10.9
1941–1960	8.0	36.2	58.0 b/	3.2 b/
1961–1980	16.61	47.1	56.5	n.a.

a/ Population growth less than immigration because of
    out-migration.
b/ Immigration from Europe only, 1946–55:

Source: Swamy, 1985.

HISTORICAL AND PRESENT DIMENSIONS OF INTERNATIONAL MIGRATION

International migration motivated by economic disparities has been a feature of the international economy for centuries. Present-day migration takes several forms. Some migrants move with their families to stay more or less permanently in their new country. Others are temporary workers who are allowed to stay only for a limited time and usually leave their dependents behind. For many countries, illegal migration is significant; such migrants include those who enter a country illegally and those who enter legally but stay beyond the permitted length of stay.

Permanent Migration and Population Growth

The nineteenth and early twentieth centuries witnessed permanent intercontinental migration on an unprecedented scale. About 50 million people left Europe for Australia, Canada, Latin America, the United States, and New Zealand. Gross immigration accounted for more than 30 percent of the population increase in the United States between 1850 and 1940, about 60 percent in Canada, 51 percent in Australia and New Zealand, and about 15 percent in Latin America (Table 8.1). This same period also witnessed emigration from the northern hemisphere to the south as colonization spread and labor movements from Asia increased, fostered by the system of indentured labor. About 8 million Chinese and over 3 million Indians, for example, are estimated to have gone to other parts of Asia and overseas between the mid-nineteenth century and World War I (Zolbert, 1983: 22), and immigrants accounted for more than 50 percent of the increase in Sri Lanka's population between 1880 and 1910 (Clark, 1954: 118).

Table 8.2
Permanent Emigration as a Percentage of Increase in Population of Emigrants' Countries

Period	Europe	Asia a/	Africa a/	Latin America
1851–1880	11.7	0.4	0.01	0.3
1881–1910	19.5	0.3	0.04	0.9
1911–1940	1.4	0.1	0.03	1.8
1940–1960	2.7 b/	0.1	0.01	1.0
1960–1970	5.2	0.2	0.10	1.9
1970 1980	4.0	0.5	0.30	2.5

Note: Numbers are calculated from data on gross immigration
        in Australia, Canada, New Zealand, and the United
        States.

a/   The periods from 1850 to 1960 pertain to emigration only
     to the United States.
b/   Emigration only to the United States.

Source: Swamy, 1985.

The impact of emigration on population growth in the sending countries was no less dramatic (Table 8.2). Emigration from Europe between 1851 and 1940 amounted to more than 15 percent of the increase in population, peaking at nearly 20 percent during the period from 1881 to 1910. For particular countries the rate was higher: nearly 45 percent of the increase in population of the British Isles during the period from 1846 to 1932 emigrated (more than 50 percent of the mid-period·population), and between 30 percent and 40 percent of the increase in population in Italy, Portugal, and Spain emigrated (Woytinsky and Woytinsky, 1953: Table 33).

In contrast to these numbers, the scale of present day permanent migration is small. Between 1960 and 1980, the United States received 7.8 million immigrants, while Australia, Canada, and New Zealand together admitted 5.7 million people (United Nations, 1983). The contribution of gross immigration to population growth in the host countries remained high because of low rates of natural increase—16 percent in the United States and much more in Canada and Oceania—but the impact on population growth in the sending countries was much reduced. Between 1970 and 1980, emigration to the major immigration countries absorbed only about 3 percent of the population growth in Europe and Latin America and less than 1 percent in Asia and Africa. Although emigration rates continued to be high for a few relatively high-income countries or those in close proximity to the United States, the rate was only 0.2 percent for India.

These figures point to one clear conclusion: permanent emigration has only a limited role to play in reducing the work force in the developing countries as a group. To take a simple example, even if 700,000 immigrants a year are admitted by the major host countries (roughly the number admitted annually during the period from 1976 to 1980) up to the year 2000, and all of them come from low-income countries, less than 2 percent of the projected growth in population in the low-income countries between 1982 and 2000 would have emigrated. By contrast, such immigration would account for 22 percent of the projected natural increase in population of the industrialized market economies and 36 percent of the projected increase in the main host countries: Australia, Canada, New Zealand, and the United States.

Temporary Worker Migration and Labor Force

Recent years have seen a marked increase in temporary migration. In Europe, beginning in the 1960s, large numbers of foreign workers were recruited by France, Germany, Switzerland, and others from the poorer neighbors like Greece, Italy, Portugal, Spain, Turkey, and Yugoslavia. By 1974, temporary foreign workers constituted 30 percent of the work force in Luxembourg, over 18 percent in Switzerland and about 8 percent in Belgium, France, and Germany (Swamy, 1981). Large-scale recruitment in the oil-rich countries of the Middle East led to even higher proportions of foreign workers. In Kuwait, Libya, Oman, Qatar, Saudi Arabia, and United Arab Emirates, foreign workers from the neighboring Arab states and from Asian countries constituted from 44 percent (Saudi Arabia) to about 89 percent (United Arab Emirates) of the work force in the early 1980s (Nagi, 1986: Table 3.1). Other countries have also admitted temporary workers on a systematic basis. During 1978, for example, the United States admitted 62,000 temporary workers, including a large proportion of professionally and technically qualified people and agricultural laborers, from the West Indies. Ghana and the Ivory Coast had about one million foreign workers in 1975, mostly from Mali, Togo, and Upper Volta (Zachariah and Conde, 1981: Table 34), while one estimate puts the number of migrant workers in Argentina (mainly from Bolivia and Paraguay) and Venezuela (mainly from Colombia) at about 2 million (ILO, 1984: Table 4.2).

The number of temporary migrant workers in Europe peaked at 6.5 million in 1974 and declined to 6.2 million in 1980. In the Middle East, foreign workers have increased from an estimated 1.8 million in 1975 to about 3 million in 1980. The total number of temporary workers—in Europe, the Middle East, South Africa, and West Africa—is probably about 13 million to 15 million.

But as is the case with permanent emigration, temporary emigrant workers constitute only a small proportion of the labor force in all developing countries although, undoubtedly, emigration is very important for a few (see Table 8.3).

Illegal Migration

By definition, it is hard to count the number of immigrants who are in a country illegally. However, the best estimates indicate that illegal migration is

Table 8.3
Emigrant Labor (legal only) as a Proportion of the Labor Force in the Emigrant Country

Country	Year	Proportion
Bangladesh	1979–80	*
India	1980	*
Pakistan	1979–80	6.0
Egypt	1980	9.0
People's Democratic Republic of Yemen	1980	34.0
Yemen Arab Republic	1981	39.0
Sudan	1975	*
Syria	1975	2.0 a/
Tunisia	1975	2.0 a/
Jordan	1975	40.2 a/
Botswana	1979	8.0
Lesotho	1978	40.0
Greece	1980	4.5
Italy	1980	4.0
Portugal	1980	11.0
Spain	1980	2.5
Turkey	1980	4.5
Yugoslavia	1980	6.0

a/   As a percentage of employed work force.
*   Less than 1 percent as a percentage of employed work force.
Source: Swamy, 1985.

often heavy. For example, between 2 million and 4 million immigrants were living illegally in the United States in 1980, half of them from Mexico (Warren and Passel, 1983). They may have constituted about 4 to 8 percent of the Mexican labor force. When the authorities in Venezuela tried to register all immigrants in 1980, they were able to identify about 270,000 illegal aliens, over 90 percent of them from Colombia. Other notable poles of illegal immigration include Hong Kong and Italy, where there may have been as many as half a million illegal workers in 1979 (United Nations, 1983).

DETERMINANTS OF MIGRATION

The basic incentive to migrate is the earnings gap between the sending and host countries. The major constraint is the immigration policy of the host country. Host countries exercise considerable (though not complete) control over the number of foreigners they admit and, in the case of temporary workers, the kind of work the foreigners do and the length of their stay. Given this overall constraint, the nationality composition of migrants is then determined by factors such as relative income differentials, distance, and cultural proximity, as well as by the sending country governments' promotional efforts.

Some Economic and Social Determinants of Immigration Policies

Immigration policies of host countries have varied over time in response to changing economic conditions, the relative bargaining strength of those who gain (employers and sometimes consumers) and those who lose (native workers) from immigration, and the social pressures that are generated by an influx of foreigners. In general, there is more resistance when the substitutability of foreign for domestic workers is high; immigration can then cause a large decline in natives' wages or, if their wages are inflexible, to an increase in their unemployment. On the other hand, buoyant economic growth characterized by large shifts in demand for labor are conducive to larger immigration, because the added supply of labor may not prevent wages from rising at a rate that the native population has been accustomed to. In all situations, however, there are constraints on social integration and assimilation; they tend to be more severe in homogeneous societies, particularly as immigrants increase as a proportion of the population and receive increasing attention and public resources.

Two studies throw some light on the economic determinants of immigration policies. One is a study of the imposition of the U.S. immigration quotas in the 1920s (Williamson, 1982). Using a general equilibrium framework, the author shows that the rise in pronativist sentiment that led to the quotas can be related to a sharp decline in America's ability to absorb immigrants. The economy-wide unskilled labor demand elasticity declined sharply between 1900 and 1929 from -3.25 to -1.6. This implied that, while in 1900 a 1 percent per annum increase in unskilled labor (as through immigration) would have caused the real unskilled wage to decline by 0.31 percent, in 1929 it would have led to a decline of 0.63 percent. Further, the derived demand for unskilled labor grew only slowly as growth of farmlands declined and biased technological change (favoring capital and skill) intensified the effect of a somewhat slower growth in capital stock.

A study (Goldfarb, 1982) of the more recent experience of physician immigration into the United States shows further that when there is a sudden increase in demand for particular skills in short supply domestically, immigration rules are eased, only to be tightened up when the scarcity declines. While there are no previously established immigration quotas (within an overall ceiling) for particular occupations or skill categories, the U.S. system has nevertheless been made to respond to shortages and surpluses of particular kinds of professionals. In 1965, the U.S. Department of Labor declared a physician shortage as the demand for medical services increased—the result of an increase in the so-called third-party payments, including public reimbursements for medical expenditures of the poor and elderly. This meant that foreign-trained medical practitioners could more readily obtain certification for permanent immigrant status. In 1970, an amendment allowed certain categories of temporary (exchange) visitors to convert to immigrant status without returning to country of origin as was previously required. As a result, the share of physicians (and related workers) in professional immigration increased sharply from 12 percent in 1969 to 25 percent in 1973. Simultaneously, medical training facilities and the output of medical graduates increased, from 7,400 in 1965 to more than 10,000 in 1973, and the number of first year medical students from 8,772 in 1963–64 to 16,000 in 1977–78. As the scarcity eased, the share of physicians in professional migration declined to 11 percent in 1979.

In the Middle East, labor importation was clearly linked to oil-related income growth and to the fact that migrant labor—largely in the construction and service sectors—did not compete with domestic labor. The determinants of the use of short-term migrants in Europe appear to be more complex. Here too, the guest worker programs coincided with rapid economic growth. In addition, it has been hypothesized (Bhagwati et al., 1984), though not fully substantiated by econometric analysis, that host country governments encouraged the use of low-cost migrant labor in industries that were losing comparative advantage. For example, foreign workers in the textile industry in Germany doubled in the late 1960s although total employment declined, and the proportion of foreign workers in the industry went up by 13 percentage points at the same time that effective protection declined.

Thus, economic factors have been shown to influence immigration policies in a number of situations. But while economic conditions vary, social resistance to immigration increases over time. The experience of the United States subsequent to the first quotas and that of Western Europe since the mid–1970s illustrates this. The U.S. immigration laws have been modified since the 1920s in several important ways, but it is worth noting that the scale of current migration is not very different from that envisioned in the 1920s, although the 1950s and 1960s were clearly more buoyant. According to the Williamson study, the annual increase in derived demand for (unskilled) labor during the period from 1948 to 1966 was nearly five times as high as in the earlier decades of the century. Another study finds that in 1970 a 1 percent increase in the number of foreign workers would have led to about 0.1 percent decline in real wages of native workers (Grossman, 1982), compared to 0.63 percent in 1929. In Western Europe most host countries began to impose restrictions on recruitment of workers in the early 1970s. Switzerland attempted to "stabilize" its migrant labor force in spring 1971, and then introduced measures to reduce it in July 1973; France, Holland, and West Germany introduced restrictions on new entrants in 1972 and 1973, culminating at the end of 1973 in a ban by the latter two countries on the entry of non-EEC (European Economic Community) workers (Paine, 1971: 1). Although these restrictions are attributed to the recession following the oil crisis, the timing of the beginning of these restrictions suggests that the social and political problems of managing a system of temporary recruitment were beginning to be felt much earlier. There had been a "maturing" of the migrant population, that is, migration had taken on a circulatory character as the same workers returned and the length of stay increased; many migrants acquired permanency status; and the age-sex composition of the migrant population began to parallel normal profiles (Swamy, 1981). The oil crisis appears to have precipitated a sharp turn in policy that would have occurred anyway. In fact, most Western European countries recovered rapidly in 1976–79; but restrictions on foreign workers did not ease.

Problems with social integration become particularly evident at the community level. There are neighborhoods in the United States and Europe where adults are predominantly first-generation immigrants (40 percent of France's 4 million foreigners live around Paris, for example). Such concentration creates stress: voters in a county in Florida in the U.S., for example, reversed an earlier policy of bilingualism in schools (Davis et al., 1983: 21). Even in the most liberal of environments, social integration is slow and delicate. As immigrants increase as a proportion of the population, they receive increasing attention and public resources. In the long run, these factors may be more important in limiting immigration than purely economic ones.

The Supply Response

Although the scale of migration is largely determined by host country policies, several questions arise regarding the supply response: what factors determine the supply from different countries, who migrates from a country, and can the government of the sending country successfully promote emigration?

As may be expected, there is a tendency, particularly evident in temporary migration, for lower-wage countries in the neighborhood of a host country to supply labor because shorter distances ease the flow of information and minimize financial and psychic costs. Host countries may for the same reasons prefer certain nationalities. Because host and sending country preferences thus often coincide, and further because migration data record actual rather than intended migration, it is difficult to empirically separate the pure supply response. Robert E. B. Lucas in three studies has managed to overcome this problem to show the importance of relative wages as well as other complementary factors in determining the intercountry pattern of supply. In a study of the nationality pattern of applications for labor certification in the United States, the ability to speak English was shown to be a significant influence along with wage differentials (Lucas, 1976). In a study of the supply of nonwhite labor to the South African mines before 1974, when mining houses had no preference for any particular source, a supply elasticity of 0.14 was estimated. Further, successful harvests or ample rainfall were found to significantly reduce the incidence of mine work, while population growth increased it (Lucas 1983a, 1983b). A study of the German guestworker program (during a period of relatively free migration) estimated that the share of incremental inflow of workers from each of the five major source countries was positively related to growth of population and negatively to wage levels in the sending countries (Bhagwati et al., 1984). Accordingly, between the mid–1960s and mid–1970s, the nationality composition of foreign workers changed in favor of the relatively poorer "new" exporters: the share of Turkey and Yugoslavia increased by 10 percentage points while the proportion of Greeks declined by 7 percentage points. In the Middle East, as well, there was a remarkable change in the nationality composition of migrant workers. The proportion of non-Arab workers increased from 12 percent to 18 percent (Choucri, 1983: 3–4), at least partly because Asian workers accepted lower wages and living conditions.

An important question in this context is whether the government of a labor exporter can increase its share of the migrant labor force by increasing the flow of information, by actively participating in the recruitment process, and by responding in a flexible way to host countries' demands. Unfortunately, although many labor exporters in Asia have attempted to do so, there has been no systematic study of the impact of such efforts. An acknowledged success story in the Middle East context is the package approach that Koreans adopted. Korean workers were hired by Korean firms that had a building or service contract in the host country. These workers were typically housed separately from the local population, and as much as 75 percent of wages was paid directly to the workers' families in Korea. By the end of 1980, nearly all Korean workers in the Middle East were employed by Korean companies, their number had increased dramatically, and the value of construction contracts had risen to $13 billion (Kim, 1986). The Korean approach appears to be unique. Less successful have been the state-operated recruitment agencies; in Bangladesh and Pakistan, for example, only a quarter to a third of all migrants had been placed through a state agency; 60 to 75 percent had found jobs through their own efforts and the assistance of friends and relatives (Swamy, 1985). Governments have also tried to regulate the operations of private recruiting agents to prevent exploitation. Unfortunately, such attempts often misfire, since one country's efforts to improve the situation of their workers abroad can lead to utilization of more labor from a less demanding neighbor.

There has been little by way of econometric analysis of migrants' characteristics, but data collected in surveys (generally of temporary workers) provide some description of economic and personal characteristics (see Swamy, 1985, for details and references). The financial costs of migration can be large and a major deterrent to emigration. These costs include the cost of passage (when employers do not pay for passage), minimum amounts of foreign exchange that migrants may be required or want to carry, payment for various documents, and, quite often, payments under the counter. Scattered evidence shows that these costs may be 50 to 100 percent of income before departure. Borrowing from friends and relatives is quite common. Surveys indicate that 40 percent of workers from Pakistan, 30 to 80 percent from India, and 25 percent from the Philippines had borrowed money to finance migration. Migration is thus difficult for the poor or unemployed, suggesting that migrants may not typically come from the lowest income groups or from the ranks of the unemployed. The few surveys that record employment status before departure show that open unemployment before migration was in fact low to moderate—4 percent in Turkey in 1971, 7 percent in Pakistan, 9 percent in the Philippines and about 12 percent in Bangladesh in the late 1970s. Larger proportions, particularly in rural areas, may have been underemployed in the sense of low productivity or few hours of work, but this is not possible to establish.

Migrant workers tend to be young adult males and married. Surveys indicate further that the majority of temporary workers are better educated than the general population, although not very highly educated (that is, not beyond secondary school). The proportion of women in migrant populations is generally small but increases as migration continues. In Germany, for example, the proportion of women in the foreign population increased for every nationality in the 1960s (by 13 to 21 percentage points), and in Ghana the number of males per 100 females among lifetime immigrants declined from 175 to 152. These changes reflect the settling of migrant populations as men establish themselves and send for their wives, often so that they can both work.

EFFECTS OF MIGRATION

Migrant workers earn substantially more than they would have at home. A few examples illustrate this. In 1971, on average, a Turkish worker in Germany earned four times as much as he did before departure (Paine, 1974). More recent information on Middle Eastern migration shows that Filipino workers in the production and construction sectors earned about six times as much, while clerical and professional personnel earned nearly seven times as much (Smart et al., 1986). A survey of 200 Bangladeshi returned migrants showed that even an unskilled worker earned, in the late 1970s, nearly ten times as much as he did before departure, while technicians and professionals earned more than ten times as much (Ali et al., 1981).

The average propensity to save is high. Surveys indicate that between 47 and 70 percent of income is saved (Swamy, 1985). The propensity to remit is high in the initial period of migration, particularly if migrants' families have been left behind, but declines over time. Thus workers in the Middle East remitted 50 percent to 80 percent of their income, while Turkish workers in 1971 remitted only 11 percent, a reflection of their longer stay and more settled circumstances. Earlier work by this author analyzing remittances of migrant workers in Europe (Swamy, 1981) showed, for example, that the greater the ratio of women to men in the migrant population, the lower is the per capita remittance, once the effect of income is controlled for.

EFFECTS OF REMITTANCES ON FAMILY EXPENDITURES

There are a number of studies that give information on how remittances affect expenditures and savings. The central questions are three: (a) what are the expenditure and saving patterns of migrant households, (b) do these patterns differ distinctly from those of nonmigrant households, and (c) do these differences conform to what may be expected from any increase in income. The first two questions are of interest to policymakers, who may be interested in altering spending and savings patterns of migrants or in understanding the impact of remittances on the economy. The last question is important because many argue that the benefits of remittances are reduced because the remittances are spent in socially unproductive ways, a criticism rarely made when income increases in other ways.

The effects of remittances on family expenditures and welfare are quite significant. They are best brought out by either comparing migrant family expenditures with those of nonmigrants (after matching for pre-emigration status) or by comparing pre-emigration and post-emigration expenditure patterns of migrants. Studies of this kind generally show a marked increase in consumption expenditures, including educational expenditures, although the proportion of income spent falls as may be expected. A Philippine survey, for example, showed that household expenditures more than doubled after migration, but the proportion of income spent declined from an average of 92 percent of income before migration to 33 percent after migration (Smart et al., 1986). An exception was found in a Bangladeshi study (Ali et al., 1981), which found no significant difference in the level or composition of consumption expenditures between migrant and nonmigrant households, nor a significant difference in the amounts spent on recreation, festivals, and ceremonies. Migrant households have a pronounced preference for investing in housing, land, and new construction. Higher proportions of migrant households in the Bangladeshi study invested in land (30 percent more in rural areas) and new construction (25 percent more in urban areas and 19 percent more in rural areas). Other surveys of migrant workers and case studies have reiterated this finding (Swamy, 1985; Arnold and Shah, 1986). Interestingly, only 11 percent of workers in the Philippine survey referred to above had acquired a house after emigration, reflecting perhaps the high price of real estate around Manila, from where the bulk of migrant workers had emigrated.

Data on the extent to which households invest in financial assets and industrial and commercial ventures are generally lacking. Three studies suggest that such investments may not be insignificant. The Philippine survey referred to above compared pre- and post-migration savings and expenditure patterns and found cash savings to be an important form of saving for migrant households. The proportion of households having cash savings increased from one-fourth to three-fourths after emigration, and the value exceeded the value of property investment. While about 30 percent reported owing a debt before departure, only 10 percent did after departure and the average value of debt declined by 30 percent. In Turkey, a substantial proportion of workers (almost equal to the proportion who bought houses or building plots) put savings into work ventures in agriculture, small commerce, and industry (Paine, 1974). An econometric analysis of miner migration to South Africa estimated indirectly that investment out of wage income made a significant contribution to increased productivity of crops and increased the size of cattle herds (Lucas, 1983b).

Since temporary migration generally means that men are away for long periods of time, there has been some interest in understanding the effects of male migration on women. In general, women seem to take more responsibility for decisions affecting children and in financial matters. A question of particular interest is whether female involvement in economic decision making and labor-force participation increases. On this the evidence is mixed. An indicator that may be examined as a "decision" variable is the use of different agricultural inputs and techniques. Analysis of data from Botswana shows that female-headed households not associated with any males used little or no modern inputs in crop cultivation, compared to 13 percent of male-headed households, which did. A higher proportion of female-headed households not associated with males, however, did adopt superior techniques of animal husbandry (Kerven, 1982: 586–9). And there was no evidence that investment in cattle or crop-production was affected by the sex of the head of the household (Lucas, 1982).

MACROECONOMIC EFFECTS OF EMIGRATION AND REMITTANCES

Important macroeconomic effects flow from the two related phenomena: departure of working-age people and inflow of remittances. In the first round, emigration affects labor market variables—the availability and cost of different kinds of labor and wage differentials—while remittances increase demand for and prices of goods, services, and assets. The first-round effects are felt most sharply in the short run, when the supply of labor and techniques of production are relatively fixed. Production and efficiency in particular sectors may suffer, especially in situations of relatively full employment of skilled workers, because vacancies are not quickly filled and complementarities between migrant and nonmigrant labor reduce production by more than the migrant's contribution. Further, the prices of commodities and assets that are in inelastic supply—land and housing, for instance—may increase sharply. Second-round effects are more complex and involve responses of households and producers to changed labor-market conditions and to increases in demand for goods and services. Participation rates may rise or fall, additional skills may be acquired, and the supply of goods may increase either domestically or through imports. Institutional factors, market imperfections, and government policies may modify these responses; poor labor mobility, for example, may accentuate wage increases in one region or sector but prevent the transmission of wage increases to other sectors and regions, and supply barriers (on housing and construction) may prevent increases in supply. While effects of migration and remittances can thus be complex, a review of consequences is limited not as much by the lack of a theoretical framework as the lack of data and systematic study. The empirical literature is extremely fragmented: While one study looks at wage effects, another looks at land prices.

Data, to the extent available and analyzed (Swamy, 1985, and references therein), do show that migration has resulted in sharp increases in real wages:

Table 8.4
Workers' Remittances [a] and Export Earnings, 1980

	Remittances (million U.S. dollars)	Proportion of exports (percentage)	Proportion of GNP (percentage)
Yugoslavia	3968	45.1	6.9
Greece	1095	27.3	2.7
Turkey	2029	71.1	3.2
Portugal	2903	64.6	12.7
Spain			
Egypt	2640	70.0	10.3
Yemen, P.D.R.	345	590.0	41.7
Yemen, A.R.	1230	n.a. [b]	40.2
Pakistan	1997	79.0	7.6
Bangladesh	281	36.0	2.5
Lesotho	270	460.0	42.0
Burkina Faso (1979)	108	83.0	11.2
Botswana	67	12.5	7.5

a/ Defined as Labor Income plus Workers' Remittances.
b/ Exports were only $12.4 million.

Source: Swamy 1985.

In some instances, however, remittances have led directly to higher

imports, often because of government schemes that provide special import

15 percent per annum and 6 percent per annum in construction wages in Pakistan and Egypt in the late 1970s and nearly 35 percent per annum in agricultural wages in the Yemen Arab Republic are examples. In Pakistan and Turkey, real wages of unskilled workers increased faster than those of skilled workers. On the other hand, survey data from Turkey and Bangladesh also show that workers having specialized skills—machinery operators in Turkey, medical specialists in Bangladesh—are difficult to replace, while less skilled workers are quite easily replaced.

Whether emigration leads to a decline in (or lower rate of growth of) production in the short run is almost impossible to assess because of lack of data. Construction sector output does seem to have increased substantially in most of these and other countries, partly because of remittances. Some case studies in Mexico have shown that in rural areas land is left uncultivated after emigration despite increased land acquisition (Richert, as reported in Weiner, 1983) while others have reported that agricultural production was not depressed. In the Yemen Arab Republic, higher wages of agricultural labor and increased demand for superior cereals coupled with investment in irrigation (financed partly through remittances) brought about significant changes in area and production—away from low-value cereals towards higher-value crops such as fruits and vegetables (Swamy, 1985).

Remittances are an important source of foreign exchange for a number of labor exporters, constituting 45 to 80 percent of export earnings for such countries as Portugal, Yemen Arab Republic, Pakistan, and Yugoslavia (Table 8.4).

In some instances, however, remittances have led directly to higher imports, often because of government schemes that provide special import facilities for migrant workers. In Turkey, the government introduced a special scheme whereby workers could import goods without prior allocation of foreign exchange. Such imports accounted for 12 to 16 percent of remittances into Turkey in the late 1970s (Paine, 1974: 135–6). In Bangladesh, a wage-earners scheme allowed migrant workers either to import goods directly or to sell foreign exchange to private importers. Workers' direct imports amounted to 19 percent of recorded remittances (Ali et al., 1981: 334–5).

As mentioned earlier, a comprehensive approach to analyzing effects of migration and remittances has been generally lacking. But one study (Choucri and Lahiri, 1983), using a macroeconomic model for Egypt, simulated that a doubling of remittances would lead to a 2 percent increase in construction sector prices. This unexpectedly small increase occurs because in this short-run model, wages were assumed to be fixed even in the construction sector, which experienced large-scale emigration.

COSTS AND BENEFITS TO SENDING COUNTRIES

The estimation of costs and benefits runs into a host of conceptual and data problems. A central question is that of whose benefits should be considered. If emigration is permanent, the group whose welfare should be considered is rightly the "domestic" population. If migration is temporary, a "national" perspective, including the welfare of migrants, may be more relevant. But since migrants are generally better off, the more immediate concern may nevertheless be with the rest of the population, that is, the domestic population. A second issue is the conceptualization of benefits and costs. Those who think of development as a matter of capital accumulation and industrialization view migration as drawing off surplus labor and stimulating technological change. Those who are concerned with distribution, local development, and social impact are quick to point out the costs: sectoral and regional imbalances, loss of skills, conspicuous consumption, and so on. A third issue is the question of how to measure costs of training, replacement, loss of production, and social externalities. Should the costs of training include the full "sunk" costs of bringing up and educating children, or should it include only public spending? How does one empirically measure the social costs of skilled emigration?

Estimating net benefits of emigration is thus a tricky business, and few if any attempts have been made to account for all the effects. Cost-benefit evaluation has generally concentrated on particular kinds of migrants; the emigration of each kind is then viewed as a "project" to be subjected to cost-benefit criteria.

Within this partial framework, case studies have shown that net benefits are likely to be higher when emigration involves unskilled, unemployed, or underemployed workers, since there is little loss of output or investment in human capital and propensities to remit are high. Using fairly detailed data on skill

Table 8.5
Skill Composition of Temporary Migration

Receiving regions/countries

Sending countries Skill categories	Middle East Temporary Workers							Germany Temporary manual workers Southern Europe & Turkey 1972	France Temporary manual workers Turkey 1968	United States Temporary Workers a/ The World 1978
	Egypt 1975	Jordan 1975	Bangladesh late 1970s	Pakistan 1975	Yemen AR 1975	Sudan 1975	India 1979			
Professional and technical	18.1	48.5	8.0	11.9	0.6	35.6	6.1	n.a	n.a	45.0
Skilled	9.7	15.7	48.9	33.2	2.9	10.7	45.0	23.0	22.0	10.7 b/
Semi-skilled	18.0	6.4	10.5	15.8	3.0	16.0		46.0	37.0	
Unskilled	54.2	29.4	32.6	39.1	93.5	37.7	48.9	31.0	41.0	44.3
Total	100.0	100.0	100.0	100.0	100.0	100.0	100.0	100.0	100.0	100.0

Note: The skill categories are not strictly comparable across regions because of different definitions and data limitations. In general, the categories indicate declining levels of training. For the United States, the first row refers to workers classified as professional, technical and kindred, and the last row includes service workers and laborers including those admitted under special programs.

a/ Includes workers of distinguished merit, and other workers including those admitted under special programs.
b/ Skilled and unskilled.

Source: Swamy 1985.

distribution and remittance flows and assigning distributional weights to consumption, a study of Bangladeshi emigration found that the benefit-cost ratio was about 3 for skilled and unskilled workers and 1.8 for professionals (Ali et al., 1981). Using a slightly different methodology, a study (Gilani et al., 1981) of Pakistani emigration found that the ratio was 1.74 for unskilled labor and 1.1 for professionals—results similar in pattern to those obtained in the Bangladeshi study. The larger the proportion of unskilled workers in the migrant labor force, therefore, the more likely it is that emigration results in positive benefits.

Available information on skill composition of temporary workers in the Middle East, Europe, and the United States shows that a substantial proportion of such workers were unskilled, ranging from 30 to 50 percent in Bangladesh, Pakistan, and India to 90 percent in the Yemen Arab Republic (Table 8.5). However, with a few exceptions, the share of the unskilled was not overwhelming. Data on permanent immigration into the United States also shows that for many developing countries, professional emigration is significant. Between 1969 and 1979, the United States admitted about half a million professional and technical workers— 75 percent of them from developing countries, nearly 50 percent from Asia. They accounted for nearly 30 percent of the rise in the employment of physicians, 12 percent of the increase in the employment of engineers, and 8 percent of the increase in employment of scientists in the United States. On the sending country side, some developing countries have experienced a heavy brain drain. During the 1970s, emigration of professionals from the Philippines to the United States constituted 12.3 percent of the increase in their number at home; for Korea the figure was 10 percent, for Egypt and India about 1 to 2 percent each (Swamy, 1985).

Social externalities, and the higher (public) costs of professional education reduce the net benefits from skilled and professional migration. In addition, the possibility of migration results in "demonstration" effects which raise salaries and prevent professionals from moving to backward areas in the sending country. It has been argued, therefore, that a country experiencing significant professional emigration should charge its trainees the full costs of education or explicitly tax foreign-earned income (Bhagwati, 1976). A tax is seen as particularly equitable since most long-term emigrants remain citizens of their home countries and immigration quotas confer on them a rent which should be appropriated by the sending country. How much would such a tax yield? If it is assumed that the bulk of all professional immigrants admitted to the United States during the period from 1966 to 1979 were still there in 1979, and that within each major occupation, their pre-tax earnings matched average earnings of Americans, their total earnings would have been about $600 million in 1979. A 10 percent tax would have yielded an amount equivalent to about 13 percent of the Official Development Assistance from the United States in that year (Swamy, 1985).

REFERENCES

Ali, S. A., A. A. Arif, A. K. Habibullah, A. R. M. Hossain, R. Islam, W. Mahmud, S. R. Osmani, Q. M. Rahman, and Amah Siddiqi (1981). *Labor Migration from Bangladesh to the Middle East*. World Bank Staff Working Paper No. 454.

Arnold F. and Shah N. M., eds. (1986). *Asian Labor Migration: Pipeline to the Middle East*. Boulder, Colo.: Westview.

Bhagwati, J. N., ed. (1976). *The Brain Drain and Taxation: Theory and Empirical Analysis*. Amsterdam: North-Holland.

Bhagwati, J. N., K. W. Schatz, and K. Wong (1984). "The West German Gastarbeiter System of Immigration." Unpublished paper (April), Harvard Migration Seminars, Cambridge, Mass.

Choucri, N. (1983). *Asians In the Arab World: Labor Migration and Public Policy*. Technology Adaptation Program. Cambridge, Mass.: Mass. Institute of Technology.

Choucri, N. and S. Lahiri (1983). *Short-Run Energy-Economy Interactions in Egypt*. Technology Adaptation Program. Cambridge Mass.: Mass. Institute of Technology.

Clark, Colin (1954). *Population Growth and Land Use*. London: Macmillan.

Davis, C., C. Haub, and J. Willette (1983). *U.S. Hispanics: Changing the Face of America*. Population Reference Bureau, Washington, D.C. (June).

Demeny, P. (1983). "Can World Population Forecasts Come True?" Population Council Notes, Washington, D.C.

Gilani, I., M. F. Khan, and M. Iqbal (1981). "Labor Migration from Pakistan to the Middle East and Its Impact on the Domestic Economy." World Bank Report (June/July), South Asia Country Programs Department, Washington, D.C.

Goldfarb, R. S. (1982). "Occupational Preferences in the U.S. Immigration Law: An Economic Analysis." In *The Gateway—U.S. Immigration Issues and Policies*. Chiswick, B. R., ed. Washington, D.C.: American Enterprise Institute for Public Policy Research.

Grossman, J. B. (1982). "The Substitutability of Natives and Immigrants in Production." *Review of Economics and Statistics* 64: 231–38.

ILO (1984). *World Labor Report*. Geneva.

Kerven, C. (1982). "The Effects of Migration on Agricultural Production." In *Migration in Botswana: Patterns, Causes, and Consequences*. Final Report of the National Migration study, Vol. 3, Central Statistics Office, Republic of Botswana, Gaborone.

Kim, S. (1986). "Labor Migration from Korea to the Middle East: Its Trend and Impact on the Korean Economy." In *Asian Labor Migration*, F. Arnold and N. M. Shah, eds. Boulder, Colo.: Westview.

Lucas, Robert E. B. (1976). "The Supply of Immigrants Function and Taxation of Immigrants' Incomes: An Econometric Analysis." In *Brain Drain and Taxation: Theory and Empirical Analysis*, J. N. Bhagwati, ed. Amsterdam: North-Holland.

———— (1982). "Outmigration, Remittances and Investment in Rural Areas." In *Migration In Botswana: Patterns, Causes and Consequences*. Final Report of the National Migration Study, vol. 3.

———— (1983a). "Mines and Migrants in South Africa." Boston University, Boston, Massachusetts. Mimeo.

———— (1983b). "Emigration, Employment, and Accumulation: The Miners of Southern Africa." Discussion paper, Migration and Development Program, Harvard University.

Nagi, M. H. (1986). "Determinants of Current Trends in Labor Migration and the Future Outlook." In *Asian Labor Migration*, F. Arnold and N. M. Shah, eds. Boulder, Colo.: Westview.

Paine, S. (1974). *Exporting Workers: The Turkish Case*. Cambridge: Cambridge University Press.

Serageldin, I., J. A. Socknat, S. Birks, B. Li, and C. A. Sinclair (1983). *Manpower and International Labor Migration in the Middle East and North Africa*. World Bank Publication. Oxford: Oxford University Press.

Smart, J. E., V. A. Teodosio, and C.J. Jimenez (1986). "Skills and Earnings: Issues in the Development Impact on the Philippines of Labor Export to the Middle East." In *Asian Labor Migration*, F. Arnold and N. M. Shah, eds. Boulder, Colo.: Westview.

Swamy, G. (1981). "International Migrant Workers' Remittances: Issues and Prospects." World Bank Staff Working Paper No. 481.

——— (1985). "Population and International Migration." World Bank Staff Working Paper No. 689.

United Nations (1983). *World Population Trends and Policies*. New York: United Nations.

Warren, R. and J. S Passel (1983). "Estimates of Illegal Aliens from Mexico Counted in the 1980 U.S. Census." Paper presented at the annual meeting of the Population Association of America, Pittsburgh, Penn.

Weiner, M. (1983). "International Emigration: A Political and Economic Assessment." Paper prepared for Harvard-Draeger Conference on Population Interactions between Poor and Rich Countries, Harvard University.

Williamson, J. G. (1982). "Immigration-Inequality Trade-offs in the Promised Land: Income Distribution and Absorptive Capacity Prior to the Quotas." In *The Gateway—U. S. Immigration Issues and Policies*. B. R. Chiswich, ed. Washington, D.C.: American Enterprise Institute for Public Policy Research.

Woytinsky, W. S. and E. S. Woytinsky (1953). *World Population and Production Trends and Outlook*. The Lord Baltimore Press.

Zachariah, K. C. and J. Conde (1981). *Migration in West Africa—Demographic Aspects*. World Bank-OECD study. Oxford: Oxford University Press.

Zolbert, A. R. (1983). "Wanted but Not Welcome: Alien Labor in Western Development." Paper prepared for Harvard-Draeger Conference on Population Interaction between Poor and Rich Countries, Harvard University.

⑨

Guest Worker Emigration and Remittances

ROBERT E. B. LUCAS

In 1981, I concluded a study of the economic causes, consequences, and evaluation of international migration by noting that: "Theoretical economic analysis of international migration far outstrips the empirical counterparts."[1] Since writing this, several, more systematic, empirical studies relating to the economics of international migration have appeared. In particular, a number of studies now exist pertaining to what are probably the three dominant guest-worker programs in the world: those in the European Economic Community, the Persian Gulf, and South Africa. The present chapter draws upon this new literature and is organized into three main sections: The first section deals with the decisions to emigrate and to remit; the second section considers certain aspects of the demand for guest workers; and the third section turns to the economic consequences for the labor-supplying countries.

THE DECISION TO EMIGRATE AND TO REMIT

Following the contributions of Todaro (1969) and Harris and Todaro (1970), most of the empirical literature on the determinants of internal migration focuses on expected wage differences between locations. In this framework, the potential migrant weighs a certain wage at home versus a gamble with respect to finding a job in town. However, particularly in a guest worker context, the role of uncertainty is often reversed. A contract is typically signed with a recruiter in the home country before departure, so that wages are known in advance.[2] Moreover, in most guest worker contexts, the migrant has a fixed-period contract and is not entitled to remain in the host country to search for a job after terminating the contract, so that there exists little uncertainty with respect to employment once recruited. The uncertainty with respect to earnings is at home. Thus, in such contexts, the Harris-Todaro framework is reversed, and one must weigh uncertain conditions at home versus a certain wage abroad. In Lucas (1987) I adopt such an approach to the supply of mine workers from Botswana, Lesotho, Malawi, and Mozambique to the mines of the South African rand. In each context, an upward-sloping supply of mine workers is found with respect to the expected earnings difference between home and the mines. Thus, although the South African mining houses often refer to the labor-supplying countries as a labor reserve, it has not in fact been a reserve of surplus labor infinitely, elastically available at the going wage.

But the role of uncertainty in the home context may be pursued further. It is perhaps natural, whenever an uncertain environment prevails, to ask whether some insurance mechanism may be found. One strategy which may be adopted by a household is to spread their risks by spreading household members across markets where income fluctuations are not positively correlated. Thus migration itself may partly be motivated by the desire to spread risks by taking advantage of geographical variations in market uncertainty. For the household as a whole to be a potential beneficiary of such a strategy, there must be some mechanism of compensation when fortunes wane. In this sense, the act of remitting may be interpreted as a stream of premium and compensation payments between various geographically spread components of the household, in a mutual understanding that help will be provided at times of hardship. The migration-remittance decision is then a simultaneous one, with both migrant and remainder of the household as beneficiaries. This idea is developed and explored empirically in Lucas and Stark (1985) and Stark and Lucas (forthcoming), with specific reference to Botswana. It is demonstrated that at times of periodic drought, migrants are called upon to increase remittances for households at risk of otherwise losing their cattle. Indeed, one can see a short-run reaction of increased propensity to sign on for a tour of duty in the South African mines whenever a drought seems imminent (Lucas, 1987). The men remain at home waiting to see if the annual rains will be sufficient to warrant plowing, but if the rains are delayed, and prospects seem increasingly risky at home, then a job in the mines is sought. The contract, at least for miners from Botswana, Lesotho, and Swaziland, is sufficiently short to permit return for plowing in the next season. Thus, the decision to migrate is tied to risk at home, and, once the worker has migrated, remittance behavior is conditioned by the understanding that insurance coverage will be provided.

Sjaastad (1962) emphasizes the view of migration as investment. The idea is that the act of migration may be costly in various ways and that the future stream of enhanced earnings in the new location may be perceived as returns on the initial capital outlay. The typical elements of cost envisioned include transportation costs, costs of initial job search, and psychic costs of leaving home. In guest-worker contexts, the relative magnitudes of such components is quite different from the typical internal migration scenario. First, as noted already, there usually is no job search after emigrating. Second, the financial costs of moving are of a different order of magnitude. Even if the substantial transportation costs are paid directly by the recruiter, personal costs to the migrant may nonetheless be large. In particular, in a number of contexts, emigration requires approval from domestic authorities, leading to substantial bribes that must be financed. In India, obtaining the required No Objection Certificate before departure is reputed to involve very considerable sums in many instances; Ali et al. (1981: 18) note that, in Bangladesh, "it is an open secret that the Recruiting Agents realize money from the job-seekers although such practices are unlawful and punishable"; and Ebiri (1985) reports similar illegal payments among Turkish guest workers leaving for Europe. Third, the psychic costs of being an alien, of not speaking the local language, of being denied permission for accompanying family members, not to mention the indignities of the South African mine compounds, surely impose greater personal costs than migrating to a nearby town at home.

Given the substantial extent to which monetary and not just psychic costs must be incurred, the question of financing arises. Typically the family, and often an extended family, incurs the cost of investing in the migrant.[3] Again, the investment in migration and the act of remitting may then be viewed as simultaneous portions of a mutual understanding between migrant and family: The family invests and the migrant repays. But the question then arises as to how such an implicit understanding may be enforced, since the migrant benefits at the initial stage and the family is only repaid thereafter. Clearly, the simple fact that the migrant cares for the family at home may obviate much of the need for other mechanisms of enforcement. Nonetheless, in Lucas and Stark (1985) evidence is presented that is consistent with a concern to inherit family property as an influence upon children's remittances. But in that account another potentially important mechanism is discussed, though not tested empirically, namely the intent to return home. Precisely in a guest-worker context the intent to return home is abnormally high, if only because contracts are often of limited duration. No doubt, this intent to return home, combined with inability to relocate one's family in the host country, helps to explain the very high propensity to remit among guest workers: they are both repaying the family's initial outlay on emigration and investing in goodwill and perhaps tangible assets to be enjoyed on return.

Of course, the intent to return home may not only reflect demand limits in the host country but also the supply choices of migrants. But not all such choices reflect failed expectations and disillusionment with life in the host country. In a target-saver model, once sufficient returns have been reaped on the initial costs of departure, the migrant fulfills the initial intent to return. This opens the possibility that the supply of guest workers may even be backward-bending with respect to the foreign wage. Lipton (1980) states that the South African mining houses have often maintained that their black workers' behavior has indeed been backward-bending with respect to mine wages, for exactly this reason, and that this was for many years cited as a reason for not raising wages. However, the evidence in southern Africa contradicts the maintained view of the mining houses, for supply has actually been significantly upward sloping with respect to the mine wage from each of the major labor-supplying countries (Lucas, 1987).

The mix of guest workers emigrating in various regions differs very substantially with respect to education and training. The mine workers in southern Africa and migrant labor from Bangladesh to the Middle East possess below-average education for their country of origin, whereas the opposite is true for European guest workers from Turkey; from Bangladesh and Turkey a comparatively large proportion of the migrants are designated as skilled or semi-skilled, whereas of the Middle East migrant workers from Pakistan some 43 percent are designated as unskilled, and in southern Africa most of the mine workers possess few industrial skills before migrating.[4] Thus, the extent of brain or skill drain embedded in the various guest-worker programs varies considerably, but to the extent such a drain does occur it is interesting to relate this to the above concepts of investment in migration.

In the longer run, not only should the decisions to migrate and to remit be seen as simultaneous, but also the decision to remain in school or to undertake training. Thus, the level of education and skills among the nation's labor force may be a function of emigration opportunities, where an appropriate training influences the probabilities and rewards from emigration, and the so-called brain drain is not then simply a drawing down of a given stock of skills. We also now possess several studies indicating that remittances rise with the level of education of the migrant.[5] A potential explanation for the latter is simply as a special case of the earlier argument: that remittances may be an act of repayment by the migrant for family investment embodied in the migrant, including the substantial costs of any schooling or training. Thus, in Lucas and Stark (1985) it is shown that remittances rise on average with respect to education for all classes of migrants, in part because education raises the migrants' earnings, but education has a larger effect in raising remittances from migrants whose educational costs are more likely to have been borne by the family. Thus, from the nation's perspective, educational costs embodied in emigrants ought not to be perceived as a deadweight loss, but as an investment in the opportunity to emigrate with remittances as the return—an investment that may or may not offer a sufficiently high social rate of return.

ELEMENTS IN THE DEMAND FOR GUEST WORKERS

Not only is guest-worker emigration selective with respect to education and skill but also with respect to other personal characteristics. For example, in each of the regional contexts cited above, the modal migrant is male and young (usually between twenty and thirty-five years old). The factors which determine the selection of emigrants are complex. Given the ability of immigration authorities to ration entry, the selectivity of international migration with respect to population characteristics depends upon attributes affecting screening for entry as well as upon attributes affecting willingness to move. In this sense, international migration is quite different from internal migration, except in such countries as South Africa, where internal migration is also very effectively restricted. In the balance, individuals' characteristics may influence the likelihood of emigrating for many reasons: because employment opportunities at home and abroad depend upon personal attributes; because attitudes towards leaving home and ability to afford the transition may be correlated with various personal characteristics; and because immigration authorities may discriminate among applicants based on listed personal information. To identify statistically these separate influences of personal attributes can be quite difficult (see Lucas 1985a).

These identification difficulties are compounded, at least in some international contexts, by the maintenance of an excess supply of guest workers. Why should this be? Why are wages of guest workers not simply lowered to clear the market? In some instances, local minimum-wage laws (Germany) and difficulties of paying differential wages between foreign and domestic workers living and working together (the South African mine compounds) are no doubt factors. But other forces may also contribute to this and lead to conscious discrimination between potential immigrants, especially along lines of national origin. This has quite clearly been the case in recruiting for the South African mines in recent years: Mozambican novices have not been recruited since the independence of Mozambique in 1975, for fear of infiltration by Marxist supporters in the mine compounds; a memorandum of understanding was drawn up with the government of Botswana, guaranteeing a minimum rate of Botswana recruitment; and some preference is given to workers from Lesotho (which is treated and often referred to as another "homeland"), for fear of creating mass unemployment and an island of discontent within the South African borders. In the Middle East, recruitment has also been selective with respect to country of origin, with a preference for foreign Arab workers (though often with reservations about admitting too many Palestinians), or at least for fellow Moslems.

These preferences may, to some extent, reflect the concerns of employers themselves. In particular, employers may wish to spread their risks and not rely too heavily upon migrant labor from a single country source. This is nicely illustrated in the South African context with respect to miners from Malawi. As of 1973, Malawi accounted for about 40 percent of South Africa's foreign mine labor force. In 1974, all recruiting in Malawi was suspended by the government of Malawi. Subsequently, in 1977, the ban was lifted but by then the mining houses no longer trusted Malawi as a stable source, and recruiting from Malawi has never again returned to the heights reached in 1973.

But probably more often, discrimination against workers from specific countries (not to mention restrictions against guest-worker immigration more generally) reflects political and social concerns, which may be in direct conflict with the interests of host-country employers. In Kuwait, for example, Russell (1987) has shown that political considerations regarding security and related preferences for worker nationality have been at odds with commercial interests. In Germany, social tensions have led to political pressures to diminish guest-worker admission. To the extent that guest-worker employment is thus discouraged in manufacturing, one may well see direct investment abroad encouraged as an alternative strategy, but in the context of construction in the Middle East, mining in South Africa, and the service industries in Europe, this alternative is not viable.

The admission of guest workers may thus be selective, not only with respect to productivity but also with respect to other attributes, and especially with respect to national origin. One mechanism through which both types of preference may be realized is via the common use of recruiting agencies in the various labor-supplying countries, who may be given job-specific numbers of workers as targets for their country. In the case of the South African mines, this recruiting is centralized in a single agency for most of the mines. The tacit purpose is to avoid competition among the mines for labor, and instead to act jointly as monopsonists in the market for black workers, a strategy which had been successful in keeping down wages at least until the early 1970s (see Lucas, 1985b). It is, however, less clear that organized recruiting has been used towards such monopsonistic ends in other parts of the globe.

The other mechanism that ultimately permits control over the size and composition of the stock of guest workers is the limited duration of contracts, frequently combined with a repatriation requirement upon contract termination. Indeed, it is precisely this feature that begins to distinguish guest-worker flows from other population movements. In a well-policed state, such as South Africa, the ability to expel contracted miners is clear. Indeed, until the mid–1970s a Master and Servants Law also prevented departure prior to contract termination, and "deserters" could be hunted and arrested. In other contexts, ability to police repatriation is less clear, and indeed a good deal of illegal migration occurs into Europe from such countries as Turkey (see Ebiri, 1985). Obtaining reliable information on propensity to return and the average duration of absence is difficult. Gilani, Khan, and Iqbal (1981: 32) report that 33 percent of Pakistani migrants to the Middle East stay abroad for less than one year, and a further 30 percent return within two years. However this measure is based on an airport survey and thus reflects a profile for the average traveller, a profile which contains more short-term migrants than does the stock of migrants overseas. The other statistical approach used is to look at length of contracts signed as a proxy for duration of residence abroad. Ali et al. (1981: 294) thus report that some 61 percent of Bangladeshi contracts specify a period of less than one year, and 95 percent are for two years or less. However, since some contract renewal occurs while in the host country (one renewal being legal in South Africa), again the duration of initial contract is not necessarily a good reflection of duration of absence. Thus, although limited contracts are meant as a device to avoid having the guests outstay their welcome, of preventing them from establishing legal rights as residents in the host countries, and of retaining the flexibility to export unemployment, it is not clear just how temporary are the guest workers in all contexts. Thus, Ebiri (1985: 207) notes that "More than a million workers went abroad [from Turkey] during the 1960s and 1970s, and about 800,000 are still working in Europe.''

Given such magnitudes of flows and especially given the selectivity of movement, no matter whether a result of supply-side or demand-side screening, it is not surprising ''in retrospect—to see the tremendous impact that the out-migration of Turkish workers to Western European countries has had on the Turkish economy and society'' (Ebiri, 1985: 207). To these impacts of guest-worker emigration, from Turkey and elsewhere, the next section now turns.

ECONOMIC CONSEQUENCES FOR THE LABOR-SUPPLYING COUNTRIES

The major economic impacts of emigration upon the labor-supplying countries potentially include consequences for output in the traditional agricultural sector, induced changes in the domestic wage labor market, and the results of remittances spent. Moreover, in each sphere, a distinction between long-run and short-run implications must be borne in mind.

The selectivity of emigrants with respect to rural versus urban origin varies considerably between the regions under consideration. From Turkey, the majority of emigrants are drawn from the urban sector, despite the fact that the majority of Turkey's population lives in rural areas, whereas from Bangladesh and throughout southern Africa, most of the emigrants originate directly from rural areas. But the mere fact that Turkish emigrants are of urban origin does not necessarily imply no loss of labor to the agricultural sector there, for internal migration into town may well be induced by departure of urban emigrants. Thus, irrespective of rural-urban selectivity, the issue arises as to whether there exists surplus labor in traditional agriculture.

In the World Bank's cost-benefit studies of emigration from Bangladesh and Pakistan, surplus agricultural labor is assumed, such that no loss in crop output occurs.[6] Ebiri (1985) makes a similar assumption for the case of Turkey. On the other hand, in direct production function estimates for the cases of Botswana, Lesotho, and Malawi, I found that labor migration significantly reduces traditional crop output in the short run (Lucas, 1987). In part, any difference in this southern African context no doubt reflects the very obvious discrepancy in population pressure on land as compared to south Asia. Yet even in very sparsely populated Botswana, there is evidence that cultivable land is far from freely available (see Lucas, 1985c).

Implications for the local wage labor market are perhaps even more varied and complex, even in the short run. In the studies of Bangladesh, Pakistan, and Turkey, it is argued that surplus unskilled wage labor prevails and that emigration of the unskilled will therefore have left wages and output unaffected. Rather, the focus of these studies is on skilled labor emigration. Ebiri (1985) reports that although even a good many of the skilled and semi-skilled migrants are apparently drawn from the construction trades in Turkey, there is no evidence of consequent slowing down in growth in this sector. Moreover, wages of skilled construction workers have risen less rapidly than those of unskilled workers, and in such related fields as metal working, "not many firms reported difficulty in finding new workers for the jobs vacated by emigrant workers" (Ebiri, 1985: 218). A somewhat different picture is, however, painted with respect to the Turkish large-scale manufacturing sector, where skilled workers could not be replaced and losses have led to more intensive use of capital, unskilled workers, and professional-level workers, though resultant effects on output are not reported. The studies of both Bangladesh and Pakistan compare the occupational distribution of skilled emigrants with demands and apparent surpluses in each category in the domestic labor market. While these studies do note the possibilities of factor substitution of the kind observed in Turkish manufacturing, and also note the potential for training replacements, there is nonetheless a presumption in those studies that costs of such adjustments will necessarily be such as to cause some significant output loss, where emigration exceeds the estimated surplus number of workers in a particular skill group. Certainly in Pakistan, wages of skilled workers have escalated quite rapidly during the major phase of emigration, and particularly so in areas with higher emigration propensities. In at least Malawi and Mozambique, mine labor recruiting for South Africa has also placed significant upward pressure on wages in commercial agriculture, leading to diminished labor input and consequent loss in production of commercial crops, even though in this context the labor withdrawn is unskilled (see Lucas, 1987).

In terms of national welfare, any output losses in traditional agriculture and in wage labor production activities may simply be added using appropriate world prices for evaluation. In terms of policy formulation, however, there may in fact be a critical distinction between impacts on these two broad sectors. In family farming, direct output losses are borne by the same household that presumably also benefits from enhanced earnings of the emigrant and, even if a distinction is made between different component portions of the household, remittances may serve to compensate the nonmovers. However, if employers must pay higher wages as a result of emigration, a conflict of interest arises between gains for the migrants and costs for employers. Since international migration is subject to policy control, in various ways, by the home-country government, there arises a fascinating political economy issue as to how this conflict will influence movement.

This fundamental conflict is very nicely illustrated with respect to the aforementioned cases of Malawi and Mozambique. During the colonial period in Nyasaland, the British authorities maintained a quota on recruiting for the South African mines, a quota that varied according to tightness of the estate labor market in Nyasaland, where the estates rested in the hands of British settlers. Following independence in 1964, the quota was lifted and recruiting for the mines rose steadily. The estates began to pass into Malawian hands, and the new owners experienced difficulties obtaining estate labor without raising wages.

Although the ostensible reason for suspending recruiting in 1974 was the crash of a plane transporting miners, evidence exists that the suspension had been previously planned and no doubt the pressure on estate wages was an important factor in this policy decision. The return of nearly 200,000 men from the mines was accompanied by a significant drop in the real wage on the estates and some, but not all, of the displaced miners were absorbed. Discontent ensued, and in 1977 the ban on recruiting was lifted but, as already noted, the mining houses no longer viewed Malawi as a stable source of recruits and recruiting has never returned to pre-cutoff levels. In colonial Mozambique, the Portuguese authorities extracted compensation from the South Africans in return for the right to recruit. This compensation took the form of a recruitment tax, an agreement that specified minimum shipments of South African goods would pass through the port of Lourenco Marques, and that deferred pay of the miners would be handed to the Portuguese in gold at the official gold price which was well below the free market value of gold. These arrangements proved extremely lucrative. Of course, the European plantation owners in Mozambique did not benefit directly from these deals, and indeed some estrangement between the authorities and planters was evident. Nonetheless, the authorities did turn a blind eye to the use of forced labor, which continued on a large scale until the early 1960s and never completely disappeared prior to independence in 1975. Thus, although mine recruiting significantly escalated plantation wages in Mozambique, some of this was offset by use of forced labor. In turn, the use of forced labor also significantly swelled the numbers seeking mine work, for the conditions of forced plantation work were even harsher than life in the mine compounds.[7] Though clearly far less dramatic than the contexts of Malawi and Mozambique, the requirement of No Objection Certificates for Middle East recruits in much of South Asia today is also designed to protect employers. Thus, in actually formulating emigration policies for guest workers, not only net benefits to the nation matter but also the distribution of the costs and benefits among classes.

"On the benefit side, remittances are the major (if not the sole) benefit from labour migration" (Gilani, Khan, and Iqbal, 1981: 72). Certainly the magnitude of remittance flows, in each of our three regional guest-worker contexts, is extremely large. In part, this reflects attempts by the various governments to encourage remitting, through such schemes as offering premium interest rates, premium exchange rates, and certain tax breaks.[8] The South African mines provide deferred pay schemes, whereby a portion of the migrants' earnings are deducted and transferred to the home country. In some instances, the government of the home country has benefitted financially from these deferred pay schemes, as in the aforementioned case of Mozambique under colonial rule, or when interest on the deposited payments accrues to the home government, and occasional attempts to render deferred pay schemes mandatory have consequently even led to mass violence among the miners.

Given the enormous magnitude of the remittance flows, their macroeconomic consequences have also been very significant. Incomes enhanced by remittances have certainly stimulated domestic demand, though this may be a mixed blessing. Ebiri (1985) concludes that in Turkey the expansion in domestic demand has served to stimulate output and employment. But in Bangladesh, it seems that inflationary pressures may have resulted from the enhanced demand and permitted monetary expansion with remittance inflows, given domestic supply constraints (see Ali et al., 1981). In the presence of domestic supply constraints, any expansion in demand is also likely to translate into a higher import bill, though obviously one of the major gains from remittances is precisely in providing the foreign exchange for import expansion. In countries suffering from foreign exchange shortages, and where the shadow value of foreign exchange exceeds the nominal rate, this effect is of particular national importance. In Turkey, Ebiri (1985) reports, foreign exchange shortages have resulted in an active black market in foreign currencies, fed to a large extent by illegal remittances from Europe. In Bangladesh, the Wage Earners Scheme has provided a legal counterpart, with remittances converted at a premium rate under a dual exchange rate regime. Whether legal or otherwise, such mechanisms may provide private incentives to remit while serving the national interest.

A large portion of the two World Bank studies of Middle East migration from Bangladesh and Pakistan is dedicated to analysis of the pattern of domestic spending induced by remittances. This is of concern for at least three reasons: because the propensity to save out of remittances influences the magnitude of any multiplier effects; because the detailed composition of demand may influence the sectoral balance of induced production or import; and, in the long run, because the composition of spending between consumption and investment affects potential growth. There exist, however, a number of methodological difficulties in gleaning empirical evidence on these issues.[9] It is clear that direct spending out of the cash brought home and the bundle of gifts transported by the returning migrant are not the central concern. Rather, one is interested in the full incidence of remittances on spending at home. A part of this might be discerned by relating expenditure patterns of households to remittances received. But this is not the approach adopted by the World Bank studies, which make, instead, a simple comparison between spending among households with and without migrants.[10] But these studies themselves also note a further methodological weakness in this approach, namely that induced spending changes are thereby ignored among households without either remittances or migrants. For example, it is frequently noted that households with income enhanced by migrants' earnings invest in land. But if the land is not thereby improved or expanded, then this represents a pure transfer, and if the seller of land consumes the capital received, then no investment occurs even though the migrant household invests.

These difficulties not withstanding, the studies of Bangladesh and Pakistan both conclude that only a small portion of remittances are spent on "productive" investment. In the Turkish case, Ebiri (1985) argues that attempts to encourage investments by migrants, through formation of "workers' companies" and "village development cooperatives" have largely failed. However, nearly half of the returned workers become self-employed in Turkey, and this probably requires at least some small investment to get started.

In southern Africa, little direct evidence exists. However, in a time series analysis, I have shown that accumulation of cattle and improvements in labor productivity in traditional crop production are significantly associated with the accumulated earnings of migrants. One cannot discern the extent to which this reflects: investments in fixed assets by migrants' households; investments by other farming households as access to capital in segmented rural markets improves with remittances; adoption of riskier, but higher yielding, farming techniques as migration provides insurance coverage; or the role of migrants' cash inputs as working capital. Nonetheless, this evidence does suggest an important feedback, at least in southern Africa, whereby labor withdrawal may hurt traditional agriculture in the short run, but accumulation out of migrants' earnings enhances output in the long run.

For the wage labor market at home, there may also be long-run implications different from those in the short run. In the long run, the domestic demand for labor will be influenced by the level, pattern, and nature of induced investments in wage labor activities. Thus far, we still possess almost no evidence with respect to this. In the long run, there may also be induced changes in labor supply. This may happen for at least three reasons. First, there may occur induced changes in labor force participation, though the direction of effect is ambiguous. Thus in Turkey, Ebiri (1985) notes a sharp drop in the labor force participation rate during the period of most rapid emigration, and suggests that this may reflect an income effect in the preference for leisure, as remittances swell incomes at home. On the other hand, Gilani, Khan, and Iqbal (1981) argue that emigration may have increased labor force participation in Pakistan, since declining unemployment means less discouraged workers. Second, circular migration may well alter the skill composition of the domestic work force as migrants return, both because of induced skill acquisition before migrating and because of any relevant skills acquired while abroad. There is, however, some evidence to indicate that the domestic labor markets do not always adjust to take advantage of these skills of returning migrants and indeed that retraining is occasionally needed (see Kubat, 1984). Third, it should be mentioned in a volume on population and development that, in the much longer run, emigration of guest workers may affect the domestic labor force through induced shifts in the fertility rate. Thus, Ebiri (1985) suggests that the simple absence of large numbers of young men from Turkey may have a direct effect in lowering fertility, though in much of southern Africa it seems only to have promoted the incidence of single mothers. Ebiri mentions other factors likely to provide a link between guest worker emigration and fertility, such as the resultant rise in income from migration and changes in attitude while abroad, while Bernheim and Stark (1986) develop a theoretical framework, simultaneously linking fertility, migration, and remittance behavior. But this returns us to a sphere in which we do not yet possess systematic empirical evidence.

CONCLUSIONS

The focus of analysis in migration decisions has perhaps begun to swing toward viewing mobility responses within a broader household strategy. In such a conceptual framework, migration becomes intimately linked with other demographic-economic household decisions, including remittances, education, and even fertility. Empirical evidence on this nexus remains very partial, both in depth and breadth. Guest-worker movements offer a potentially rich area for future research in this vein, since they typically involve separation of families, often require substantial educational and other investments, and consequently result in large-scale remittances. Such evidence as does exist, thus far, indeed begins to suggest that at least migration, remittances, and education are important components in intrafamilial, intertemporal understandings, designed as investment and risk-spreading strategies. But much remains to be done in this sphere.

At the macroeconomic level, I have tried to emphasize that it is important to bear in mind the long-run effects of emigration on development and not just the short-run impact. In fact, even the evidence on the short-run consequences is very limited, and a number of studies simply assume the existence of surplus unskilled and agricultural labor. Indirect evidence, in a few guest-worker contexts, does indicate a rise in domestic wages of skilled workers as a result of emigration. Moreover, econometric evidence demonstrates a similar effect even for unskilled labor in parts of southern Africa, plus a short-run reduction in traditional crop output. Thus, where evidence actually exists, it seems to suggest that, given the type of guest worker actually emigrating, there probably are some short-term national losses in production. How large these losses may be depends, in part, on ability to switch technique of production, but at least in Turkey shifts in technique have been induced to a significant extent.

A key component in the link to long-term consequences of emigration, and of guest workers in particular, is accumulation induced by remittances. Unfortunately, a number of methodological difficulties plague compilation of systematic evidence in this regard. However, existing studies do indicate that households with migrants tend to invest somewhat more than nonmigrant households. I have also shown that cattle accumulation and enhanced labor productivity in traditional agriculture are significantly associated with accumulated earnings of migrants in southern Africa. Thus, although emigration may generate short-term production losses, in the long run this strategy may well enhance domestic production through accumulation.

In my survey article, mentioned at the outset, I outlined how some of the consequences of emigration might be assembled into a cost-benefit framework. This has now been undertaken in two major projects for the World Bank, looking at Bangladesh and Pakistan. The implicit objective in most cost-benefit studies, and of these in particular, is maximization of national welfare. But it seems clear that this is not always the objective when actually formulating migration policies, and international migration is obviously susceptible to control. The relative political influence of various groups, who are helped or hurt by migration, is critical to policy outcomes with respect to international population movements. This is true with respect to the countries of immigration, where conflicts often emerge between the commercial interests of employers on the one hand, and concerns over social tensions, competition for jobs, and even security issues on the other hand. But it is also true with respect to some of the labor-supplying countries, where the interests of the migrants and of local employers may be at odds, and in some instances this has led to prohibitions on emigration.

NOTES

1. Lucas, 1981: 109.

2. Recently, there has been quite widespread violation of contracts in Middle East recruiting, in the sense that wages are cut after the migrant arrives. However, it is difficult to believe that word of this has not now spread and that potential recruits undertake appropriate discounting of promised wages.

3. Indeed, in a broader sense, the family may also invest in psychic costs of separation, especially perhaps when the husband emigrates, leaving the wife alone at home with their children, which is quite typical of many guest-worker programs. Ebiri (1985), for example, reports that the majority of Turkey's emigrant guest workers are married, though this is untrue of miners in southern Africa.

4. See Ali et al., 1981; Ebiri, 1985; Gilani, Khan, and Iqbal, 1981; and Lucas, 1985a. Note, however, that the studies for Bangladesh and Pakistan are based on the occupational profile of migrants as documented in their exit forms, and it is not altogether clear whether this really reflects occupation prior to departure or the contracted occupation at destination.

5. See Rempel and Lobdell, 1978; Knowles and Anker, 1981; Lucas and Stark, 1985.

6. See Ali et al., 1981; and Gilani, Khan, and Iqbal, 1981.

7. For statistical evidence on these effects, see Lucas, 1987.

8. On the other hand, the official mechanisms set up to facilitate remittances do not always function terribly well. See, for example, Ali et al., 1981: 68–70.

9. A number of these difficulties are well described in Gilani, Khan, and Iqbal, 1981: 74–87.

10. Adopting this strategy does bypass a further methodological difficulty, namely that spending patterns of migrant's household may change even though no actual remittances occur. In particular, from the previous argument that migration can provide insurance for the household, more risky investment strategies may well be permitted, even though current remittances are not observed.

REFERENCES

Ali, S. A., et al (1981). *Labor Migration from Bangladesh to the Middle East*. World Bank Staff Working Paper No. 454. Washington, D.C.

Bernheim, B. D., and O. Stark (1986). "The Strategic Demand for Children: Theory and Implications for Fertility and Migration." Discussion Paper No. 25, Migration and Development Program, Harvard University.

Ebiri, K. (1985). "Impact of Labor Migration on the Turkish Economy." In *Guests*

Come to Stay: The Effects of European Labor Migration on Sending and Receiving Countries, R. Rogers, ed. Boulder, Colo.: Westview.

Gilani, I., M. F. Khan, and M. Iqbal (1981). *Labour Migration from Pakistan to the Middle East and Its Impact on the Domestic Economy*. Final Report, South Asia Country Programs Department. Washington, D.C.: World Bank.

Harris, J. R., and M. P. Todaro (1970). "Migration, Unemployment and Development: A Two-sector Analysis." *American Economic Review* 60: 126–42.

Knowles, J. C., and R. Anker (1981). "An Analysis of Income Transfers in a Developing Country: The Case of Kenya." *Journal of Development Economics* 8: 205–26.

Kubat, D., ed. (1984). *The Politics of Return: International Return Migration in Europe*. New York: Center for Migration Studies.

Lipton, M. (1980). "Men of Two Worlds." *Optima* 29: 72–201.

Lucas, Robert E. B. (1981). "International Migration: Economic Causes, Consequences and Evaluation." In *Global Trends in Migration: Theory and Research on International Population Movements*, M. M. Kritz, C. B. Keely and S. M. Tomasi, eds. New York: Center for Migration Studies.

——— (1985a). "Migration amongst the Batswana." *The Economic Journal* 95: 358–82.

——— (1985b). "Mines and Migrants in South Africa." *American Economic Review* 75: 1094–1108.

——— (1985c). "The Distribution and Efficiency of Crop Production in Tribal Areas of Botswana." In *The Household Economy of Rural Botswana*, D. Chernickovsky, R. E. B. Lucas and E. Mueller, eds. World Bank Staff Working Paper No. 715.

——— (1987). "Emigration to South Africa's Mines." *American Economic Review* 77: 313–30.

Lucas, R. E. B., and O. Stark (1985). "Motivations to Remit: Evidence from Botswana." *Journal of Political Economy* 93: 901–18.

Rempel, H., and R. A. Lobdell (1978). "The Role of Rural-to-Urban Remittances in Rural Development." *Journal of Development Studies* 14: 324–41.

Russell, S. S. (1987). "Interactions of Economic and Political Considerations in Migration Policy Formulation: The Case of Kuwait." Paper presented to the Joint MIT-Harvard Seminar on Migration and Development, Cambridge, Mass., March 5, 1987.

Sjaastad, L. A. (1962). "The Costs and Returns of Human Migration." *Journal of Political Economy* 70: 80–93.

Stark, O., and R. E. B. Lucas (forthcoming). "Migration, Remittances and the Family." *Economic Development and Cultural Change*.

Todaro, M. P. (1969). "A Model of Labor Migration and Urban Unemployment in Less Developed Countries." *American Economic Review* 59: 138–48.

10

International Labor Migration and Development

THOMAS STRAUBHAAR

From the previous contributions to this volume, it has become clear that to overcome the problem of rapid population growth two potential solutions are basically available: efforts to reduce the birth rate significantly and emigration. The first solution is often quite difficult to execute. Effectively reducing the birth rate during early stages of economic development is limited by individual attitudes, desires, motivations, knowledge, and income levels, which prevent large changes in fertility patterns in the short run. Emigration, on the other hand, can be seen as a powerful policy for reducing the population growth in the short run. The economic consequences of emigration are, however, less obvious once we look at them in more detail.

Despite the growing literature about the phenomenon of international labor migration, there is still great controversy about its economic effects on the country of emigrants' origin [for a detailed presentation see Straubhaar (1987)]. On one side, there is the neoclassical approach referring back to Adam Smith's idea that migration tends to equalize the differences in economic opportunities between the home country and abroad that motivate workers to migrate. Therefore, according to this neoclassical view, international migration of labor should narrow the development gap between the country of emigrants' origin and abroad. On the opposite side, the Swedish Nobel laureate Gunnar Myrdal and his scholars argue that international labor migration tends to increase the inequality. Therefore, according to this view, emigration harms the economic development of the home country and strengthens the polarization in poor (home) and rich (foreign) countries.

This controversy is caused especially by a lack of empirical research. While the ''brain drain''—the migration of highly skilled manpower from poor to rich countries—attracted some welfare theorizing in the 1960s and early 1970s [for a survey see the collection of articles by Bhagwati (1983: 44–195)], the mass movements of temporary migrants with few skills have for a long time only generated a rather descriptive literature [for an overview see Swamy (1985), Böhning (1984), and Stahl (1982)]. Sadly lacking in support were formal economic treatment or econometric studies.

Since international organizations have supported research programs such as the "International Migration for Employment Project" by ILO, the "SOPEMI"-project (Continuous Reporting System on Migration) by the OECD, and the World Bank migration model (World Bank 1983, 1985), econometric approaches are now used more often for explaining international labor migration. In this chapter, we support these efforts to remedy the lack of empirical studies in international labor migration. We will look for the empirical evidence about whether international labor migration tends to help or to harm the economic development of the country of emigrants' origin.

This chapter relies on empirical work on modeling internal migration flows done by Salvatore (1980, 1981a, 1981b, 1984). It is a first attempt of modeling international labor migration flows in the context of a simultaneous-equations model based on time-series data. The discussion is organized as follows: First, we will set up a simultaneous-equations model. Then, we are going to estimate such a model for the European South-North migration flows in the years 1960 to 1984. Finally, we will look at the knowledge which we might gain by such an exercise.

SETTING UP A SIMULTANEOUS-EQUATIONS MODEL

Since Muth (1971) asked his "chicken or egg" question (Which came first, the chicken or the egg?), simultaneous-equations techniques have become more prominent in theory, models, and empirical studies on migration (for a survey see Greenwood 1985). Such models have been applied, however, to migration within the same country. In the field of international migration, research has maintained its strong orientation toward the determinants as opposed to the consequences, of migration. Sadly lacking in support of the growing theoretical literature on international labor migration were empirical studies, analyzing the effects of migration within the context of an appropriate simultaneous-equations model.[1] No wonder that in such an absence the discussion of the effects of international labor migration has often reverted to meaningless, endless, and emotional controversy.

By reason of high interdependence between the causes and the consequences of migration, the effects of international labor migration can only be analyzed within the context of an appropriate simultaneous-equations model. Setting up and estimating such a simultaneous-equations model of international labor migration, however, is extremely complex, since migration influences, and is in turn influenced by, many social and demographic factors, as well as more purely economic variables.

How many endogenous and exogenous variables should we include in our simultaneous-equations model? The size of the simultaneous-equations model has to be in accordance to the function of the migration process, to the availability of (labor) migration data (especially the number of observations in the time series), and to the insight we expect to get out of the model. Additionally, by including too many endogenous variables in the model, the model can no longer be estimated econometrically.

Like most of the simultaneous-equations models on internal migration based on time-series data, the number of variables that could reasonably be employed in our model was restricted by the degree of freedom constraints. Accordingly, the structural form of our simultaneous-equations model is given by:

$$m^e_t = a_0 + (a_1 {}^* e_t) + (a_2 {}^* g^a_{L,I,t}) + (a_3 {}^* g^a_{y,t}) + (a_4 {}^* m^e_{t-1}) \tag{1}$$

$$u_t = b_0 + (b_1 {}^* m^n_t) + (b_2 {}^* g_{P,t}) + (b_3 {}^* g_{y,t}) + (b_4 {}^* g^{EC}_{y,t}) + (b_5 {}^* u_{t-1}) \tag{2}$$

$$y_t = c_0 + (c_1 {}^* m^n_t) + (c_2 {}^* r_t) + (c_3 {}^* g^{EC}_{y,t}) + (c_4 {}^* y_{t-1}) \tag{3}$$

where,

m^e_t = Rate of gross bilateral emigration flows from a country of origin to a country of destination. Expressed as a percentage of L_t, the size of the labor force in the country of origin in year t.

m^n_t = Rate of net overall migration flows from and to a country of origin to all destination countries (including the flows of returning migrants). Expressed as a percentage of P_t, the size of the population in the country of origin in year t.

e_t = $(1/u^a_t) {}^* y^r_t$ = expected net gains in year t from migration abroad, calculated by the probability of obtaining a higher paid job, times $y^r_t = y^a_t/y_t$, the ratio in the real income per capita abroad (y^a_t) and at home (y_t) in year t.

y_t, y^a_t, y^{EC}_t = Real income per capita in the country of origin, destination, and the European Economic Community (EC) in year t (in constant U.S. dollars with exchange rates and prices for 1980).

$g_{y,t}, g^a_{y,t}, g^{EC}_{y,t}$ = Rate of growth in the real income per capita in the country of origin, destination, and in the EC in year t.

u_t, u^a_t = Rate of unemployment in the country of origin, and destination in year t (number of unemployed workers in year t as a percentage of L_t).

$g_{P,t}$ = Rate of change in P_t, the population of the country of migrants' origin (where migrant people are not included in the population figure).

r_t = Real rate of remittances to the country of origin in year t per capita in the home country (in constant U.S. dollars with exchange rates and prices for 1980).

$g^a_{L,I,t}$ = Rate of change in $L_{I,t}$, the labor force in the industrial sector of the destination country in year t (where migrant workers are not included in the labor force).

The reason for choosing these three endogenous variables out of the pool of potential endogenous variables is given by the existing simultaneous-equations models of internal migration. Almost all of these studies have taken the in, out, or net migration rate, the unemployment rate, and the real income per capita (or real wage) rate as the endogenous model variables: "Since migration, incomes and rates of unemployment are interdependent, a simultaneous-equations model [including these three endogenous variables] is an absolute theoretical necessity" (Salvatore, 1981b: 507).

The reasoning for choosing our specific exogenous variables to explain the emigration equation is given by Bhagwati's (1983, 1984) request to take the international migration flows as demand-determined. Differently from the internal migration flows, which are generally free, international migration flows are constrained by controls. In the presence of immigration restrictions, migration flows are mainly demand-determined. The existence of migration-willing workers becomes a necessary condition for emigration but it is not a sufficient condition. The opportunity to emigrate depends on the demand for immigrant labor.

For contemporary international migration to occur it is necessary and sufficient that, first, there is a demand for foreign labor in the immigration country, and, second, that there are no immigration restrictions to prevent the immigration of active foreigners. An approach that does not take into account the dominance of the demand-determined causes is of no value in explaining the international labor migration flows, as we have shown in detail in Straubhaar (1986).

Equation 1 describes the rate of gross bilateral labor emigration as depending on

- An attractivity index, given by the real income per capita ratio between the countries of emigrants' origin and (potential) destination times the emigrants' probability of getting a (higher-paying) job in the destination country (measured by the inverse of the unemployment rate in the destination country). In that formulation, we incorporate Todaro's (1969, 1980) basic idea that people move to maximize their expected gains from migration or stay, into a simple aggregated form.

  Contrary to the Todaro approach with a linear formulation of the probability function $(1-u_r^a)$, our index takes the inverse of the unemployment rate abroad $(1/u_r^a)$ as a proxy for the strictness of the immigration restrictions in the destination country. It is easy to show that, for low rates of unemployment, this hyperbolic formulation of the probability function leads to more demand-determined migration flows than with the linear formulation by Todaro.

  While on theoretical grounds the present discounted value of the real income ratio (or difference) should be used as an explanatory variable in the Todaro model, almost all migration studies use the ratio (or the difference) in current real income in their empirical estimations. It is assumed that the difference in current real income is a good proxy for present and future income per capita ratios (or differences), which also avoids the controversial choice of discount rates (Salvatore, 1981a: 20; 1981b: 501–502).

  In this simplified form, needed to test the model empirically, the Todaro model differs from a neoclassical approach only by combining the independent variables, analyzed separately in the neoclassical approach, into a single composite index.[2] From an analytical point of view, the income part of our composite index represents the necessary condition (the potential supply on migrant labor), while the inverse of the unemployment rate in the destination countries stays for the decisive condition (the demand for foreign labor in the immigration country).

- The growth of employment opportunities in the industrial sector of the destination country. Including this independent variable, we are going to test Fields' (1975, 1976) expectation that labor turnover variables (such as rates of new hires) might play an important part in the explanation of migration flows. In taking the employment in the industrial sector we assume that foreign labor is absorbed by this sector especially.

- The growth of the real income per capita in the destination country as a measure to express the need and demand for foreign labor and the overall performance of the economy in the destination country.

- The one-period lagged emigration flows. The lagged dependent migration variable among the explanatory variables stays for the often mentioned chain migration (i.e., the self-feeding process by which potential migrants are stimulated by friends and relatives already living abroad). While, from an analytical point of view, the stock of migrants living in the destination country would be the appropriate variable to describe the chain migration, Shaw (1975) has indicated the limited explanatory power of this variable in a migration equation, because it is highly related to the other explanatory factors. We confirm, therefore, Salvatore's (1981a: 18) statement that the alternative to using the stock of migrants in time series studies "is the inclusion of the lagged dependent migration variable among the explanatory variables."

It is expected that a_1, a_2, a_3, and $a_4 > 0$. That is, the higher

- the attractivity difference between the potential emigrants' home and destination countries,
- the job turnover,
- the need for foreign labor and the overall growth in the destination country, and
- the gross bilateral emigration flows in the previous year that might provide help, information, and knowledge to potential migrants among relatives and friends,

the higher we expect to be the outflow of workers emigrating from their home country to a specific destination country.

In the two other model equations, it is the effect of emigration on the variations in the endogenous variables only that we are interested in. For that reason, we concentrate on the econometrically most significant rather than on the economically most meaningful model specification. Thereby, the inclusion of the lagged dependent variable is supposed to "pick up the effects of unmeasured factors that may have affected net migration rates and rates of employment and wage change" in the previous period, but that were not included in the structural equations due to the incomplete model specification (Greenwood et al., 1986: 228). In following this procedure, it is the intention to isolate most of the migration effects from other determinants of the variations in the endogenous variables.

Equation 2 describes the rate of unemployment in the country of migrant's origin as depending on

• current movements on the labor market as the growth of the labor force (measured by the rate of change in the population of the home country without the migrant workers) and the overall (out or in) flow of migrant workers,
• the past situation on the labor market (measured by the previous rate of unemployment as a proxy),
• the general economic situation in the home country and in the average of the EC-destination countries (measured by the rate of growth in the real income per capita as a proxy).

It is expected that b_3, $b_4 < 0$, while b_2, $b_5 > 0$. That is, the smaller

• the number of potential new entrants into the domestic labor market, and
• the rate of unemployment at the beginning of the period,

the more

• the outflow of migrant workers relieves the domestic labor market, and
• the overall growth of the domestic economy and the average growth of the potential destination economies requires additional labor force,

the lower is the rate of unemployment in the country of migrant's origin.
If $b_1 < 0$ ($b_1 > 0$), we would assume a relief (an increase) of unemployment by emigration, that is, the higher the outflow of migrant labor the lower the unemployment rate.

Equation 3 describes the real income per capita (as a measure for the overall standard of living in the country of migrant's origin) as depending on

• the net flow of migrant workers,
• their remittances to relatives,
• the rate of growth of income per capita abroad as a proxy for the dependence of the domestic on the international economic situation, and
• the standard of living in the past (measured by the real income per capita in the period before).

It is expected that c_2, c_3, $c_4 > 0$. That is, the more

• a remaining person is (in the average) supported by money earned abroad by migrant workers,

and the higher

- the growth rate of the most important foreign economies, and
- the standard of living in the past,

the higher is the actual real income per capita in the country of migrant's origin.

Given the general subject of our study, the sign for c_1 is of special interest. It leads to the crucial question, which we asked in the previous section: Does labor migration help or harm the country of worker's origin? If $c_1 \geq 0$ ($c_1 \leq 0$), then there exists no reason to argue that migration harms (helps) the countries of origin. On the contrary, it can be expected that migration increases (decreases) the real income per capita of the remaining population.

PROS AND CONS OF THE MODEL

The simultaneous-equations model has several pros and cons.

As a model based on aggregated migration data, it does not reflect at all the heterogeneous characteristics of the individual migrants composing the aggregate flows. Microeconomic factors had, however, influenced the selection of some explanatory variables. That is, the operational formulation of the macroeconomic migration equation is oriented toward the microeconomic behavior of a single migrant.

The model is highly aggregated not only in the motivational dimension (by the single migrant), but also in the geographical (by single regions) and in the economic activity dimension (by single sectors). It differs neither for rural or urban nor for agricultural or industrial areas, but takes the migrants' home economy as a homogeneous region. Because migration is known to be a selective process, such an aggregation causes a bias of the expectation on migration. Results for the economy as a whole are likely to obscure specific regional or sectoral patterns, and there is no doubt that a disaggregation of national to regional (migration) data would increase the insight of our analysis. But it is almost impossible to obtain reliable data, controlling for either the regional or sectoral dimension. In addition to the pure statistical problems, a disaggregation of the national to the regional level would have to include aspects of internal (labor) migration. Finally, migration politics is almost exclusively a matter of nations and not single regions.

Due to the lack of appropriate time-series data or the problems of specification, our simultaneous-equations model is a relatively small model. On the other hand, the more variables we would have included, the higher the degree of misspecification and the more difficult it would be to obtain statistically significant results controlled for so many more variables.

Formulating the migration equation in a dynamic way is a likely source of inappropriate model specification. The higher the probability of a misspecified migration equation and the less reliable the available migration data, the higher the probability of a "wrong" dynamic behavior of a migration model (as compared to the real world) and the more carefully we should interpret the model outcomes. That is, our model may indicate an explosive, cyclic, or stable time path, even though the real world itself had no such tendencies.

For simplification, in our simultaneous-equations model some explanatory variables are substituted by proxies. For example, we have taken the average income per capita as an explanatory variable. From an analytical point of view, to explain international labor migration, it would have been desirable to take (sector-specific) wage rates. But what more does an officially recorded wage rate tell us? It is well known that the wages of immigrants cannot be measured by sector-specific average wage rates. Immigrants are very likely to be paid a wage far below the average level.

Another example is the interpretation of Todaro's statement "that the job probability variable appears to have 'independent' statistical significance and to add to the overall explanatory power of the regression when isolated from the relative or absolute income differential variable" (Todaro, 1980: 380).

While the concept is straightforward and has become a strong theoretical background in the labor turnover discussion, measuring the probability of obtaining employment is a key problem in empirical migration research. To calculate that probability (which depends on the supply and demand for jobs), we need data on the number of job vacancies and the number of people seeking employment. Unfortunately, these data are hardly available, and we had to represent the turnover approach by the growth in the labor force in the industrial sector of the destination country. This proxy takes into account the fact that the immigrant labor force is concentrated in the industrial sector of the destination country. On the other hand, to reflect the whole idea of the turnover approach, we should also have included an explanatory variable describing the number of layoffs (i.e., quits, discharge, disability, death, retirement, and entrance into the military service).

Finally, our simultaneous-equations model does not respect the effects of migration in the country that receives the migrants or their repercussion on the country of worker's origin. That is to say, we are looking at the case of a small economy that must take the international relations as a condition. This assumption is justified by the findings that the European guest-worker migration flows were determined by the demand of the destination countries (Straubhaar, 1986).

EMPIRICAL ESTIMATION OF THE MODEL

The Data

In order to be able to empirically test our hypotheses on international migration, we had to look for a research area for which we judged the migration data to be more reliable than in any other area. As a result of that search, we ended up taking the migration flows from the European Mediterranean countries of Greece,

Italy, Portugal, Spain, and Turkey into the EC-destination countries between 1960 and 1984.

There are many reasons which justify this choice: Compared to migration flows in other areas, the mass emigration from Southern to Northern Europe started earlier, at the end of the 1950s, providing us with longer time series. Additionally, they are characterized by a lower proportion of illegal or undocumented migrants. Finally, thanks to the OECD-SOPEMI-Reports (OECD, 1973–1985), statistical data on international migration from Southern to Northern Europe are available that find a high level of accord among researchers of migration.

In our procedure we include two types of migration variables. To empirically test the determinants of international labor migration, we are relying on the gross bilateral emigration flows, while for the consequences we are looking at the total net migration flows. Taking the gross out-migration flows as the dependent variable in the equation describing the causes of international labor migration is highly preferable to taking net migration flows, because first, there is no such thing as a "net" migrant, and second, emigration flows may be compensated by remigration flows, both caused by different factors.

To indicate the intensity of migration flows, all migration data in our study are expressed as migration rates. Thereby, the gross emigration flows are divided by the number of the domestic labor force (without emigrants), while the net total migration flows are divided by the total population of the home country (without the emigrants but including the returning migrants).

Measuring the migration rate as computed in our study neglects the fact that migration is a renewable phenomenon. For that reason, a better method would include the average intensity and tempo of migration in the framework of cohort analysis. In the absence of longitudinal data on migration, however, estimations of the average intensity and tempo of migration for a given cohort is not possible.

The Method

An appropriate econometric technique for empirically estimating our simultaneous-equations model is the technique of two-stage least squares (TSLS) (Johnston, 1984: 472–83). Though TSLS is not as efficient as three stage least squares, only the incorrectly specified equation is inconsistently estimated if misspecification is present (Hausman, 1978: 1264–65). Because of the lagged dependent variables m_{t-1}, u_{t-1}, y_{t-1} in each of the three structural equations, the Durbin-Watson statistic is not valid for testing our model for serial correlation. Instead, an easy alternative test provided by Durbin had to be used, which we will call h-statistic in the empirical test of our model (see Pindyck and Rubinfeld, 1981: 194). If this h-statistic indicated a serial correlation problem, either we have reformulated our structural equations to the difference form

$$dm^e = m_t^e - m_{t-1}^e, \quad du = u_t - u_{t-1}, \quad \text{and} \quad dy = Y_t - Y_{t-1}$$

or we have used the Cochrane-Orcutt method.

The presence of serial correlation in the residuals gives some evidence of dynamic misspecification. On the other hand, the adoption of a serial correlation adjustment in the estimation technique imposes untested and unnecessary restrictions on the dynamic structure of the model and is plagued by econometric inefficiency and bias.[3] While in principle our model may be further developed in order to remove these problems by the adoption of more general distributed lag specifications, experiments in this direction indicate that the general framework does not lend itself very readily to the analysis of migration dynamics, since the resulting model may reflect severe and rather intractable residual serial correlation problems.

For these reasons, we will concentrate on the validity of the simulated dynamic outcome of our simultaneous-equations model as compared to the actual historical data, rather than on overcoming the serial correlation problem completely. Nevertheless, when the historical simulation of the dynamic behavior of our model deviated largely from the actual historical data, and, therefore, we had to correct for serial correlation in our model equations, we followed Fair's (1970) advice that the lagged dependent and independent variables must be in the instrument list in order to obtain consistent estimates when doing instrumental variable estimation with a serial correlation correction.

The Results

From Table 10.1 we can see that about two fifths of the estimated coefficients show the expected sign with a statistical significance of 1 percent.[4] About two-thirds of the estimated coefficients are statistically significant at a level of 10 percent or higher, and only one-seventh of the estimated signs are "unexpected."

While this first step gives some insight into the performance of each single regression equation, it does not indicate much about the validity of the model as a whole.

In a multiple-equation model each individual equation may have a very good statistical fit, but the model as a whole may do a very bad job in reproducing the historical data. The converse may also be true; the individual equations of a simulation model may have a very poor statistical fit, but the model when taken as a whole may reproduce the historical time series very closely. (Pindyck and Rubinfeld, 1981: 355).

This difficulty arises because the construction of a simultaneous-equations model often involves understanding the dynamic structure of the system that results when individual equations are combined. Additionally, the goodness of

Table 10.1
Empirical Performance of Our Simultaneous-Equations Model

A) EMIGRATION EQUATION

COUNTRY	EMIGRATION TO	INDEP.VARIABLE	e_t	$g^a_{L,I,t}$	$g^a_{y,t}$	m^e_{t-1}	h	rho	$\bar{R}^2$
		EXPECTED SIGN	+	+	+	+			
GREECE	GERMANY		0.09 ***	-0.97	1.70 *	0.53 ***	0.55		0.98
		T=	5.44	-0.48	1.46	8.73			
ITALY	GERMANY		0.02 **	-0.65	0.66 **	0.74 ***	0.26		0.97
		T=	2.05	-1.19	2.21	7.56			
ITALY	FRANCE		0.04 ***	-0.07	-0.04	0.34 ***	0.18		0.97
		T=	4.94	-0.31	-0.46	2.97			
PORTUGAL	FRANCE		0.01	-0.62	5.69 *	0.80 ***	0.77		0.95
		T=	0.22	-0.07	1.54	14.21			
SPAIN	GERMANY		0.02 ***	-0.10	0.17 **	0.40 ***	0.30		0.98
		T=	6.26	-0.69	2.08	5.09			
SPAIN	FRANCE		0.03 **	-0.53	0.22	0.71 ***	-2.03	-0.38	0.98
		T=	1.89	-1.15	1.16	6.66			
TURKEY	GERMANY		0.09 ***	0.06 ***	-0.01	0.83 ***	2.23	0.45	0.94
		T=	3.21	3.90	-1.30	11.81			

Table 10.1 (continued)

B) UNEMPLOYMENT EQUATION

COUNTRY	INDEP.VARIABLE DEP.VARIABLE	m_t^n ?	$g_{p,t}$ +	$g_{y,t}$ -	$g_{y,t}^{EC}$ -	u_{t-1} +	h (DW)	rho	$\bar{R}^2$
	EXPECTED SIGN								
GREECE	du_t	0.01 **	1.79 ***	-0.14 **	-0.21 *		(2.03)		0.42
	T=	2.55	3.63	-1.99	-1.65				
ITALY	u_t	0.03		-0.11		1.10 ***	0.11		0.89
	T=	0.42		-0.96		16.47			
PORTUGAL	du_t	0.00	0.44 **	-0.04	0.08		(2.36)		0.45
	T=	-0.08	2.28	-0.36	0.50				
SPAIN	du_t	0.04	2.42 ***	-0.44 ***			(1.12)		0.27
	T=	1.67	4.22	-3.06					
TURKEY	du_t	0.16	0.30 ***	-0.09 **	-0.07 **		(1.10)		0.42
	T=	0.42	2.85	-1.98	-1.78				

Table 10.1 (continued)

C) REAL INCOME PER CAPITA EQUATION

COUNTRY	DEP.VARIABLE		m_t^n	r_t	$g_{y,t}^{EC}$	y_{t-1}	h (DW)	rho	$\bar{R}^2$
INDEP.VARIABLE									
EXPECTED SIGN			?	+	+	+			
GREECE	ln y_t		0.03	0.02	1.22	0.95 ***		-0.61	0.99
		T=	-0.24	0.84	4.21	30.13			
ITALY	ln y_t		0.33	0.06	0.38	1.00 ***		0.15	0.98
		T=	0.25	0.47	0.16	14.50			
PORTUGAL	ln y_t		0.01	0.11	0.79 **	0.69 ***	-0.68		0.99
		T=	0.49	2.01	1.95	4.36			
SPAIN	g_t		0.12 ***	0.03 ***	0.00		(1.66)		0.58
		T=	2.91	2.94	0.94				
TURKEY	ln y_t		-0.11 **	0.00 ***	0.05	0.80 ***	0.19		0.98
		T=	-2.27	2.63	0.12	13.19			

* = SIGNIFICANT AT THE 10%-ERROR-LEVEL
** = SIGNIFICANT AT THE 5%-ERROR-LEVEL
*** = SIGNIFICANT AT THE 1%-ERROR-LEVEL

SOURCES : For the income data: OECD (1986b); for the labor market data: OECD (1986a); for the migration data: OECD (1973-).

fit of single structural equations cannot be measured by the R^2 statistics, because it may become negative even when a correct model has been used (Basmann 1962). A replacement of the R^2 statistics and a test of the model's validity are provided by the simulation of our simultaneous-equations model over the sample period. Only by a simulation test can we find out something about the performance of the model as a whole in reproducing the historical data.

The results of this exercise are presented in Table 10.2. We can see that in the long run the simulated time paths closely follow the actual ones. Accepting the average annual percentage error as a proxy for the quality of the performance of our model, we measured rather small annual average deviations of the simulated bilateral emigration flows from the actual ones in most of the cases.[5] The deviation reached more than 20 percent in only one case. For the real income per capita, the simulated annual averages deviated from the actual ones by about 1 percent in four out of five cases, and for Greece only it deviated by about 8 percent. The simulated unemployment rates differed from the actual ones in the annual average by about 5 percent in the cases of Greece, Portugal, and Turkey; by about 20 percent in the case of Italy; and by about 30 percent in the case of Spain.

To evaluate the long-run performance of our model, we also calculated the root-mean-square percent (rms-%) simulation error. For the gross bilateral emigration flows, this measurement indicates a small deviation of the simulated emigration flows: in the case of Greece, Italy, and Portugal of about 65 percent, 30 percent, and 50 percent, respectively. It indicates low deviations in the case of the real income per capita in the range of 3 percent for Italy, Portugal, Spain, and Turkey and of about 8 percent in the case of Greece. For the unemployment rates the model does best in the case of Turkey with a rms-% error of less than 10 percent and worst for Spain with a rms-% error of about 50 percent.[6]

Explaining why the emigration equations indicate larger deviations than the real income per capita and the unemployment rates, two facts are of special importance:

- The gross bilateral emigration flows were much more unstable in their annual variations than the real income per capita flows or the unemployment rates.
- In many cases, the bilateral emigration flows had very low absolute values. Small absolute simulation errors provided, therefore, large relative deviations.

To measure the short-run performance of our simulation model we have calculated Theil's inequality coefficient (Row "Total" in Table 10.2). This statistic indicates for the gross bilateral emigration flows that the simulated variations correspond to the actual variations by about 85 percent in the cases of the Greek and Spanish emigration flows to Germany and the Italian and Spanish flows to France, and by about 75 to 80 percent in the other cases. For the real income per capita, the variations in the actual time paths are reflected by the simulated time paths almost completely. Less than 5 percent of the short-run changes in

Table 10.2
Short- and Long-Run Performance of the Model, 1963–1984

COUNTRY	END.VAR.	LONG-RUN PERFORMANCE ANNUAL AVERAGE		SIMULATION ERROR		SHORT-RUN PERFORMANCE THEIL'S INEQUALITY COEFFICIENT			
		SIMULATED	ACTUAL	MEAN %	RMS-%	TOTAL	TM	TS	TC
GREECE	m^e_t to GER	0.899	0.873	19.8%	64.9%	0.149	0.006	0.152	0.841
	u_t	0.036	0.040	-1.1%	27.9%	0.133	0.132	0.395	0.473
	y_t	2991	3254	-7.6%	8.2%	0.047	0.756	0.125	0.119
ITALY	m^e_t to FRA	0.029	0.029	-1.7%	29.6%	0.129	0.001	0.048	0.951
	m^e_t to GER	0.111	0.184	-44.8%	50.2%	0.243	0.647	0.015	0.338
	u_t	0.051	0.065	-19.7%	23.3%	0.129	0.747	0.050	0.203
	y_t	5831	5753	1.3%	3.2%	0.015	0.203	0.021	0.776
PORTUGAL	m^e_t to FRA	0.712	0.700	1.6%	48.0%	0.252	0.001	0.252	0.747
	u_t	0.047	0.047	4.8%	19.2%	0.060	0.009	0.458	0.533
	y_t	1972	1946	1.1%	3.7%	0.019	0.118	0.106	0.776
SPAIN	m^e_t to FRA	0.052	0.047	10.6%	0.022	0.142	0.053	0.000	0.947
	m^e_t to GER	0.056	0.055	1.8%	0.016	0.112	0.006	0.095	0.900
	u_t	0.073	0.067	27.7%	51.2%	0.102	0.131	0.298	0.571
	y_t	4821	4793	0.3%	2.7%	0.014	0.042	0.331	0.627
TURKEY	m^e_t to GER	0.003	0.003	0.0%	0.002	0.201	0.010	0.318	0.672
	u_t	0.129	0.122	6.3%	7.8%	0.033	0.737	0.027	0.236
	y_t	1082	1092	-0.9%	3.1%	0.015	0.052	0.008	0.900

For Spain and Turkey: Emigration Mean % error = %-Difference between simulated and actual average;
Emigration RMS-% error = RMS error.

the Greek and less than 2 percent in the Italian, Portuguese, Spanish, and Turkish real income per capita are not predicted by its simulation with our model. For the unemployment rate, less than 15 percent of the short-run variations in the actual data are not reflected in our simulation results in the cases of Greece, Italy, and Spain. For Portugal and Turkey, about 5 percent of the short-run changes remained unpredicted.

The decomposition of Theil's inequality coefficient into proportions of inequality (see the row "T^M, T^S, T^C" in Table 10.2), with few exceptions, shows neither a systematic error (indicated by T^M) nor a variance problem (T^S). Most of the simulation errors are due to the unsystematic error (indicated by T^C). This breakdown of the simulation errors into their characteristic sources shows, therefore, in most cases, the ideal (and not worrisome) distribution of inequality over the three sources. To summarize, we can learn from the different statistics, mentioned only briefly, that our model is useful to explain the time paths of the endogenous variations both in the short run and in the long run.

An Interpretation of the Results

Once the validity of our three simultaneous-equations model is accepted, we can start looking at the signs and values of the estimated coefficients in an analytical sense. In summarizing the results by country, we would assume that the gross bilateral emigration flows

- from Greece to Germany were driven mostly by the attractivity difference between Greece and Germany, and less strongly by the dynamics of the emigration movement and by the German demand for foreign labor;
- from Italy to Germany and to France have followed a similar pattern in regard to the attractivity difference to the destination country. In regard to the variations in the economic situation in the destination countries (proxied by the growth rate of the real income per capita), the Italian emigration flows have been elastic in the case of Germany but not in the case of France. Thereby, the emigration flows to Germany had a much stronger self-feeding element than in the French case;
- from Portugal to France were driven mostly by the French demand pattern for foreign labor. The more (or less) the French economy was in need of migrant workers, the more (or less) Portuguese emigrated to France. Additionally, the high value of the parameter for the lagged dependent variable indicates a strong dynamic chain migration effect;
- from Spain to Germany and to France have followed a very similar pattern, where the attractivity differences were the most important determinants. The Spanish-French emigration pattern was more elastic to changes in its determinants than the Spanish-German emigration flows. The snowball effect of the emigration dynamics was twice as strong in the Spanish-French emigration flows than in the Spanish-German emigration flows;
- from Turkey to Germany were characterized by the high elasticity of the Turkish emigration pattern to changes in the German attractivity and by the low (and negative) elasticity to the changes in the German real income per capita. These results might

indicate that the Turkish-German emigration pattern has followed a path not only determined by the economic factors included in our model. The high value of the parameter for the lagged emigration variable supports this expectation. It indicates that factors causing emigration in a previous period (and not necessarily reflected by the exogenous variables included in our simultaneous-equations model) participate to a large extent in the explanation of the actual Turkish emigration flows to Germany.

In the unemployment equation, we are most interested in the sign of the estimated coefficient for m_i^n. The very low value of the parameters of the net migration variables and their low statistical significance suggest that on an aggregated (national) level, migration is not a powerful labor market policy. Its magnitude (as compared to the total unemployed labor force in the home countries) is small, and it relieves the labor market pressure of unemployment to a marginal extent only.

Given the basic question of our research—does migration harm or help the development of the country of migrants' origin—a look at the sign of the estimated coefficient of m_i^n allows us to answer this key question. If the sign is positive, we would expect that emigration stimulated the development of the country of origin and that remigration rather harmed this development process. If the sign is negative, we would expect the opposite.

According to our results, migration did not strongly affect the variations in the real income per capita. In the cases of Greece and Portugal, the estimated coefficients are near nil and statistically insignificant, and therefore not reliable for quantitative interpretation. The same is true for Italy, where the estimated value, indicating that an increase of the net migration rate by 0.1 percent (in absolute terms, for example, from a rate of 1 percent to a rate of 1.1 percent) would increase the real income per capita by about 3 percent. For Turkey this estimated parameter is statistically negative, indicating that an increase of the net migration rate by 0.1 percent (in absolute terms) would decrease the real income per capita by about 1 percent. For Spain, we may fairly assume that an increase of the net migration rate by 1 percent would stimulate the growth of the real income per capita by about 0.12 percent (in absolute terms, for example, from a rate of 1 percent to a rate of 1.12 percent).

In our model, the influence of migrants' remittances on the real income per capita of those remaining is also included. According to our estimated parameters, this relationship is positive in the cases of Spain and Turkey with a statistical significance at the 1 percent level and in the case of Portugal with a statistical significance at the 5 percent level. An increase by 1 percent of the average amount of remitted money per remaining person increased the average real income per capita by about 0.1 percent in the case of Portugal, and by less than 0.01 percent in the case of Turkey. For Spain, an increase by 1 percent of the average amount of remitted money per remaining person stimulated the growth of the real income per capita by about 0.03 percent.

Taking together these two migration-related variables, our model allows the

Table 10.3
Simulated and Actual Averages for the Real Income Per Capita and the Unemployment Rate for Greece, Italy, Portugal, Spain, and Turkey, 1963–1984

COUNTRY	VARIABLE	SIMULATED W/O EMIGRA	ACTUAL	DIF % MEAN %
GREECE	u_t	8.4%	4.0%	4.4%
	y_t	2903	3254	-9.4%
ITALY	u_t	5.0%	6.5%	-1.5%
	y_t	5881	5753	1.9%
PORTUGAL	u_t	6.0%	4.7%	1.3%
	y_t	1490	1946	-21.2%
SPAIN	u_t	10.5%	6.7%	3.8%
	y_t	4332	4793	-9.6%
TURKEY	u_t	12.5%	12.2%	0.3%
	y_t	932	1092	-11.8%

W/O EMIGRA = Without Emigration

$$\text{DIF \%} = u_t^{sim} - u_t^{act}; \qquad \text{MEAN \%} = \frac{1}{T} \sum_{63}^{84} [(y_t^{sim} - y_t^{act})/y_t^{act}] * 100$$

conclusion of a positive influence of emigration on the economic development of the home country in the cases of Italy, Portugal, and Spain. In the cases of Greece and Turkey, with one of the two variables showing a negative sign, this conclusion cannot be drawn yet. Additional investigation has to be made.

To get some more insight about the development effect of international migration on a migrant's home economy, we can simulate our model under the assumption that there was no international migration from these countries. From our results presented in Table 10.3, we learn that under the assumption of no migration,

- in Greece, the real income per capita would have been lower by about 10 percent, and the unemployment rate might have been about 8 percent instead of the actual 4 percent;

- in Italy, the real income per capita would have been slightly higher, and the unemployment rate might have been lower and reached about 5 percent instead of the actual 6.5 percent;

- in Portugal, the real income per capita would have been significantly lower by about 20 percent, and the unemployment rate might have been about 6 percent instead of the actual 5 percent;

- in Spain, the real income per capita would have been smaller by about 10 percent, and the unemployment rate might have been lower and reached about 10 percent instead of 7 percent;

- in Turkey, the real income per capita would have been smaller by about 10 percent, while the unemployment rate might not have changed much and reached a level of about 12 percent.

In summary, we suggest that, according to our data and results, migration has not negatively affected the development of the Southern European countries of migrants' origin, but it has stimulated the economic development of these countries (measured in terms of real income per capita and the unemployment rate in the home country).

CONCLUSIONS

In testing our simultaneous-equations model empirically, we have applied it to the migration flows from the Southern European countries Greece, Italy, Portugal, Spain, and Turkey to the EC-destination countries Germany and France. From the outcome of this application, we learn that a composite attractivity index, as it has been used in the context of the Todaro model for internal migration, is a very powerful explanatory variable also in the case of international labor migration. Todaro's basic idea that the ratio between the real income per capita abroad and at home, weighted by the probability of obtaining a higher-paying job abroad, is an important determinant of migration flows acquired some empirical evidence. Formulated in slightly modified form (to reflect the fact that European migration flows were demand-determined), the migration equation based on Todaro's idea explained the European migration patterns well.

It also turned out that the immigration control systems of the EC-destination countries have closely followed economic lines, drawn by the domestic demand for foreign labor. The strictness of the immigration restrictions were inversely related to the domestic labor surplus. The higher the unemployment rate in the EC-destination countries (and the more restrictive, therefore, their immigration control systems), the less immigrants have been admitted and the more foreign workers have been sent back.

Contrary to our expectation, the job turnover in the destination country (proxied in our model by the labor force employed in the industrialized sector of the destination country) did not determine the migration patterns. Because these variables were statistically significant in most of the internal migration models that were using a job turnover approach, further research is indicated before we may reject the validity of such an approach in the case of international labor migration.

The estimated parameters of the lagged emigration variable showed values in the range of 0.3 to 0.8. This variance may be explained in different ways. From an analytical point, in our demand-determined Todaro approach, the addition of the lagged endogenous variable takes the gross bilateral emigration flows as a function of the expected values of the explanatory variables, with expectations generally formed on the basis of a distributed lag of current and past values of the explanatory variables. A low value of the parameter may reflect, therefore, a lower expected net gain of migration; a high value, a higher expected net gain of migration. Within a dynamic view of the migration pattern, a high value of the parameter of the lagged emigration variable indicates a high self-feeding element in the emigration flows. It reflects a high tendency towards a chain migration process. A low value indicates the opposite. From an econometric point of view, a high value of the parameter of the lagged emigration variable may indicate a tendency towards a not especially well specified migration equation. That is, most of the present variation in the dependent emigration variable is explained by the lagged dependent emigration variable but not by current variations in the other explanatory variables.

In asking for the consequences of international labor migration, our simultaneous-equations model indicates no empirical evidence that international labor migration has harmed, but some support that international labor migration has influenced positively, but rather weakly, the overall economic development of the countries of workers' origin. The quantitative results of our simultaneous-equations model and of the simulation exercise suggest a contribution of international labor migration to the overall economic growth of the countries of emigration by 10 percent of total growth in the maximum.

Apart from the Sapir (1981) paper, there does not appear to be any published work on international labor migration flows that uses a similar simultaneous-equations model based on time series data.[7] Checking our results with other work is not possible, therefore, and we can compare the outcome of our simultaneous-equations model to Sapir's work only. In his conclusion, Sapir (1981: 173–74) gives strong support to our feeling about the impact of international labor migration for the countries of workers' origin: "The model suggests that the large scale labor emigration that took place in Yugoslavia during the period from 1966 to 1972 has been beneficial to this economy, at least on an aggregate level. Indeed, it appears to have increased the gross domestic product. . . . Also, it has decreased the unemployment rate." The correspondence of our results to Sapir's conclusions is an important confirmation for the validity of the empirical outcome of our simultaneous-equations model.

NOTES

1. As an exception we mention Sapir (1981). He has analyzed the impact of international migration on the Yugoslav economy, using a macroeconomic model and time series data for the period from 1965 to 1972.

2. Salvatore (1981b) has even shown that for the internal migration flows in Italy it was theoretically and empirically preferable to take the explanatory variables separately and independently, rather than within a single composite Todaro index.

3. Here, we may only mention the limited applicability of the Cochrane-Orcutt procedure to correct for serial correlation in the case of small samples (Harvey, 1981: 198). In following Greenwood and Hunt (1984: 962), we had to look, therefore, for the validity of our model by a fully dynamic historical simulation.

4. Following Greenwood (1975b: 804), we will classify the signs of our estimations in the categories "not unexpected" and "unexpected," where we mean by "not unexpected" either expected a priori or not specified. We will also follow his procedure that "when a coefficient has a 'wrong' sign (or when a sign is not specified), a two-tail test of the null hypothesis is applied" and use a one-tail test otherwise (i.e., when a sign is expected). For better model specification y_i and r_i are expressed in their logarithmic form.

5. Due to the fact that the actual emigration rates were lower than 0.001 in some years, for Spain and Turkey the figures in Table 10.2 reflect respectively the percentage difference between the simulated and actual mean, and the rms error.

6. While these rms percentage-errors may seem large, they are encouraging as compared to the rms percentage-errors of some of the simultaneous-equations model on internal migration (see as an example Greenwood and Hunt 1984: 967).

7. The World Bank research study on labor migration in the Middle East and North Africa analyzes labor migration using a simultaneous-equations model (Serageldin et al., 1983; the complete model was described in World Bank, 1983). The results of that study, however, were of interest rather on the level of model techniques, indicating "avenues" for further studies in the "development of an alternative and better algorithm for the solution of the systemic model" (World Bank, 1985: 38) than in the context of carrying out "detailed field work and econometric studies which could be used to predict migration flows among countries in response to economic and other social variables" (World Bank, 1985: 2).

REFERENCES

Basmann, R. L. (1962). "Letter to the Editor." *Econometrica* 30: 824–26.

Bhagwati, J. N. (1983). *Essays in International Economic Theory*. R. C. Feenstra, ed. Vol. 2. Cambridge, Mass.: MIT Press.

——— (1984). "Incentives and Disincentives: International Migration." *Weltwirtschaftliches Archiv* 120: 678–701.

Böhning, W. R. (1984). *Studies in International Labour Migration*. New York: St. Martin's Press.

Fair, R. C. (1970). "The Estimation of Simultaneous Equation Models with Lagged Endogenous Variables and First Order Serially Correlated Errors." *Econometrica* 38: 507 16.

Fields, G. S. (1975). "Rural-Urban Migration, Urban Unemployment and Underemployment, and Job-Search Activity in LDCs." *Journal of Development Economics* 2: 165–87.

——— (1976). "Labor Force Migration, Unemployment and Job Turnover." *Review of Economics and Statistics* 61: 21–32.

Greenwood, M. J. (1975a). "Research on Internal Migration in the U.S.: A Survey." *Journal of Economic Literature* 13: 397–433.

————— (1975b). "A Simultaneous-Equations Model of Urban Growth and Migration." *Journal of the American Statistical Association* 70: 797–810.

————— (1985). "Human Migration: Theory, Models, and Empirical Studies." *Journal of Regional Science* 25: 521–44.

Greenwood, M. J., and G. L. Hunt (1984). "Migration and Interregional Employment Redistribution in the United States." *American Economic Reveiw* 74: 957–69.

Greenwood, M. J., et al. (1986). "Migration and Employment Change: Empirical Evidence on the Spatial and Temporal Dimensions of the Linkage." *Journal of Regional Science* 26: 223–34.

Harvey, A. C. (1981). *The Econometric Analysis of Time Series*. Oxford: Philip Allan.

Hausman, J. A. (1978). "Specification Tests in Econometrics." *Econometrica* 46: 1251–71.

Johnston, J. (1984). *Econometric Methods*. 3d ed. Tokyo: McGraw-Hill.

Muth, R. F. (1971). "Migration: Chicken or Egg?" *Southern Economic Journal* 37: 295–306.

OECD (1973–1985). *SOPEMI* (Système d'Observation Permanente des Migrations), various reports yearly from 1973 to 1985. Paris: OECD.

————— (1986a). *Labour Force Statistics 1963–1983*. Paris: OECD.

————— (1986b). *National Accounts 1971–1983*. Vol. 1. Main Aggregates. Paris: OECD.

Pindyck, R. S., and D. L. Rubinfeld (1981). *Econometric Models and Economic Forecasts*. 2d ed. New York: McGraw-Hill.

Salvatore, D. (1980). "A Simultaneous Equations Model of Internal Migration with Dynamic Policy Simulations and Forecasting." *Journal of Development Economics* 7: 231–46.

————— (1981a). *Internal Migration and Economic Development*. Washington, D.C.: University Press of America.

————— (1981b). "A Theoretical and Empirical Evaluation and Extension of the Todaro Migration Model." *Regional Science and Urban Economics* 11: 499–508.

————— (1984). "An Econometric Model of Internal Migration and Development," *Regional Science and Urban Economics* 14: 77–87.

Sapir, A. (1981). "Economic Reform and Migration in Yugoslavia (An Econometric Model)." *Journal of Development Economics* 9: 149–81.

Serageldin, I., et al. (1983). *Manpower and International Labor Migration in the Middle East and North Africa*. New York: Oxford University Press.

Shaw, R. P. (1975). *Migration Theory and Fact (A Review and Bibliography of Current Literature)*. Bibliography Series No. 5. Philadelphia: Regional Science Research Institute.

Stahl, C. W. (1982). "Labor Emigration and Economic Development." *International Migration Review* 16: 869–99.

Straubhaar, T. (1986). "The Causes of International Labor Migration—A Demand-Determined Approach." *International Migration Review* 20 (Winter Issue).

————— (1987). *On the Economics of International Labor Migration*. Bern/Stuttgart: Paul Haupt.

Swamy, G. (1985). *Population and International Migration*. World Bank Staff Working Paper No. 689. Washington, D.C.: World Bank.

Todaro, M. P. (1969). "A Model of Labor Migration and Urban Unemployment in Less Developed Countries," *American Economic Review* 59: 138–48.

————— (1980). "Internal Migration in Developing Countries: A Survey." In *Population and Economic Change in Developing Countries,* R. A. Easterlin, ed. Chicago: University of Chicago Press.

World Bank (1983). *Tools for Manpower Planning.* Vols. 1–4. World Bank Staff Working Papers No. 587–590. Washington, D.C.: World Bank.

———— (1985). *Simulating Flows of Labor in the Middle East and North Africa.* World Bank Staff Working Paper No. 736. Washington, D.C.: World Bank.

PART THREE

Population Size and Growth, Technical Change, Status of Women, and International Responsibility

Population Density and Farming Systems: The Changing Locus of Innovations and Technical Change

PRABHU L. PINGALI and HANS P. BINSWANGER

Rapid population growth since the turn of the century has led to an exhaustion of the land frontier in most countries across the world, causing a decline in arable land per capita. Traditional societies across the world have devised remarkably similar means of coping with reductions in per capita land availability. This chapter highlights the farmer-based and modern technological options available to societies for achieving growth in agricultural output through increases in land and labor productivity.

The farmer's means of coping with increasing population densities or increased demand for agricultural output is usually an expansion of the area under cultivation. Additional land is brought under cultivation either through a reduction in fallow periods or through the cultivation of virgin land. With the exhaustion of the land frontier, intensive cultivation of permanent fields becomes the norm. Permanent cultivation systems are characterized by land investments for terracing, drainage, and irrigation; intensive manuring systems; and a change from hand cultivation to the use of animal draft power. All of Europe and East Asia and most of South Asia made this transition to permanent cultivation of land before this century, while most of Sub-Saharan Africa is still under fallow systems today. By comparing Sub-Saharan Africa with Asia, we are able to illustrate the process of agricultural intensification and the associated changes in agricultural technology.

Farmer-generated technical change is capable of sustaining slow and steadily growing populations with modest increases in agricultural output. It appears, however, to be incapable of supporting rapidly rising agricultural populations or rapidly rising nonagricultural demand for food. It is at this stage that large-scale irrigation systems and science- and industry-based technical changes must become major sources of the rate of growth in agricultural output. State-supported large-scale irrigation systems have been in existence for centuries in China and Egypt and have become prominent in India in the late nineteenth and early twentieth centuries. Inputs such as high-yielding seed varieties and chemical fertilizers not only increase the productivity of land but also increase the productivity of labor, thus leading to increases in per capita output and therefore generating surpluses that can be transferred to the nonagricultural populations. However, the transition to science- and industry-based inputs is costly, especially in terms of establishing an institutional structure and an industrial base that is capable of generating and supplying these technologies. The ability of a country to achieve rapid growth in agricultural output is therefore constrained by the size of its physical and human capital base.

The first section of this chapter discusses the determinants of the intensity of land use, emphasizing the consequences of population concentration and improvements in transport infrastructure. Section two discusses the farmer-based innovations in response to agricultural intensification, and section three analyzes the role of science and industry based innovations in achieving rapid increases in agricultural output.[1]

DETERMINANTS OF THE INTENSITY OF LAND USE

Population Density

The existence of a positive correlation between the intensity of land use and population density has been shown by Boserup (1965, 1980). She argues from the premise that during the neolithic period forests covered a much larger part of the land surface than today. The replacement of forests by bush and grassland was caused by (among other things) a reduction in fallow periods due to increasing population densities. "The invasion of forest and bush by grass is more likely to happen when an increasing population of long fallow cultivators cultivate the land with more and more frequent intervals" (Boserup, 1965: 20).

Table 11.1 presents the relationship between population density and the intensity of the agricultural system. At very sparse population densities, up to four persons per square kilometer, the prevailing form of farming is the forest fallow system. A plot of forest land is cleared and cultivated for one or two years and then allowed to lie fallow for twenty to twenty-five years. This period of fallowness is sufficient to allow forest regrowth. An increase in population density will result in a reduction in the fallow period, and eventually the forest land degenerates to bush savannah. Bush fallow is characterized by cultivation of a plot of land for two to six years followed by six to ten years of fallowness. The period of fallow is too short to allow forest regrowth. Increasing population densities are associated with longer periods of continuous cultivation and shorter fallow periods. Eventually the fallow period becomes too short for anything but grass growth. The transition to grass fallow occurs at population densities of around sixteen to sixty-four persons per square kilometer. Further increases in population result in the movement to annual and multi-cropping, the most intensive systems of cultivation.

Table 11.1
Food-Supply Systems in the Tropics

System[a]	Farming intensity (R value)[b]	Density of population[c] (persons per square kilometer)	Tools used[d]
Gathering (G)	0	0–4	None
Forest-fallow (FF)	0–10	0–4	Axe, machete, and digging stick
Bush-fallow (BF)	10–40	4–64	Axe, machete, digging stick, and hoe
Short-fallow (SF)	40–80	16–64	Hoe, animal traction
Annual cultivation (AC)	80–120	64–256	Animal traction and tractor

a. Description of food-supply systems:
Gathering—wild plants, roots, fruits, nuts
Forest-fallow—one or two crops followed by fifteen to twenty years of fallow
Bush-fallow—two or more crops followed by eight to ten years of fallow
Short-fallow—one or two crops followed by one or two years of fallow; also known as *grass-fallow*
Annual cultivation—one crop each year
Multiple cropping—two or more crops in the same field each year. These systems are not mutually exclusive. Two or more may very well be practiced concurrently—cultivated in concentric rings of various lengths of fallow, for example, as in Senegal.
b. R = (number of crop cycles per year × number of years of cultivation × 100) ÷ (number of years of cultivation + number of years of fallow). *Source:* Ruthenberg (1980, 16).
c. These figures are only approximations, the exact numbers depending on location-specific fertility of the soil and agroclimatic conditions. *Sources:* Boserup (1981, 19, 23); Ruthenberg (1980).
d. *Sources:* Ruthenberg (1980); Boserup (1965).

The above discussion leads to the broad generalization that, for given agro-climatic conditions, increases in population density will gradually move the agricultural system from forest fallow to annual cultivation and even multi-cropping. The reasons for population concentration or growth and the consequent decline in arable land per capita are discussed subsequently.

Since the turn of this century, we have observed a substantial increase in the natural rate of population growth across the world, mainly due to a sharp decline in the death rates caused by rapid advances in public health services. At the worldwide level, and at the level of a specific country, the decline in arable land per capita must be attributed primarily to this general increase in population. Within a country and within regions, however, population concentrations vary by soil fertility, altitude, and market accessibility. These intracountry variations are briefly discussed below using examples primarily from Sub-Saharan Africa. Table 11.2 provides the major causes and consequences of population concentration.

Soil Fertility

The marginal productivity of labor is relatively higher on more fertile soils; hence one would expect immigration from less endowed areas leading to reductions in cultivable areas per capita. Ada district, Ethiopia, Nyanza Province, Kenya, and the southern province of Zambia are a few examples of fertile areas that are relatively densely populated and intensively cultivated. High-altitude areas are similarly densely populated due to immigration from the lowlands because of lower disease incidence (notably malaria and sleeping sickness). Population concentrations on the Ethiopian and Kenyan highlands are examples of this phenomenon.

Transport Infrastructure and Market Access

Given suitable soil conditions, areas with better access to markets, either through transport networks or those in the proximity of urban centers, will be more intensively cultivated. Intensification occurs due to two reasons:

1. Higher prices and elastic demand for exportables implies that marginal utility of effort is higher, hence farmers in the region will begin cultivating larger areas.
2. Higher returns to labor encourage immigration into the area from neighboring regions with higher transport costs.

Intensive groundnut production in Senegal, maize production in Kenya and Zambia, and cotton production in Uganda have all followed the installation of the railway and have been mainly concentrated in areas close to the railway line. Similarly, agricultural production around Kano, Lagos, Nairobi, Kampala, and other urban centers is extremely intensive compared to other parts of these countries.

Other Causes

Finally, it should be noted that inter- and intra-country variations in population densities, especially in Sub-Saharan Africa, have historically been caused by tribal warfare and slave trade resulting in population concentrations in relatively inaccessible highlands. Population concentration on the high plateau of Rwanda and Burundi was in response to the incursions of slave traders as well as for health reasons. Similar migrations from the lowlands to the Mandara Mountains in Cameroon, the Jos Plateau in Nigeria, and the Rift Valley in Kenya and

Table 11.2
Causes and Consequences of Increased Population Density

Condition	Cause	Consequence	Action taken
Natural growth of population	Improved public health and lack of emigration	Reduction in available area per capita	*Reduction in fallow periods* Movement from shifting to permanent cultivation
Soil fertility	Immigration to capture the benefits of higher returns to labor input		*Mechanization* Plowing—where agroclimatic and soil conditions make it profitable
Transport facilities[a]	Immigration to capture the benefits of reduced transport costs		Transport—where markets exist for food and other crops
Urban demand[a]	Immigration to capture the benefits of proximity to markets		Milling—in response to higher opportunity cost of time for female household members
Health	Immigration to cooler highlands to avoid malaria and the tsetse fly		*Investments in land* For soil fertility, drainage, terracing; increase in the marginal lands brought under cultivation
Historic	Immigration to inaccessible highlands to avoid tribal warfare and the slave trade		
Land laws, rights	Restrictions on the right to open new land		*Land rights* From communal to private ownership of land

a. With improved transport facilities and urban demand and in the absence of immigration, the area under cultivation will expand.

Tanzania have been based on the desire for security. Subsequent population growth has made many of these areas the most densely populated parts of Africa.

FARMER-BASED INNOVATIONS IN RESPONSE TO INTENSIFICATION

Traditional societies across the world have devised remarkably similar means of coping with reductions in agricultural land per capita. Farmer-initiated adjustments to growing land scarcity are: a reduction in fallow periods and the concentration of cultivation on soils most responsive to intensification; an increase in land investments, such as destumping, terracing, drainage, and irrigation; an increase in labor input for more intensive manuring techniques; and a switch from hand hoes to animal-drawn plows and then to tractors.

Changes in Land Use

The intensification of agricultural systems is constrained by climatic and soil factors. Table 11.1 illustrates the impact of climatic factors on the intensification of the agricultural system. For given agroclimatic conditions, the extent of intensification is conditional on the relative responsiveness of the soils to inputs associated with intensive production, such as land improvements, manure, and fertilizers. The responsiveness of intensification is generally higher on soils with higher water- and nutrient-holding capacity. This is primarily because higher water-holding capacity reduces drought risk. Water-holding capacity is higher the deeper the soils and the higher their clay content. It is low on shallow sandy soils.

Figure 11.1 presents a stylized picture of the differences in soil types across a toposequence for given agroclimatic conditions. Soils on the upper slopes are relatively light and easy to work by hand; tillage requirements are minimal on these soils. The clay content of the soils increases as one goes down the toposequence; consequently power requirements for land preparation increase. Higher clay content also reduces yield risks due to increased water retention capacity of the soils. The soils are heaviest in the depressions and marshes at the bottom of the toposequence. These *bas-fonds* or bottomlands are often extremely hard to prepare by hand and are often impossible to cultivate in the absence of investments in water control and drainage. The high labor requirements for capital investments and land preparation make the bottomlands the least preferred for cultivation under low population densities, and they are often found to be fallow. As population densities increase, however, the bottomlands become intensively cultivated, due to the relatively higher returns offered to labor and land investments, especially in rice cultivation. Also, as population densities increase, labor supply increases, making it possible to undertake the labor-intensive investments in irrigation, drainage, and so forth.

For instance, Grove (1961) cites the case of *fadama* (flood land) use in Northern Zaria, Nigeria. This land was not cultivated by the local farmers, who preferred

Figure 11.1
Toposequence and Soil Type

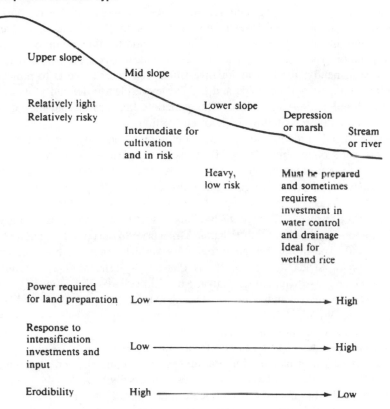

the lighter soils of the mid-slopes. Seasonal migrants from the densely populated areas near Kano, however, chose to cultivate this land, as they had long been accustomed to bottomland cultivation. The "stranger farmers" from Kano cultivated the *fadamas* in the dry season until the population densities in Zaria became high enough to induce the local group to undertake this type of cultivation as well. *Fadamas* in Zaria are now fully utilized and are scarce, being bought, sold, and rented.

Soil type differences across a toposequence that are characterized here could be microvariations limited to a few hundred meters or a few kilometers, or they could be macrovariations where entire regions are part of one level of toposequence. For example, the northeastern part of Thailand can be characterized as being the upper slopes, while the central plains of Thailand are the lower slopes and valley bottoms.

Land Investments

In the early stages of agricultural intensification—forest and early bush fallow—there are almost no investments made in land. Tree cover is cleared by felling and fire and the stumps are left in the ground to allow quick regeneration of vegetation when the plots are returned to fallow. As a plot of land is used more permanently, the first major investment that takes place is to remove all the tree stumps from the fields and to have more clearly defined plots of land on which cultivation takes place. This generally happens around the late bush fallow and early grass fallow stage of cultivation.

As discussed in the previous section, cultivation generally starts on the easy-to-work soils of the mid-slopes. These soils are also the most susceptible to erosion as the farming system intensifies. Accordingly, systems of land use in Africa developed protective devices against erosion as population densities increased, such as: ridging and tie-ridging, silt traps, and elaborate systems of stone-walled terraces. These protective land investments were in use in the more densely populated parts of Sub-Saharan Africa prior to the colonial period (Allan, 1965: 386). The hilltop refuges provided several historic examples of terrace cultivation in Africa, for instance: Jos Plateau, Nigeria; Mandara Mountains, Cameroon; Kikuyu Highlands, Kenya; Mt. Kilimanjaro, Tanzania; Kigezi District, Uganda; and Rwanda-Burundi (Okogbo, 1977; Morgan, 1969; and Gleave and White, 1969).

Anti-erosion investments in land are becoming increasingly common in the more recently intensified areas of Africa. Machakos District of Kenya, for example, was a site of increased migration from the highlands, and between 1955 and 1965 the farmers in the district almost universally accepted the practice of bench terracing the intensively cultivated mid-slopes (Ahn, 1979).

As population densities increase, one observes a movement from the mid-slopes to the hard-to-work soils of the lower slopes and depressions. This movement to the valley bottoms creates a need for drainage without which the heavy, waterlogged soils cannot be brought under cultivation. The investment in draining is labor intensive and is generally avoided until population pressure makes the cultivation of this land remunerative. The use of the valley bottoms for rice cultivation, which is very common and a very important source of food supply in South and Southeast Asia, is rare in tropical Africa. Floodland cultivation of rice in Guinea, Sierre Leone, the Senegal and Niger valleys, and the basin of Lake Victoria has been increasing, and one would expect this trend to continue throughout Africa. For instance, in Sukumaland, Tanzania, the flood plain land that forty years ago was left for grazing is now completely cultivated with rice, and the demand for this land is extremely high (Rounce, 1949).

In Asia, small-scale irrigation and water-control techniques that reduce water stress or allow dry-season cultivation are very common. In semi-arid India, the gently rolling hills are intensively used for rainfed crops, the run-off being stored in tanks and used for irrigated wet rice cultivation in the valley bottoms. While some of these tank systems have been in operation for hundreds of years, the majority of the investment in these systems was made in the late nineteenth and early twentieth centuries. Since the 1950s, tank irrigation has been surpassed by investment in wells for cultivating a second crop on the mid-slopes. Water is drawn from the wells with the help of electric or diesel pumps (Engelhardt, 1984). The ultimate in water-control structures is seen in the meticulously terraced hillsides of Java and the Philippines where in each rice field the required depth of water is stored and the excess drained into the field immediately below (Ruthenberg, 1980).

As the land frontier becomes exhausted, farmer-initiated irrigation systems have to be complemented by state-supported, large-scale irrigation systems. Large-scale irrigation systems are of great antiquity in Egypt, China, and Japan. They have become very important in India, Korea, and Taiwan in recent decades. The building of such large-scale systems is induced by high population density when adequate labor supply is available and when the demand for expanding cultivated area through irrigation is high. The failure of large-scale irrigation systems in Sub-Saharan Africa can be attributed to labor scarcity and the lack of demand for expanding cultivated area. The Office du Niger scheme in Mali is a case in point. The 50,000 hectares that were actually developed by 1964 fall far short of the initial target of several hundred thousand hectares; and even in this area the density of settlement is insufficient to yield an output that would meet all costs of both the settlers and the management of the scheme, provide the settlers with good livelihood, and earn some return on the large amount of capital invested (de Wilde, 1967: 288).

Development of Organic Fertilizer Use

Under forest and bush fallow cultivation, long term soil fertility is maintained by periodic fallowing of land. Renewed vegetative growth on fallowed land helps to return fresh organic matter to the top soil and therefore recharges it with nutrients. When fire is used for clearing vegetation, the burnt ashes return to the soil the nutrients taken up by trees and bush cover. This closed cycle of nutrient supply is disrupted when long fallow periods are replaced by grass fallows. Accordingly, at this stage the farmer starts complementing fallow periods with additional organic wastes from the household, mainly in the form of vegetative waste and dung from cattle and livestock. At first these fertilization techniques are fairly rudimentary, often involving no more than a periodic transport of household refuse to the plots to be cultivated. Sometimes, as in the case of the farmers on the Mandara mountains and the Ethiopian highlands, the dwellings are situated at a high point so that the refuse washes down to the fields below. In the lower rainfall zones, where vegetative cover is lower, more labor input may be required to augment the supplies from the household. The Bemba in Zambia, for instance, used to cut branches from surrounding trees and carry them onto the plot of land to be cultivated and burn the pile of branches to provide nutrients for the plot (Chitemene techniques). Richards (1961) reported that branches were cut from an area up to six times as large as that to be planted.

As farming intensities increase more labor intensive fertilizing techniques such as composting and then manuring evolve. The Fipa of Tanzania collect fallen and cut vegetation and bury it in mounds. Beans, manioc, cowpeas, and so on are planted on these mounds, which are rich in nutrients due to rotting vegetation. This system of composting is common in Tanzania, Zambia, and Zaire (Miracle, 1967).

The use of animal manure is common in most of the densely settled, intensively cultivated pockets of Sub-Saharan Africa. Farmers in the hill refuges, mentioned earlier, have for generations used manure on their terraced fields. The inhabitants of the very densely populated Ukara Island in Lake Victoria laboriously collect three tons of manure per year from each adult cattle and transport it to the fields by headloads. In addition to this, they practice green manuring with legumes (Allan, 1965: 201). The use of manure is also characteristic of the densely populated parts of Northern Nigeria. In the villages of Katsina Province, livestock are kept tethered in the compound and the manure is collected in heaps. Household refuse and ashes are added to the heaps. Those farmers with large holdings usually supplement their supplies through an active manure market. In the villages near Kano city, farm manure was complemented by night soil transported from the city (Gleave and White, 1969: 284). In areas where livestock herding has traditionally been separate from farming, one tends to observe contracts between herders and farmers as farming intensities increase. The typical case being a farmer inviting a herder to graze his stock on the fallow land and thus benefit from the cattle droppings. Toulmin (1983) describes such contracts in central Mali. Farmer-herder contracts are also common in India.

Finally, one observes the incorporation of legumes such as green manure in a crop rotation cycle. Green manuring, along with other fertility-restoring measures, is a common practice in several parts of India and China. The use of cowpeas in the rotation cycle is becoming increasingly common among the permanently cultivated areas of Africa. All of the manuring techniques discussed above were and continue to be very important in China, Japan, and most of Europe.

As agriculture intensifies, one observes a sharp decline in yields due to a drop in soil fertility, which can only be reversed by more labor intensive fertility restoring techniques. Pingali and Binswanger (1984), using data from fifty-two specific locations in Africa, Asia, and Latin America, show a significant positive association between manure use and farming intensity. It is important to note that farmers at lower agricultural intensities are already familiar with the more evolved manuring techniques, since many of them use these techniques on their garden plots. The reason they do not use these techniques on all their fields is that there are other alternatives, such as fallowing, that require much lower labor input than intensive manure production. It is only when land pressure makes it inevitable that general use of these techniques is resorted to.

The Evolution of Tool Systems

, The transition from digging sticks and hand hoes to the plow is closely correlated with the intensity of farming. The simplest form of agricultural tool, the digging stick, is most useful in the very extensive forest and bush fallow systems where no land preparation is required. As the bush cover begins to recede, the ground needs to be loosened before sowing and at this stage hand hoes replace digging sticks. Hand hoes are used for land preparation and weeding in the latter stages of bush fallow, grass fallow, and even some instances of annual cultivation. Land preparation using the hoe becomes extremely labor intensive and tedious by the grass fallow stage. This is especially true because of the persistence of grass weeds. "The use of a plow for land preparation becomes indispensable at this stage" (Boscrup, 1965: 24). A switch to the plow during grass fallow results in a substantial reduction in the amount of labor input required for land preparation. The net benefits in switching from the hoe to the plow are conditional on soil types and topography. The benefits are lower for sandy soils and for hilly terrain.

The preceding discussion on the evolution from hand hoes to animal drawn plows is formalized in Figure 11.2. This graph compares the labor costs under hand and animal-powered cultivation systems and shows the point where animal traction becomes the dominant technology.

The overhead labor costs in the transition from hand to animal power are: the cost of training animals, the cost of destumping and leveling the fields, and feeding and maintaining the animals on a year-round basis. The cost of training the animals is independent of the intensity of farming. The cost of destumping is extremely high under forest and early bush fallow system, owing to the high density of stumps per unit area. As the length of fallow decreases the costs of destumping decline because of reduced tree and root density. Destumping requirements are minimal by the grass fallow stage. The costs of feeding and caretaking of draft animals is also very high during forest and early bush fallow, primarily due to the lack of grazing land and due to the prevalence of diseases such as trypanosomiasis. As the fallow becomes grassy, grazing land becomes prevalent and so does animal ownership; hence the costs of maintaining draft animals decline. By the annual cultivation stage, however, grazing land becomes a limiting factor, necessitating the production of fodder crops, which in turn lead to an increase in the cost of feeding and maintaining draft animals. The total cost of using draft animals for land preparation, early season weeding, and manuring is given by the curve, T_p.

The labor costs for cultivation using hand tools rise rapidly as farming intensity increases. This is mainly due to the increased effort required for land preparation, weeding and for maintaining soil fertility. T_h shows total labor costs using hand hoes for land preparation and weeding, while T_h' adds in the cost of maintaining soil fertility. The T_h' curve becomes flatter as cheaper chemical fertilizers are substituted for labor intensive manure production.

Figure 11.2
A Comparison of Labor Costs with the Practice of Hand Cultivation and Animal-Powered Cultivation

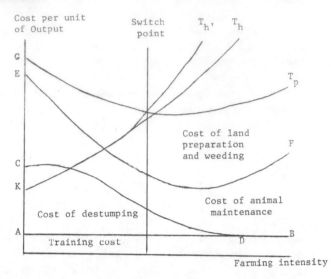

T_p = Total labor costs for land preparation, early season weeding, and manuring, using animal traction

T_h = Labor costs for land preparation and early season weeding, using the hand hoe

T_h' = T_h plus labor costs for maintaining soil fertility without manure from draft animals

Switch point = Farming intensity at which animal traction becomes the dominant technology

Animal-drawn plows are the dominant technology at the point where the costs of hand cultivation exceed the costs of transition to animal power. This switch is shown in Figure 11.2.

The transition from animal plows to tractors is explained better in the context of choice of techniques rather than in terms of the evolution of farming systems. Factors that determine this transition are capital availability, economic efficiency of tractor use, labor cost, and peak season labor scarcity. Tractors generally emerge as feasible alternatives to animal-drawn plows at the stage of permanent cultivation of land. Land preparation and transport are usually the first operations for which tractors are used.

A detailed analysis on the evolution of tool systems using information from field visits to approximately fifty locations in Sub-Saharan Africa is provided in Pingali, Bigot, and Binswanger (1987). Empirical evidence on the labor-saving benefits and the increases in yields per man hour through a change to animal-drawn plows and tractors is provided in Pingali and Binswanger (1984).

SCIENCE- AND INDUSTRY-BASED INNOVATIONS

In the previous section we showed how societies have coped with increasing population densities or increased market demand for food output through more intensive use of farmer-generated inputs, mainly land and labor. Such intensification can and often does increase agricultural output, but it is important to remember that the rate of growth in output is low in the absence of science- and industry-based inputs.

The remainder of this chapter concentrates on the potential role of science- and industry-generated innovations and inputs.

Population Density and the Rate and Direction of Science-Based Technical Change—The Induced Innovation Hypothesis

The history of agricultural growth of the developed world illustrates that the rate and direction of technical change are influenced by an economy's land and labor endowments, by the non-agricultural demand for labor, and by conditions of demand for final agricultural products. In agriculture the constraints imposed on development by an inelastic supply of labor may be offset by advances in mechanical technologies while the constraints imposed by an inelastic supply of land may be offset by biological technology. This responsiveness of science-based invention and innovation to economy-wide factors has come to be known as the process of induced innovation (Hayami and Ruttan, 1971; Binswanger and Ruttan, 1978).

A comparison of agricultural development in the United States and Japan illustrates clearly the influence of land and labor endowments on the direction of technical change. This comparison highlights the extremes in land and labor endowments. In 1880 Japan had only 0.65 hectares of land per male worker, while the United States had 25.4 hectares, that is, about forty times as much. By 1970 this difference in land/labor ratio increased: Japan had 1.57 hectares per worker while the United States had 160.5 hectares per worker, 100 times as much. These differences in land/labor endowments are reflected in massive differences in factor prices. For instance, in 1880 a worker in Japan had time period to work nearly 2,000 days to buy a hectare of land, while his U.S. counterpart could buy land after working roughly one-tenth that time. However, the rate of growth in agricultural output has been remarkably equal for these two countries in the ninety-year period 1880 to 1970, roughly 1.6 percent per annum. Japan and the United States have relied on entirely different technological paths to achieve growth in output. Japan emphasized biological, yield-raising technology supported by heavy irrigation investments, along with intensive manuring techniques while the United States emphasized mechanical technology. Careful historical and econometric enquiries by Hayami and Ruttan (1971) and Binswanger and Ruttan (1978) substantiate this conclusion.

The induced innovation literature has several implications for the rate and direction of technical change in agriculture of the developing countries. The obvious case is in countries where population pressure increases against land resources, making land increasingly scarce and expensive relative to labor. Here the development of biological and chemical technologies is the most efficient way to promote agricultural growth. Recent technical change in Indian and Philippine agriculture are cases in point (Hayami and Ruttan, 1988). Up until the end of the 1950s, growth in agricultural output was brought about primarily by expansion of the cultivated area in response to increased world demand for export crops and domestic demand for food crops. With the rapid growth of population after World War II, the supply of unexploited land became progressively exhausted. Towards the end of the 1950s, expansion of cultivated land stagnated, but the number of workers in agriculture continued to grow, leading to a decline in cultivated area per worker. In the 1960s, in response to increasing land prices and falling wages the Philippine agriculture made a transition from the traditional growth pattern, based on an expansion of the cultivated area, to a modern pattern based on an increase in land productivity. Increases in land productivity were achieved through expansion of the irrigation system, modern varieties of rice fertilizers, and other chemical inputs. Taiwan (China) went through a similar transition from area expansion to improvements in land productivity in the 1930s (Hayami and Ruttan, 1988). Innovations in biological technology that led to the rapid diffusion of the green revolution, or seed-fertilizer technology, in South Asia after the mid–1960s were induced by changes in relative resource endowments and factor prices similar to changes that occurred in Japan and Taiwan (Binswanger and Ruttan, 1978: 360). One could expect similar development in the more densely populated parts of Sub-Saharan Africa in the future, for example, as is happening in the Kenyan highlands today.

Agriculture in the United States, in contrast, emphasized mainly mechanical technology in the period 1880 to 1970. Innovations in biological technology did not become important until the 1940s, well after the land frontier had been exhausted. Developing country examples of technical change emphasizing mechanical technology are not common. Presumably such change is possible where labor rather than land is a constraint on agricultural growth and where export markets make the cultivation of larger areas profitable. Expansion in the area under sugar cane production in the South and Central West Regions of Brazil were closely associated with the substitution of labor with tractor power. The rapid adoption of tractor power in these regions during the 1960s was induced by rising wages under conditions of land abundance (Sanders and Ruttan, 1978). Mechanization of European farms in Sub-Saharan Africa during the colonial period was similarly induced by severe labor constraints. Europe and Japan made the transition to mechanical inputs after the wage explosion of the 1950s caused by a rapid increase in the non-agricultural demand for labor. In the late 1960s and 1970s, one has come to observe partial mechanization of agriculture under low-wage conditions—for instance, in the Indian Punjab, Thailand, and Philippines. Mechanization under low-wage conditions is selective, concentrating only on the power-intensive operations such as tillage, transport, and processing. In all these cases, mechanical inputs for power intensive operations co-exist with human and animal power for control-intensive operations such as weeding and interculture. Binswanger (1986) shows that it pays to mechanize the power-intensive operations even under low wages, while control intensive operations are mechanized when wages are high or rapidly rising.

This discussion indicates that the land and labor endowments of an economy are important determinants of the direction of technical change. The rate of technical change, however, is conditional on the economy's ability to generate or adapt innovations to match its specific environmental and economic conditions. In other words, the rate of technical change is determined by an economy's capital base (both industrial and human capital) and on its ability to provide institutional support for rapid technical change. To be complete, therefore, any discussion of induced technical change has to consider the environmental and institutional framework in which innovation, development, and adoption of new technology takes place.

The Generation of Innovations and the Development of an Industry

The Agricultural Machinery Industry. Mechanical technology is sensitive to agroclimatic factors such as soils, terrain, and rainfall regimes, and economic factors such as capital availability, farm size, and materials available. Where there is a divergence in either environmental or in economic conditions, direct transfer of mechanical technology is limited. Accordingly, where factor endowments warrant it, one observes a great deal of invention or adaptation of mechanical technology to meet local conditions. In the early phases of mechanization, such work is usually done by small manufacturers or workshops in close association with farmers. This process provides direct solutions by mechanically minded individuals to problems perceived by farmers. For instance, in 1880 there were 800 distinct models of plows advertised for sale in the United States. Early machinery innovation in the developing world reveals similar reliance on small workshops and direct farmer contact. The emergence of a diversified machinery industry out of small shops in the Indian Punjab and the power tiller industry in Thailand and the Philippines all followed similar patterns. In the early phases small workshops have a distinct advantage over large corporations because of the location-specificity of the innovations and the producer's ability to capture the gains of their innovative effort through sales.

The contribution of large corporations increases over time but continues to be most important in the area of engineering optimization. It is at this stage that engineering staffs of corporations are most effective. For instance, it was only around the start of the twentieth century that the plow industry in the United

States consolidated with the large firms, such as John Deere, purchasing the patents and assets of small firms.

Given this dominant role of individual initiative in the development of agricultural machinery, what are the appropriate government policy interventions towards mechanization? The government should encourage small-scale innovation and adoption through: patent laws for the enforcement of innovator's rights; testing, standardization, and information dissemination; and support of agricultural engineering education and some university-based research. Finally, it should be noted that efforts to protect the domestic agricultural machinery industry through import controls have not generally been successful. This is because the small innovators no longer have access to models or a wide range of engines to design locally adapted machines. For a more complete account of the historical patterns in development of the agricultural machinery industry, see Binswanger (1986).

The Agricultural Chemical Industry. Agricultural chemical innovations are generally in the form of fertilizers, pesticides, and herbicides. The demand for agricultural chemicals (with the exception of pesticides) is induced by factor prices in the same way as the demand for biological and mechanical technology. A substitution of chemical fertilizers for farm-produced manure would occur only when the price of fertilizers declines relative to the price of labor. Similarly, a decline in the price of herbicides relative to the price of labor leads to a substitution of herbicides for hand weeding. For instance, given the low wage rates in semi-arid India, the use of herbicides is uneconomical compared to hand weeding (Binswanger and Shetty, 1977). No particular labor-saving bias is associated with the use of pesticides, since pest damage to outstanding crops cannot usually be prevented by hand labor. Pesticides, of course, protect the higher output obtained through the use of fertilizers and high-yielding seeds against insects and disease and can therefore be considered a complementary (insurance) input.

Unlike in the case of mechanical technology, small entrepreneurs do not play a major role in the generation of chemical innovations. This is because the innovators require special skills acquired through university training and specialized facilities too expensive to provide for an individual researcher. Accordingly, most research and development of agricultural chemicals is conducted by large corporations. These corporations can accrue the returns to their investment in research through the sale of the final product, which is protected by patents. Chemical innovations have to be adapted to agroclimatic differences, such as soils and rainfall regimes, but here again adaptive research is more easily done by the parent corporation. The parent company may set up experimental fields in different environments as part of its sales effort.

As in the case of mechanical technology, private corporations have a comparative advantage in the research, development, and production of chemical technology. Here again the role of government should be restricted to enforcing patent laws, testing, and supporting university education and basic scientific research.

Agriculture Research Institutes

Not all agricultural research can be left to individual or private sector initiative and innovativeness. There are several areas of research where incentives for private sector research have not been adequate to induce an optimum level of investment. In these areas the social rate of return exceeds the private rate of return because a large share of the gains from research are captured by other firms and by consumers rather than by the innovating firm (Ruttan, 1982). The most obvious case is basic or supporting research in genetics, plant pathology and physiology, soil science, and so on, which has implications for the development of chemical and biological innovations. Applied research by private corporations uses the results of basic scientific enquiry without having to fully compensate the basic researcher who produced the results.

The second case is where the search for solutions is very expensive and very risky but once the solutions are obtained they can be easily reproduced by the users or other firms. For instance, research and development of new crop varieties is complex, having to consider a wide variety of parameters ranging from agroclimates and soil types to consumer tastes. Yet once a suitable variety is developed, it can be reproduced by individual farmers. Seed companies, therefore, have not been able to capture more than a small share of the gains from the development of new crop varieties. Hybrid varieties are an exception to this generalization.

Public-sector agriculture research institutes are therefore an essential part of a strategy for rapid growth in agricultural output through science- and industry-based inputs. Public research effort in agriculture should concentrate mainly on the provision of basic research and on research leading to advances in biological technology. Public research on mechanical and chemical technology should be minimal and mainly university-based, since the private sector has greater initiative to conduct research in this area.

It is important to remember that the role of the public sector in the production of agricultural technology is enhanced only when agriculture intensifies and technologies (such as high-yielding varieties) that increase the productivity of land are demanded. Agricultural Experiment Stations became important sources of growth in the United States only after the land frontier was exhausted. Japan's National Agricultural Station became prominent earlier in 1904 when it began initiating a crop-breeding project in the face of stagnation in agricultural output. Much of the post-independence consolidation and realignment of the Indian agricultural research system took place in the 1960s, coinciding with the initiation of major crop improvement programs. And finally, agricultural research capacity in Brazil began to develop in the 1960s and 1970s as the pressure on land and the demand for land productivity in the Northeast Region began to increase. (All the above examples were obtained from Ruttan, 1982.)

CONCLUDING REMARKS

Over the past century, agricultural output in the developed world has grown at a rate of around 2 percent, no matter what the initial factor endowments or technologies used. In addition to accommodating population growth, this growth rate has been able to accommodate the increases in final demand for food associated with rapidly rising per capita incomes. And it has been associated, by and large, with falling real food prices.

Developing countries are experiencing rates of population growth of between 1 to 4 percent. If their per capita incomes were to grow at rates comparable to those experienced by the developed world, food demand would grow at rates of between 2 to 5 percent. Sustained rates of growth of food supply that exceed 2 or 2.5 percent per year are, however, unprecedented in the history of the developed world. Of course, there exists the possibility of expanding supply via trade. But for countries where still a large proportion of the economy is in agriculture, such a strategy implies truly staggering rates of nonagricultural growth. The nonagricultural growth rates must be high enough to satisfy both increased domestic nonagricultural demand as well as increased exports to trade for food. Since such high nonagricultural growth rates are hard to achieve, a combination of agricultural policies and programs must be found that will raise growth rates of agricultural supply to substantially higher levels than what we are accustomed to. Such a strategy needs to encourage investment and innovation on the part of all the actors involved in the technology generation, investment, and production process.

We have seen the truly impressive role which farmer innovation and investment has played historically, even in continents that are not normally associated with a dynamic agriculture. The research on the recent experience of developed countries has perhaps not sufficiently emphasized that farmer innovation and investment continue to be of major importance in interaction with science- and industry-based innovations. Indeed, the increasing complexity of science- and industry-based innovation places an ever higher burden of technology screening and adaptation on farmers, and it is not, therefore, surprising to find that human capital is becoming an ever more important input into the agricultural production process. While farmer innovation and farmer investment can be driven by the necessity of increasing subsistence food production, favorable price policies are a necessary condition to provide greater incentives to accelerate the farmer-based investment and innovation processes. But the discussion of this chapter also shows that favorable prices are only one necessary condition for rapid agricultural growth. They are simply not sufficient. In the current climate of tight or shrinking development budgets, there is a danger that budgets for the core agricultural activities of the government may be cut too much.

First of all we have seen the important role of infrastructure investments in speeding up the process of intensification. High border prices in Zaire, for example, could not be transmitted to the interior of the country via the deteriorating interregional road network. And local rural roads have as much to do with the level of farmgate prices as border price.[2]

Direct government investment is also required into medium- and large-scale irrigation and drainage systems. History shows that such investments become necessary long before area growth comes to a halt. In India, for example, the late nineteenth century and early twentieth century was a major period of investment into small-, medium-, and large-scale irrigation, but area growth continued to contribute substantially to output growth until 1965. Nevertheless, as the experience with large-scale irrigation in much of Africa shows, one can also invest in irrigation too early, when land resources are too large to make labor intensive irrigated agriculture attractive.

In land-abundant countries, strategies based on area expansion are the lowest-cost sources of growth to even a poor agricultural population. At the opposite extreme are countries like Bangladesh, where the required resources for large-scale irrigation and drainage schemes are truly daunting. And the scale of projects required simply exceeds what farmers, or even local governments, can undertake on their own.

Improved incentives for private research and development are also required: patent systems, other forms of protecting innovators' rights, and absence of arbitrary government interference are a must. Too many countries are excessively fearful of private seed companies, for example, or of international competition in the agricultural machinery area.

But again historical experience and research such as Evenson's or Ruttan's show that no country has been able to benefit from science-based technical change in the absence of an agricultural research system capable of doing both basic and applied scientific research. Even borrowing of technology has been shown to be difficult without a public sector capacity of adaptive research. In passing, it is well worth noting that most external donors have, until recently, not provided support for research systems on a sufficiently long-term basis but distracted from strengthening national systems by building research components into short-term projects. Project trends are fortunately changing, but perhaps not sufficiently fast.

Apart from these core government activities there are areas where the role of government is less well documented. Available evidence on extension suggests that rates of return to extension activities justify the cost, and rates of return to well managed extension system may be very high (Lau, Feder, and Slade, 1984). On the other hand, governments and donors have, by and large, overemphasized public distribution of credit over the past two decades, probably at the expense of more important long-term investment in sources of growth, and while governments certainly have regulatory functions in areas of marketing and trade (such as the establishment of auction markets, the fostering of competition, or the stabilization of highly volatile prices), many governments have excessively intervened in the marketing and storage processes themselves by attempting to perform functions better performed by traders and transport entrepreneurs.

Given the amount of knowledge and research about the agricultural development process, two current debates seem rather pointless. The first is about whether it is sufficient to "set prices right" to get agricultural development going. Of course, it is not. It is only a necessary condition. The second debate is the one about private versus public sector activities. Both are required and the knowledge base is sufficient in most circumstances to be quite clear about where private enterprise is sufficient and where it is not. Only by harnessing private initiative wherever possible and by actively pursuing the core government activities can the extraordinary rates of growth of agricultural output be achieved that are required of developing countries over the next thirty to fifty years. While these countries probably do not face starvation even under low agricultural growth scenarios, the goal is not avoiding starvation but raising per capita incomes and drastically improving nutrition levels.

NOTES

1. This chapter was originally prepared as a paper for the 5th Agricultural Sector Symposium of the World Bank, January 7–9, 1985. It was also presented at the Seminar on Population and Rural Development at New Delhi, India, December 15–18, 1986, organized by the International Union for Scientific Study of Population. The authors are consultant and staff member of the World Bank. However, the World Bank does not accept responsibility for the views expressed herein, which are those of the authors and should not be attributed to the World Bank or to its affiliated organizations. The findings, interpretations, and conclusions are the results of research supported in part by the Bank; they do not necessarily represent official policy of the Bank. The designations employed and the presentation of material in this document are solely for the convenience of the reader and do not imply the expression of any opinion whatsoever on the part of the World Bank or its affiliates concerning the legal status of any country, territory, area, or of its authorities, or concerning the delimitation of its boundaries, or national affiliation.

2. For a discussion of the role of railroad and road investments in the very successful agricultural development of Thailand, see IBRD, 1982.

REFERENCES

Ahn, Peter (1979). "Erosion Hazard and Farming Systems in East Africa." In *Soil Conservation and Management in the Humid Tropics*, D. J. Greenland and R. Lal, eds. Chichester: John Wiley.

Allan, William (1965). *The African Husbandman*. Edinburgh: Oliver and Boyd.

Binswanger, Hans P. (1986). "Agricultural Mechanization: A Comparative Historical Perspective." *The World Bank Research Observer*. Vol. 1, no. 1 (January): 27–56.

Binswanger, Hans P., and Vernon Ruttan (1978). *Induced Innovation: Technology, Institutions and Development*. Baltimore: Johns Hopkins University Press.

Binswanger, Hans P., and S. V. R. Shetty (1987). "Economic Aspects of Weed Control in Semi-Arid Tropical Areas of India." Economics Program, Occasional Paper No. 13. Hyderabad: ICRISAT.

Boserup, Ester (1965). *The Conditions of Agricultural Growth*. Chicago: Aldine.

——— (1981). *Population and Technological Change: A Study of Long-Term Trends*. Chicago: University of Chicago Press.

De Wilde, John C. (1967). *Experiences with Agricultural Development in Tropical Africa*. Vol. 2. Baltimore: Johns Hopkins University Press.

Engelhardt, Thomas (1984). "Economics of Traditional Smallholder Irrigation Systems in Semi-Arid Tropics of South India." Ph.D. Thesis, Universitat Hohenheim.

Gleave, M. B., and H. P. White (1969). "Population Density and Agricultural Systems in West Africa." In *Environment and Land-Use in Africa*, M. F. Thomas and G. W. Whittington, eds. London: Methuen.

Grove, A. T. (1961). "Population and Agriculture in Northern Nigeria." In *Essays on African Population*, K. M. Barbour and R. M. Prothero, eds. London: Routledge and Kegan Paul.

Hayami, Yuhiro, and Vernon Ruttan (1971). *Agricultural Development: An International Perspective*. Baltimore: Johns Hopkins University Press.

——— (1988). *Agricultural Development: A Global Perspective*. Baltimore: Johns Hopkins University Press.

IBRD (1983). "Growth and Employment in Rural Thailand." Country Programs Department, Report No. 3906-TH. Washington, D.C.: World Bank.

Lau, Lawrence J., Gershon Feder, and Roger Slade (1984). "The Impact of Agricultural Extension: A Case Study of the Training and Visit Method in Harayana, India." Draft, Agriculture and Rural Development Department, Research Unit. Washington, D.C.: World Bank, September.

Ludwig, H. D. (1968). "Permanent Farming on the Ukara." In *Smallholder Farming and Smallholder Development in Tanzania*, Hans Ruthenberg, ed. Munich: Weltforum Verlag.

Miracle, Marvin P. (1967). *Agriculture in the Congo Basin*. Madison, Wisc.: University of Wisconsin Press.

Morgan, W. B. (1969). "Peasant Agriculture in Tropical Africa." In *Environment and Land-Use in Africa*, M. F. Thomas and G. W. Whittington, eds. London: Methuen.

Norman, M. J. T. (1979). *Annual Cropping Systems in the Tropics*. Gainesville, Fla.: University of Florida Press.

Okogbo, B. N. (1977). "Farming Systems and Soil Erosion in West Africa." In *Soil Conservation and Management in the Humid Tropics*, D. J. Greenland and R. Lal, eds. Chichester: John Wiley and Sons.

Pingali, Prabhu L., and Hans P. Binswanger (1984). "Population Density and Agricultural Intensification: A Study of the Evolution of Technologies in Tropical Agriculture." Agriculture and Rural Development Department, Research Unit, Report No.: ARU 22. Washington, D.C.: World Bank, October.

Pingali, Prabhu L., Yves Bigot, and Hans P. Binswanger (1987). *Agricultural Mechanization and the Evolution of Farming Systems in Sub-Saharan Africa*. Baltimore: Johns Hopkins University Press.

Richards, A. I. (1961). *Land, Labour and Diet in Northern Rhodesia*. London: Methuen & Co.

Rounce, N. V. (1949). *The Agriculture of the Cultivation Steppe*. Capetown: Longmans, Green & Co.

Ruthenberg, Hans P. (1980). *Farming Systems in the Tropics*. 2d ed. Oxford: Clarendon Press.

Ruttan, Vernon (1982). *Agricultural Research Policy*. Minneapolis: University of Minnesota Press.

Sanders, John H. and Vernon Ruttan (1978). "Biased Choice of Technology in Brazilian Agriculture." In *Induced Innovation*, H. P. Binswanger and V. W. Ruttan, eds. Washington, D.C.: World Bank.

Schapera, I. (1943). *Native Land Tenure in the Bechunaland Protectorate*. Capetown: Lovedale Press.

Toulmin, Camilla (1983). "Herders and Farmers or Farmer-Herders and Herder-Farmers?" London: Overseas Development Institute, Pastoral Network Paper, January.

Trapnell, C. G. and J. N. Clothier (1937). *Soils, Vegetation and Agricultural Systems of Northwestern Rhodesia*. Lusaka: Government of Northern Rhodesia.

Von Rotenham, D. (1968). "Cotton Farming in Sukumaland." In *Smallholder Farming and Smallholder Development in Tanzania*, Hans Ruthenberg, ed. London: Muchen.

12

Development and the Status of Women: Indicators and Measures

MARY G. POWERS

The extent to which women participate in and benefit from economic development is determined in part by the nature and type of development initiatives, some of which may dramatically alter their status in society. Accurate description of the relative status of men and women is, therefore, a prerequisite to understanding the relationship between the status of women and economic development. Evaluating whether the changes associated with development result in benefits or costs to women requires unequivocal measures or indicators of the status of women relative to that of men at different points in time.

Attempts to assess the status of women are not new; there is a voluminous literature of varying quality and focus (Powers, 1984). With respect to the link between the status of women and development, much of the literature has sought a link between the status of women and their fertility (Powers, 1984, 1985; Mason, 1984). Interest has focused on ways to reduce fertility in those developing countries where high fertility and consequent high growth rates are seen as impediments to development. More recently, concern has shifted to the effects of development on the situation of women.

This chapter discusses (1) the change in development emphases giving rise to increased concern for the status of women during the past two decades; (2) some conceptual and methodological issues underlying efforts to measure the status of women; and (3) a series of indicators of the situation of women developed as part of a large ongoing project at the United Nations Statistical Office.

CONCERN WITH THE STATUS OF WOMEN AND THE DEVELOPMENT PROCESS

During the 1970s, criticisms of earlier approaches to development gave rise to several new emphases including a "basic needs" approach to development. The latter emphasized the components necessary to provide a decent standard of living for all members of society and for particular groups within societies, including women. It focused on the central role of work, broadly defined, in meeting basic needs for shelter, clothing, food, and other goods. That is, work is viewed as contributing to the basic needs of a population, either by generating income with which to purchase goods or by the direct production of goods for self and family consumption. This definition encompasses paid employment and also the performance of non-remunerated but required work such as gathering firewood for cooking, tending a garden or animals for family food consumption, and so forth.

In developing countries, particularly in rural areas, women are heavily concentrated in the non-remunerative work sector, fetching water, gathering fuel or firewood, and tending animals and the family food crop. The basic needs approach to development pays more attention than earlier emphases to the type and extent of work done by women and to changes in the standard of living of women and their families when changes are introduced, such as those associated with the modernization of agriculture (Boserup, 1970).

A body of literature concerned with "women in development" issues has grown that focuses on the effects on women of the introduction of modern economic practices (Buvinic, 1981; Ware, 1981). A number of studies have demonstrated that the modernization of the economy, particularly agriculture, has tended to increase employment opportunities for men and, at the same time, reduce the opportunities and markets for the type of work women traditionally have done (Boserup, 1970; Ware, 1981).

While it is necessary to identify key problems and areas of concern both in relatively stable and changing societies, the situation of women in agriculture is illustrative of the negative effects development programs may have on women. The changing roles of women in agricultural production have been described in several countries undergoing "modernization" of agriculture (Boserup, 1970; Safilios-Rothschild, 1974, 1980). In many societies based on subsistence agriculture, food production was often dominated by women, and, in fact, patterns of "female farming" have been contrasted with later "male farming" (Boserup, 1970). That the subordination of women increases when a society moves from a pattern of female farming to male farming has been well documented (Boulding, 1976). When women were the primary producers of food, they had considerable authority with respect to disposing of family resources. As crop production moved towards new commercial crops, the family unit, which once consumed most of its own product, instead sold it in a market situation, resulting in new social and economic relationships.

Commercial farming requires access to credit and technical information in order to achieve higher productivity and to sell to new markets. In most cases, male heads of household became sellers or managers of the agricultural holding, and women tended to lose control over family agricultural output (Palmer and von Buchwald, 1980). The introduction of cash crops in areas where women have done much of the farming is often used as a case in point to demonstrate the negative effects development programs may have for women. In many areas of Africa it is expected that women will continue to provide most of the food for their families, yet, once cash crops and modern farm equipment are introduced, men become the equipment operators, receivers of credit, and, ultimately, control whatever cash the crop produces. In such cases, development provides opportunities for men that in fact may reduce the standard of living for women and their children.

The situation of women in agriculture in developing countries is but one illustration of broader problems of inequity that exist in all sectors of developing nations and, indeed, in all societies. Interest in the participation of women in development has arisen as a result of increased awareness of the negative impact that economic development may have on the status of women, specifically on the resources and opportunities available to them in both agriculture and industry.

MEASURING THE STATUS OF WOMEN

International strategies for improving the status of women or for decreasing existing inequities place great importance on developing statistics on women that show where the inequities exist and permit researchers to monitor changes over time. Such measures must quantify women's participation in development relative to that of men and identify groups for whom the processes of social and economic change associated with development have had a negative impact. Such an effort is already underway and has produced a number of indicators from existing data.

Relevant indicators of the situation of women have been developed as part of a joint project on improving statistics and measures of the situation of women, sponsored by the Statistical Office of the Department of International and Economic Affairs of the United Nations Secretariat and the International Research and Training Institute for the Advancement of Women. That project produced two publications, *Compiling Indicators on the Situation of Women* and *Improving Concepts and Measures for Statistics and Indicators on the Situation of Women*, which suggest measures and indicators that might be used to relate changes in the status of women to development programs (United Nations, 1985).[1] The first report is a practical guide to developing statistics and indicators on the situation of women from existing national data systems. The second report suggests improvements needed in the quality and relevance of data pertaining to women. In addition, an international microcomputer data base on women was developed and used in the preparation of *Selected Statistics and Indicators on the Status of Women*, the report of the Secretary-General for the 1985 World Conference on the United Nations Decade for Women (United Nations, 1985). A compilation of thirty-nine statistical indicators on the situation of women for 172 countries or areas of the world was presented as shown in Table 12.1 for Trinidad and Tobago. The indicators were developed from existing national statistical sources discussed in *Compiling Social Indicators on the Situation of Women*. A large

Table 12.1
The Status of Women: Indicators and Measures

		TRINIDAD AND TOBAGO				
Indicators	1970		1980		2000	
POPULATION COMPOSITION, DISTRIBUTION & CHANGE						
1 Total population (000s)	508	519	535	533	664	657
2 Percentage total population age 0-14	20	21	17	17	14	14
3 Percentage total population 15-59	26	27	29	29	31	31
4 Percent.60+ fem; percent. pop. 60+	54	6	52	8	54	11
5 Percentage total population rural	..	..	38	41	..	..
6 Pop. change p. yr. (%):rural, urban	1.1	0.7	-0.4	0.1	0	3.6
Pop. change p. yr. (%):total	1		-0.3		1	
EDUCATION, TRAINING AND LITERACY						
7 Percentage age 15-24 illiterate	1	1	1	1	..	..
8 Percentage age 25-44 illiterate	9	3	3	2	..	..
9 Percent. age 25+ entered secondary level	14	17	24	26	..	..
10 Primary level enrolment (000s)	111	115	82	83	76	76
11 Second level enrolment (000s)	27	25	45	47 a	..	..
12 Percent. second. enrol. vocational	3	8	5	12 a	..	..
13 Third level enrolment (000s)	0.9	1.5	3.1	4.8	8.1	9
14 Combined primary-second. enrol.ratio	84	82 b	80	77 b	..	..
ECONOMIC ACTIVITY						
Labour force participation rates (%):						
15 Females, males (overall)	19	47	24	52	30	59
16 Females, males, ages 25-44	39	96	43	96	49	96
17 Females, males ages 45-59	40	95	44	94	51	94
18 Percent. lab. force fem: rural, urban	..	..	..	..	..	..
Percent. lab. force fem: total	25					
Employment status, occupation, industry:						
19 Percent.total pop. unpaid fam.wkrs	..	..	2	2	..	..
20 Percent. total pop. employees	..	..	21	45	..	..
21 Percent. total pop. prof.-adm.wkrs	..	..	..	..	..	..
22 Percent. total pop. clerical-sales	..	..	..	..	..	..
23 Percent.lab.force in industry	19	42	19	46	20	48
24 Percent.lab.force in agriculture	17	19	10	13	5	7
25 Male/female wage ratio, non-agric.	..		..		..	
HOUSEHOLDS, MARITAL STATUS AND FERTILITY						
26 Percentage age 15-19 never married	..	..	..	..	..	..
27 Percent. age 45-59 not currently mar'd	..	..	..	..	..	..
28 Percent. age 60+ not currently married	..	..	..	..	..	..
29 Total fertility rate	3.89		3.07		2.28	
30 Mar'd women using contraceptives (%)	44		54 c		..	
31 Average household size: rural, urban	..	..	..	..	..	..
Average household size: total	4.8		3.98		2.9	

Table 12.1 (continued)

	TRINIDAD AND TOBAGO					
Indicators	1970		1980		2000	
HEALTH AND NUTRITION						
32 Life expectancy at birth	67.7	63.7	71	66.5	76	70.6
33 Child survival age 0 to 5	96	95	..	..	..	..
34 Survival rate, age 15 to 45	94	93	..	..	..	..
35 Maternal mortality rate	135.7		78.9 c		..	
36 Anaemia: pregnant, non-preg. fem.(%)	..	..	56	21	..	..
37 Percentage births trained attendants	..		90 c			
38 Percentage deaths from infectious and parasitic diseases	6	7 d	5	5c	..	..
POLITICAL PARTICIPATION						
39 Members national legislative bodies	..	..	..	..	..	..

Separate figures for each year refer to females and males respectively unless other-
wise indicated. a 1978. b Age 5-16. c 1977. d 1972.
Source: United Nations, Selected Statistics and Indicators on the Status of Women.
Report of the Secretary General to the World Conference, 1985, No. a/Conf.116/10.
Page 122. (Note) A wall chart showing 13 of the indicators available for most
countries was also prepared for the Conference and is available from the United Nations.

body of data concerning the situation of women is now routinely collected by national and international statistical services, but the data were not systematically compiled in one place until the development of the data base.

A third text in the series also has been completed, *Improving Statistics and Indicators of Women Using Household Surveys* (Ware, 1986). It suggests data collection methodologies that can be immediately incorporated into household survey programs to improve the collection of data on women. It is especially concerned with improving household surveys in developing countries. The three reports and the data base provide a useful and practical framework as well as general guidelines for the development of national and international indicators on the situation of women. It is no longer possible to say there are no data available to examine the impact of various development strategies on women.

A discussion follows, dealing with some of the premises underlying the selection of indicators, as well as some of the remaining conceptual and methodological problems, as illustrated by the indicators of economic activity and labor force participation.

BASIC PREMISES OF INDICATOR DEVELOPMENT

Several basic premises underlie the selection of the indicators developed as part of the project described above. The first is that, for most purposes, the status of women in any area of life is best described relative to that of men. The illustrative indicators are designed to compare the situation of men and women with respect to employment, education, family status, and other significant areas of social life. The disaggregations suggested are designed to identify and compare the situation of men and women in terms of access to or control over significant societal resources.

A second premise is that no single indicator best describes the multiple dimensions of the status or situation of women in any one society, let alone in all societies. Moreover, improvement in one aspect of life for women is not necessarily associated with improvement in all other areas. For example, equal access to education is not necessarily followed by equal access to employment. Consequently, any evaluation of change in the status of women must incorporate several measures.

A third premise is that even though no single indicator adequately describes the status of women in any society, the primacy of economic indicators in most societies is assumed. As noted, much previous research in the social sciences focused on the reproductive and family roles of women. Yet their disadvantaged position in every society in the world is linked to the lack of recognition of the economic or productive roles they perform and to the disadvantaged positions they occupy when they are economically active. Positions in other major institutions are often influenced by economic roles because access to economic roles determines whether women can provide for themselves or are dependent upon men for their survival. Inequality frequently results from the division of labor into routine household sustenance and maintenance functions on the one hand and "productive" economic functions on the other. The former are not generally defined as work and are usually assigned to women, whereas the latter are usually assigned to men. The underlying assumption has been that there is a basic incompatibility between "productive" economic roles, defined as "work," and those activities required to sustain and maintain the household and family on a daily basis. Because of the time spent on such sustenance activities as gathering fuel and caring for children, some incompatibility between the two types of work inevitably exists (Vanek, 1974). The extent of incompatibility is not the same in every setting, however. In fact, there is considerable evidence that rural women in developing countries spend considerable time as agricultural workers intermittently working in the fields and in processing agricultural produce (Ware, 1986: 62–73).

A final premise was that useful, policy-relevant indicators of the situation of women and of gender inequality can be extracted from existing national data systems. The illustrative indicators developed thus far draw on existing data in censuses, surveys, and registration systems. As such, there are some key indicators that are broadly comparable for many societies, making it possible to measure aspects of gender inequality among different societies as well as within different regions and areas of individual societies. The sources for selected indicators are not the same in all countries because of variations in quality in the different sources of data. A survey may be used for labor force data in one country, a census in another, for example. Each of the major data sources has advantages and limitations. Each also has some clear sex biases associated with underlying concepts, data collection, and processing.[2] Taken together, however, existing sources provide a considerable amount of data from which macro-level indicators of the situation of women may be developed. These include indicators of the situation of women in the labor force, in the educational system, and in families and households, as well as in other less central areas. It is recognized that many aspects of women's lives cannot be described with existing data. Other types of in-depth investigations in individual communities undergoing modernization will produce other measures appropriate to particular cultural contexts. They are not included here, however.

ILLUSTRATIVE INDICATORS OF THE SITUATION OF WOMEN

In recent years, there has been no shortage of lists of indicators of levels of living, social well-being, and other policy-relevant areas of social concern (United Nations, 1978; McGranahan, et al., 1979; OECD, 1982). With some adaptation and disaggregation, many of these are useful for understanding the situation of women. The problem with simply recommending disaggregation by sex is that not all indicators are equally relevant to concern over equality between the sexes and its relationship to development. Moreover, it should be noted that while disaggregating existing data by sex is a necessary step in the direction of describing the situation of women, it is not entirely sufficient because many existing statistical systems describe an essentially male view of reality rather than a human view. Therefore, some indicators, even from existing data, require rethinking and perhaps redefining the concepts and methods underlying their construction, so that they accurately describe the changing reality of women's participation in the economic, political, and social life of society.

As noted, the disadvantaged position of women in every society in the world is linked to the lack of recognition of the economically productive roles they perform and to the disadvantaged positions they occupy when they are counted as economically active. The situation of women in the labor market is, of course, linked to their access to appropriate education and to their positions in households and families. It is important, however, to emphasize the primacy of the economic, or goods- and income-producing, roles of women when seeking to understand the extent to which their status is affected by development. The remainder of this chapter focuses on the economic indicators and refers the reader to the reports cited earlier for more detailed discussion of indicators in other areas.

INDICATORS OF ECONOMIC ACTIVITY AND LABOR FORCE PARTICIPATION

A considerable body of data from censuses and surveys describes the economic activity and labor force participation of men and women in most countries. In

general, the 1960, 1970, and 1980 rounds of population censuses defined economic activity or work largely in terms of whether a person engaged in an activity
for which she or he was paid directly or indirectly. This included unpaid family
workers but not housework done in one's own home. National practices have
been anything but consistent, however, and the various concepts and definitions
have been altered to suit the particular conditions and situations of individual
countries. Major differences occur in the specification of requirements for clas-
sifying someone as in the labor force or not in the labor force, and in the treatment
of unpaid family workers.

The unpaid family worker has been one of the categories particularly discriminatory toward women. Unpaid family workers are often wives working in small
family businesses in urban areas and on agricultural holdings in rural areas. In
many countries, in order to be counted as an unpaid family worker (and to be
included in the labor force) one must have worked at least one-third of the normal
working hours without pay in some kind of enterprise operated by a relative.
Yet persons who define themselves as employees or own account workers and
report working one hour during the reference period (often the previous week)
are counted as in the labor force. The one-third time requirement was dropped
in the 1982 international recommendations. The new definition may have been
implemented in the collection of official statistics in some countries by 1985,
but most existing statistics are based on the old definition.

The enumeration of women as unpaid family labor is important to the situation
of women in two contrasting ways. On the one hand, if they are not accurately
counted, women's contribution to the economic product of the nation is inade-
quately measured. On the other hand, classification as unpaid family labor may
contribute to the hidden unemployment of women to the extent that women who
would prefer and would accept a paid labor force position if they found one,
are classified as unpaid family labor and hence as employed rather than as
"looking for work" or unemployed. Indicators of unemployment, in particular,
must be sensitive to such classification problems.

The extent of unemployment among women may also be underreported because many workers are not, strictly speaking, unemployed in the sense of looking
for work. Frequently, they might be more appropriately described as underemployed, as they are involuntarily working part-time or for a shorter than normal
period. Frequently, also, there is a mismatch between the jobs they hold and
the skill level capacity they have. Few countries report data on underemployment,
but such measures may be calculated if one has access to public use tapes with
appropriate basic statistics. Unemployment and underemployment may be affected differently by development processes and programs.

Entering the labor market and finding employment is the first step in the
process of acquiring a suitable position, in terms of qualifications and rewards.
A notable feature of labor markets in many countries at all stages of development
is the segregation of men and women in terms of the industries in which they
work and the occupations they hold. The segmented labor market most women

enter leads to low-paying, less secure jobs in the economy. The earnings or income gap between men and women, which has been noted in many countries, is, in large part, a result of this segregation and segmentation.

Recognition of the conceptual difficulties which exist with respect to labor force data does not imply they cannot be used. Several indicators of the economic activity of women may be developed simply by disaggregating by sex already existing data. These include the following:

1. labor force participation rates by sex and selected age groups and by urban and rural residence;

2. unemployment rates (especially in the paid labor force) by sex and age and a ratio of female to male unemployment levels;

3. the proportion of unpaid family workers in the labor force by sex and a ratio of female to male proportions;

4. the proportion of professional and managerial jobs by sex and a ratio of female to male proportions;

5. male/female wage or earnings ratio in non agricultural employment.

Measuring income or earnings presents real problems in all developing countries, where large proportions of the population are not wage earners and where written records of financial transactions are not common. There are additional problems with measuring income for women, as relatively few of them are wage-earners. Also, when self-employed, they tend to be part of a family or group enterprise and estimating their share of the total income is difficult. Development of relative income or earnings indicators is the area most in need of field research. Nonetheless, it is possible to obtain some measures for nonagricultural employment in a number of developing countries.

In addition to the above indicators, census and survey data for most developed countries and many developing countries permit construction of an "index of occupational segregation." The index indicates the percentage of men or women who would have to change their jobs in order for the occupational distribution of men and women to be the same (Shyrock and Siegel, 1971; Blau and Hendricks, 1979; Beller, 1982). This indicator of inequality is of interest in many developed countries, but of limited value in developing countries. The above indicators should provide a reasonable indication of how men and women function in the labor markets of individual countries.

OTHER RELEVANT INDICATORS

Illustrative indicators of gender inequality with respect to education, family and household status, health and other areas were developed after a similar review of available data, underlying biases, etc. They include the following lists:[3]

INDICATORS OF LITERACY AND EDUCATION:

1. Literacy rates for men and women and a ratio of female to male literacy;
2. Percentage of the population age six to twenty-four enrolled in school, by sex and age, and female to male enrollment ratios;
3. Percentage of all persons enrolled who are in the second level, by sex;
4. Percentage of women and men twenty to twenty-four years old who have completed secondary school and a ratio of women to men twenty to twenty-four years old who have completed secondary school.

INDICATORS OF FAMILY STATUS AND FERTILITY:

1. Female headship rates compared to male headship rates;
2. Households with women fifteen to forty-nine years of age and children under age fifteen, and no adult male, as a proportion of all households;
3. Single-person households by sex (and selected age categories);
4. Median age at first marriage for women and men;
5. Legal minimum age at marriage for women and men;
6. Proportion of women and men in each marital status category by age;
7. Average (mean) age difference between husbands and wives;
8. Number of children ever born to women fifteen to forty-nine years of age (by marital status when possible);
9. Child-woman ratio for all women age fifteen to forty-four and for all women age fifteen to forty-four in the labor force.

INDICATORS OF HEALTH AND NUTRITION:

1. Ratio of infant mortality per 1,000 female births to infant mortality per 1,000 male births;
2. Ratio of the mortality rate of female children one to four years old to the mortality rate of male children one to four years old;
3. Female life expectancy at birth compared to male life expectancy at birth;
4. Maternal mortality rate;
5. Percentage of live births under 2,500 grams;
6. Percentage of pregnancies delivered by trained personnel;
7. Tabulation of weight by age for male and female children up to five years. Index of relative "normalcy";
8. Per capita consumption of calories or animal protein per day by sex for countries having such estimates by sex;
9. Relative proportions of men and women who have been immunized against specific diseases (diphtheria, tetanus, whooping cough, measles, poliomyelitis, and tuberculosis).

Illustrative indicators in other less central areas are also suggested in the sources cited earlier.

CONCLUSIONS

Several conclusions follow from the review of current work on indicators of the situation of women.

1. Even though much more work needs to be done in this area, recognition of the multiple dimensions of women's status makes it possible to measure selected aspects of the status of women such as labor force participation, education, and family status, which affect, and are affected by, the development process.

2. Even with existing limitations and sex biases, a number of data sources (censuses, surveys, etc.) are available for use in the construction of such indicators. A data base, developed by the United Nations Statistical Office, brings together in one source indicators of women's situation which are derived from several disparate sources.

3. Using such indicators along with compatible indicators of the development process, it is possible to know with greater precision than in the recent past how various dimensions of the status of women are related to development.

NOTES

1. United Nations, *Compiling Social Indicators on the Situation of Women and Improving Concepts and Methods for Statistics and Indicators on the Situation of Women*, United Nations Publications, Series F, Nos. 32 and 33, Sales Nos. E84, IVII2 and E.84.XVII.3. The first report was drafted by Mary G. Powers and the second by Nadia Youssef. More detailed information and sources of data for the measurement of women's status and on the conceptual and methodological issues involved may be found in *Compiling Social Indicators on the Situation of Women*.

2. These problems are discussed in detail in *Compiling Social Indicators on the Situation of Women*.

3. These are described in detail in *Compiling Social Indicators on the Situation of Women*.

REFERENCES

Beller, A. (1982). "Occupational Segregation by Sex: Determinants and Changes." *The Journal of Human Resources* 17: 371–92.

Blau, F. and W. E. Hendricks (1979). "Occupational Segregation by Sex: Trends and Prospects." *The Journal of Human Resources* 14: 197–210.

Boserup, E. (1970). *Women's Role in Economic Development*. London: Allen and Unwin.

——— (1975). "Employment of Women in Developing Countries." In *Population Growth and Economic Development in the Third World*, Leon Tabah, ed. Belgium: Ordina Editions.

Boulding, E. (1976). *The Underside of History: A View of Women Through Time*. Boulder, Colo.: Westview Press.

Buvinic, M. (1981). "Introduction." *Women and Development: Indicators of Their*

Changing Role. Socioeconomic Studies 3. Paris: United Nations Educational, Social and Cultural Organization.

Mason, K. O. (1984). *The Status of Women: A Review of its Relationships to Fertility and Mortality*. New York: The Rockefeller Foundation.

McGranahan, D., E. Pizarro and Richard C. Pizarro (1979). *Methodological Problems in Selection and Analysis of Socioeconomic Development Indicators*. Report No. 79:4. Geneva: United Nations Research Institute for Social Development.

OECD (1982). *The OECD List of Social Indicators*. Paris: Organization for Economic Cooperation and Development.

Palmer, I. and U. Von Buchwald (1980). *Monitoring Changes in the Conditions of Women—A Critical Review of Possible Approaches*. Geneva: United Nations Research Institute for Social Development.

Powers, M. G. (1982). "Introduction" to *Measures of Socioeconomic Status*, Mary G. Powers, ed. Boulder, Colo.: Westview Press.

——— (1984). *Compiling Social Indicators on the Situation of Women*. Studies in Methods. Series F, no. 32. New York: United Nations.

——— (1985). *Measures and Indicators of Women's Status: Some Recent Developments*. Women and International Development, Joint Harvard/MIT Group, WID Working Paper No. 8, Cambridge, Mass.

Safilios-Rothschild, C. (1974). *Women and Social Policy*. Englewood Cliffs, N.J.: Prentice-Hall.

——— (1980). "The Persistence of Women's Invisibility in Agriculture: Theoretical and Policy Lessons from Lesotho and Sierra Leone." *Policy Studies Working Paper No. 88*. New York: The Population Council.

Shyrock, H. and J. Siegel (1971). *Methods and Materials of Demography*. U.S. Bureau of the Census, vol. 1, Washington, D.C.: U.S. Government Printing Office, pp. 232–33.

United Nations (1978). *Social Indicators: Preliminary Guidelines and Illustrative Series*. Statistical Papers, Series M, no. 63. E. 78, XVII.8. New York: United Nations.

——— (1985). *Selected Statistics and Indicators on the Status of Women*. Report of the Secretary General to the World Conference to Review and Appraise the Achievements of the United Nations Decade for Women: Equality, Development and Peace. Nairobi, Kenya: A/Conf.116/10.

Vanek, J. (1974). "Time Spent in Housework." *Scientific American* 231 (November): 116–20.

Ware, H. (1981). *Women, Demography and Development*. Canberra: Australian National University.

——— (1986). *Improving Statistics and Indicators on Women Using Household Surveys*. Draft Working Paper. New York: International Research and Training Institute for the Advancement of Women and United Nations Statistical Office.

Youssef, N. H. (1984). *Improving Concepts and Methods for Statistics and Indicators on the Situation of Women*. Studies in Methods. Series F, no. 33. New York: United Nations.

13

The Economic and Social Performance of Small Nations

CLIVE DANIEL

There are now more than 100 nations that are members of the United Nations or the World Bank and that have populations of less than 10 million.[1] Of these, approximately seventy have populations of less than 5 million and thirty-four have populations numbering less than one million. Almost all of the very small nations are generally categorized as underdeveloped.

The existence of these small nations, many of which became independent in the post–World War II era, raises a number of interesting questions for policymakers and professional economists. There are questions such as, do these small nations have the potential to become viable economic units? Are they capable of sustaining reasonable rates of growth over long periods of time? Are the tools of economic theory, whether of the keynesian, monetarist, or supply-side varieties relevant for very small countries? In general, can the policies of governments of very small countries have positive, affirmative impacts on their economies? Or are these countries simply sometimes the beneficiaries, and at other times the victims, of external economic developments or disturbances over which they have no control?

Of course, it is true that no nation, not even the United States of America, nor the Union of Soviet Socialist Republics, is totally immune to external economic conditions. The worldwide impact of the increases in the price of oil in 1973–74 and 1979 makes that fact absolutely clear. Yet, the case can certainly be made a priori that small nations are much more likely to be vulnerable to external disturbances than larger ones. In this chapter an attempt is made to answer some of the questions that have been raised by the emergence of this large number of small and underdeveloped nation-states. The number of people in a population is only one of the several ways in which the size of a nation may be measured. Other possible valid measurements of a nation's size are the value of gross national product (GNP) and the geographic size of the area occupied by the nation. There are situations in which one or the other of these two possible measurements would be a more appropriate method of determining national size. In this chapter, however, the number of people is used as the indicator of national size. The literature provides good precedent for the use of population size in this way.[2]

In this chapter, a nation is defined as small if its population at the midpoint of 1984 was less than 20 million. A total of 75 underdeveloped nations, for which at least some of the data were available, falls into this category. This group of nations is divided into four groups: nations with populations of between 10 and 20 million; nations with populations of between 5 and 10 million; nations with populations of between one and 5 million; and the mini-states with populations of less than one million. The unavailability of data for the mini-states with populations of less than one million requires that they be omitted from most parts of the study.

The point can be made that setting the dividing line at a population of 20 million, as well as the dividing lines within the sample, is arbitrary. Some may argue, with justification, that a nation with a population of 20 million is not small. However, this group of relatively large nations is included in the study in an effort to determine the similarities and differences between them and the undeniably small nations.

THE NATURE OF THE STUDY

In this study no attempt was made to develop a complete growth model for small, underdeveloped countries. In such a model, the contribution to growth of each explanatory variable would be independently identified and measured. As Landau has correctly stated, there are no such models which have found general acceptance.[3] Here, instead, very simple statistical tools were used to analyze and compare some of the characteristics of the countries in the sample. A preliminary attempt was also made to test the suggestion by Kuznets that structural change might be a more important ingredient in the growth process of small than large nations.[4] He had argued that, in spite of the problems of limited domestic markets, some small countries were able to achieve and maintain high growth rates by quickly adjusting their economies to take advantage of new opportunities as they occur in the international marketplace.

In addition to the examination of strict economic variables, an attempt was made to see if any significant correlations existed between nation size and the provision of social services on a per capita basis. The rationale for these tests was that if there were economies of scale in the provision of social services, their higher per unit cost in small countries would reduce their production. In this case small countries might be found to provide fewer social services than larger countries at a comparable level of development.

The study was conducted because it was thought that a focus on size might reveal some interesting insights. It is true that in a cursory examination of the data released by such organizations as the United Nations and the World Bank, one would find examples of low and high growth rates by both large and small nations. One would also find periods of high as well as low inflation rates by both kinds of nations. Although economic theory does acknowledge the importance of economies of scale, it would require a heroic assumption, even for an economist, to conclude that a large nation would at all times grow more rapidly than a small nation. Economic theory also recognizes the importance of factor endowments and the efficiency with which factors are allocated and utilized as important determinants of the growth process. Unfortunately, it is very difficult to measure the efficiency of factor utilization, and especially so at the national level. An examination of the efficiency of factor utilization is beyond the scope of this study. It is readily acknowledged that size is only one factor, and not the most important factor in determining the economic performance of nations.

THE DATA

The data for this study were taken primarily from the *World Development Report 1986* and the *International Financial Statistics Yearbook 1986*.[5] Countries included in the study were those with populations of less than 20 million at the mid-point of 1984 and which were classified as low income, middle-income, and upper-middle-income in the *World Development Report*. Countries in the study are listed in Appendix I. Of the seventy-five countries, twenty-one had populations of less than one million, twenty-five had populations of between one and 5 million, nineteen had populations of between 5 and 10 million, and ten had populations of more than 10 million. Most of the variables tested were taken directly from the "World Development Indicators" in the annex of the *World Development Report*. The variable for structural change was constructed by summing the differences between the percentage contributions to output of the agricultural, industrial, and service sectors between 1965 and 1984. The negative signs were ignored.

THE RESULTS

One of the interesting, although not surprising, findings of the study provided at least partial support for the argument that countries that pursue export-oriented policies are more likely to achieve high rates of growth than those with inward-oriented policies. This support came from the finding that there was almost always a strong and significantly positive correlation between high import growth rates and high rates of growth of gross domestic product (GDP). The results of this part of the study are presented in Table 13.1. The correlation between export growth and growth of GDP was sometimes only moderate. The lower values for the correlation coefficients between export growth and GDP growth should not be taken to denigrate the importance of exports. It is well known that it is through exports that countries earn the necessary foreign exchange to pay for imports. The very strong and significant correlations between import growth and

Table 13.1
Correlations between Growth of Trade and Growth of Gross Domestic Product

Countries with populations larger than one million

	EXP 65-73		EXP 73-84
GDP 65-73	.3924 (42) P = .005	GDP 73-84	.4702 (42) P = .001
	IMP 65-73		IMP 73-84
GDP 65-73	.4286 (42) P = .002	GDP 73-84	.71 (42) P = .000

Countries with populations between one and five million

	EXP 65-73		EXP 73-84
GDP 65-73	.3642 (48) P = .069	GDP 73-84	.4525 (19) P = .026
	IMP 65-73		IMP 73-84
GDP 65-73	.2964 (18) P = .116	GDP 73-84	.6978 (18) P = .001

Countries with populations between 5 and 10 million

	EXP 65-73		EXP 73-84
GDP 65-73	.4131 (15) P = .063	GDP 73-84	.4714 (15) P = .038
	IMP 65-73		IMP 73-84
GDP 65-73	.5976 (15) P = .009	GDP 73-84	.8290 (15) P = .000

Countries with populations of more than 10 million

	EXP 65-73		EXP 73-84
GDP 65-73	.6250 (9) P = .036	GDP 73-84	.5270 (8) P = .090
	IMP 65-73		IMP 73-84
GDP 65-73	.7762 (9) P = .007	GDP 73-84	.6688 (8) P = .070

EXP 65-73: Average annual percentage growth rate of exports 1965-73.
EXP 73-84: Average annual percentage growth rate of exports 1973-84.
IMP 65-73: Average annual percentage growth rate of imports 1965-73.
IMP 73-84: Average annual percentage growth rate of imports 1973-84.
GDP 65-73: Average annual percentage growth rate of GDP 1965-73.
GDP 73-84: Average annual percentage growth rate of GDP 1973-84.

The numbers in parentheses are the numbers of countries in the tests.

P = The two-tailed level of significance.

GDP growth were obtained in the test in which all of the countries in the study were included, as well as the tests on the subgroups of countries of similar size.

In this part of the study, Pearson's correlations were run between the average annual percentage growth rates of exports and imports and the average annual growth rates of GDP. The tests covered the 1965 to 1973 and 1973 to 1984 time periods. In six of the eight correlations conducted between import growth and GDP growth, the coefficients were significant at the 99 percent level. The more moderate correlations between GDP growth and export growth were significant at the 99 percent level in two of the eight tests, and significant at a greater than the 95 percent level in three other tests.

The greater values for the correlations and levels of significance between imports and growth than exports and growth suggest that for the countries in the study, in the periods covered, it was the greater ability of the outward-oriented economies to import capital goods, technology, and raw materials that allowed them to achieve higher growth rates. This conclusion is further supported by the fact that the values for the coefficient and the levels of significance were generally greater in the later of the two time periods. It was during the later period that two major increases in the price of imported oil strained the ability of both developed and underdeveloped nations to maintain or increase their levels of imports.

The fact that correlation coefficients between trade and growth were consistent for all the groups of countries suggests that export orientation is important for medium-sized as well as small countries.

STRUCTURAL CHANGES

Some correlations were run on the relationship between structural change and economic growth rates. These were done to test the suggestion by Kuznets that small countries could achieve high growth rates by quickly adjusting their economies to compete in changing international markets.[6] He had also suggested that sometimes the greater "community of feeling" among smaller populations might help in facilitating the necessary adjustments. These results are presented in Table 13.2.

The results offer some tentative support to the hypothesis by Kuznets. In the test conducted for all of the nations in the study, there was a weak but positive and statistically significant (at the 91 percent level) correlation between structural change and growth. However, when tests were conducted on nations grouped according to size, the value of the correlation coefficient and the level of significance increased for nations with populations of less than 5 million. In the tests for the two groups of nations with larger populations, the correlation coefficients were not significant and even had the "wrong" signs. Thus, structural change had a significant and positive correlation with growth in the smaller, but not the larger nations, in the study.

Table 13.2
Correlations between Structural Changes and Growth

Populations greater than one million

STRUCT 65-84

GNP 65-84   .2646
                      (42)
                  P = .090

Populations between one and 5 million

GNP 65-84   .4836
                      (19)
                  P = .036

Populations between 5 and 10 million

GNP 65-84   -.0605
                      (15)
                  P = .830

Populations greater than 10 million

GNP 65-84   -.1506
                      (8)
                  P = .722

STRUCT 65-84:   Structural changes between 1965 and 1984.
GNP 65-84:   Average annual percentage growth rate per
                 capita GNP.

The numbers in parentheses are the number of countries in the
tests.

P = The two-tailed level of significance.

THE PROVISION OF SOCIAL SERVICES

In addition to the examination of strict economic variables, some tests were
conducted to determine the relationships between the level of development and
the rate of growth on one hand and some indicators of social welfare on the
other. Per capita GNP in 1984 was used as the measure of development, and
the average annual percentage growth rate of per capita GNP between 1965 and
1984 was used as the measure of growth. Variables used as indicators of social
welfare were life expectancy at birth, population per physician, per capita daily
calorie supply as a percentage of daily requirements, and primary and secondary
school enrollments as percentages of their age groups. The data for each variable
were the latest available at the time that the study was conducted. The results
of this part of the study are presented in Table 13.3.

It was not surprising to find that the richer countries, those with larger per

Table 13.3
Correlations between the Level of Development and the Provision of Social Services

Populations greater than one million

	PHYSI	CALORI	PRIMSC	SECSCH	LE 84
GNP-84	-.4748	.5982	.4743	.7055	.6717
	(40)	(54)	(52)	(52)	(54)
	P = .002	P = .000	P = .001	P = .000	P = .000

Populations between one and five million

GNP-84	-.6646	.6646	.4462	.7470	.6160
	(25)	(25)	(24)	(24)	(25)
	P = .000	P = .000	P = .029	P = .000	P = .001

Populations between 5 and 10 million

GNP-84	-.4277	.6289	.4362	.7760	.8302
	(13)	(19)	(18)	(18)	(19)
	P = .145	P = .004	P = .070	P = .000	P = .000

Populations greater than 10 million

GNP-84	-.6493	.4521	.5723	.4401	.7182
	(9)	(10)	(10)	(10)	(10)
	P = .058	P = .190	P = .084	P = .203	P = .010

Correlations Between the Rate of Growth and
the Provision of Social Services

Population Greater than one million

	PHYSI	CALORI	PRIMSC	SECSCH	LE 84
GNP 65-84	-.2322	.4173	.3491	.2993	.3658
	(38)	(52)	(50)	(50)	(52)
	P = .161	P = .002	P = .013	P = .035	P = .004

Populations between one and five million

GNP 65 84	-.3701	.3806	.4089	.2841	.2491
	(16)	(23)	(22)	(22)	(23)
	P = .158	P = .073	P = .059	P = .200	P = .126

Populations between 5 and 10 million

	PHYSI	CALORI	PRIMSC	SECSCH	LE 84
GNP 65-84	-.2144	.3409	.4405	.5510	.5710
	(13)	(19)	(18)	(18	(19)
	P = .482	P = .153	P = .067	P = .018	P = .005

Populations of greater than 10 million

GNP 65-84	-.0750	.7546	.1143	-.1387	.4177
	(9)	(10)	(10)	(10)	(10)
	P = .048	P = .012	P = .753	P = .702	P = .115

PHYSI: Population per physician.
CALORI: Calori supply as a percentage of daily requirement.
PRIMSC: Primary school enrollment as a percentage of age group.
SECSCH: Secondary school enrollments as a percentage of age group.
LE 84:   Life expectancy at birth in 1984.
GNP 84:   Per capita GNP in 1984.
GNP 65-84:   Average annual growth rate of per capita GDP
between 1965 and 1984.¹
The numbers in parentheses are the number of countries in the test.

P = the two-tailed level of significance.

capita GNPs, were almost universally associated with better standards of social welfare. Life expectancy at birth and per capita GNP were 0.6717 for all the nations in the study; 0.6160 for nations with populations of between one and five million; 0.8302 for nations with populations of between 5 and 10 million; and 0.7182 for nations with populations of more than 10 million. They were all significant at least at the 99 percent level.

Similar results were obtained for the correlation coefficients between per capita GNP and the other welfare variables. It might be of interest that the correlation coefficients between secondary school enrollments and per capita GNP were higher than those between primary school enrollments and per capita GNP for the groups of nations with populations of less than 10 million. The coefficients for secondary school enrollments were 0.7470 for nations with populations of less than 5 million, and 0.7760 for nations with populations of between 5 and 10 million. Both were significant at the 99 percent level. For nations with populations of more than 10 million, the coefficients were greater for the correlations between per capita GNP and primary school enrollments.

Perhaps of more interest than the relationship between wealth and the provision of welfare services is the relationship between the rate of growth and the provision of welfare services. While richer countries can afford to allocate more resources to welfare than poorer ones, it might be expected that countries in the pursuit of high growth rates might make sacrifices in the provision of social services. One might therefore expect to find a weak or even an inverse relationship between the rate of growth and the provision of welfare services. The results of this part of the study are also presented in Table 13.3.

As might have been expected, the relationship between growth rates and the provision of welfare were not as strong as those between wealth and the provision of social services. Yet the results do not provide support for those who believe that fast growth can be achieved only at the expense of social welfare. Of the five welfare variables tested—life expectancy at birth, population per physician, calorie supply as a percentage of the daily requirement, and primary and secondary school enrollments as percentages of their respective age groups—for all of the countries in the study and the subgroups, only one "wrong" sign resulted, and that correlation was not significant. On the other hand there was a strong positive correlation between high growth rates and daily calorie supply for nations with populations of more than 10 million. There was also moderate and positive correlations between high growth rates and calorie supply as well as high growth rates and primary school enrollments in the test for all the nations. The coefficient for secondary school enrollments and fast growth was 0.5510 for nations with populations of between 5 and 10 million. All these correlations were significant at least at the 98 percent level.

It is possible that the countries with high growth rates might be highly correlated with the countries that had higher per capita GNP. In order to test for that possibility I ran correlation tests between GDP and growth rates. The coef-

Table 13.4
Correlations between GNP in 1984 and the Growth Rate of GNP between 1965 and 1984

```
                    Populations Greater than one million

                            GNP 84
                             .4583
                GNP 65-84    (52)
                             P = .001

                Populations between one and five million

                            GNP 84
                             .4187
                GNP 65-84    (23)
                             P = .047

                Populations between five and ten million

                            GNP 84
                             .6180
                GNP 65 84    (19)
                             P = .005

                Populations greater than 10 million

                            GNP 84
                             .1661
                GNP 65-84    (10)
                             P = .647
```

```
GNP 84:          Per capita GNP in 1984 dollars.
GNP 65-84:       Average annual percentage growth rate of per
                 capita GNP
                 between 1965 and 1984.
```

The number in the parentheses are the number of countries in the test.

P = the two-tailed level of significance.

ficients were larger than 50 percent only for the countries with populations of between 5 and 10 million. See Table 13.4.

OTHER RESULTS

In the only statistically significant results from the countries with populations of less than one million, there was an inverse relationship between population size and life expectancy at birth. The value of the coefficient was $-.6086$. It was significant at the 99 percent level. There are no obvious economic explanations for this result.

There was a statistically significant relationship at the 95 percent level between debt as a percentage of exports and population size in the nations with populations of less than 5 million. The value of the coefficient was 0.4261. The relationship was not significant for any of the other groups of nations.

No statistically significant relationships were found between the size of populations and rates of growth or rates of inflation. These results were not entirely surprising. As was mentioned above, factor endowments and the efficiency of factor utilization are better determinants of growth than mere population size. This is not to say that the size of the population is not an important economic variable for a country, but only that population size must be considered in the context of several other important economic variables.

CONCLUSIONS

It was mentioned at the beginning of this chapter that there are now several small and some very small nations in the world. An attempt was made to test for the importance of relative size among a sample of nations of what may be called medium and small size. Although different results were sometimes obtained for groups of countries of varying sizes, generally, the correlation coefficients did not change significantly when tests were run for different groups of countries.

These results should not be taken to downplay the importance of the size of the population as an economic variable. The size of the domestic market remains an important consideration in the decision-making of many firms. Even if international protectionism is not a factor, many firms become competitive internationally only after learning how to produce and to compete in the domestic market. A small home market could prevent the creation of some new business enterprises.

APPENDIX

COUNTRIES IN STUDY	POPULATION (in millions)
Antigua and Barbuda	.08
Bahamas	.23
Barbados	.25
Belize	.16
Benin	3.83
Bolivia	6.25
Botswana	1.05
Burundi	4.54
Cameroon	9.47
Cape Verde	.32
Central African Republic	2.52
Chile	11.88
Congo, People's Republic of the	1.70
Costa Rica	2.53
Cote D'Ivoire	9.47
Cyprus	.65

Dominica	.08
Dominican Republic	6.10
Ecuador	9.11
El Salvador	4.78
Fiji	.69
Gabon	.81
Gambia, The	.72
Ghana	13.15
Greece	9.90
Grenada	.09
Guatemala	7.74
Guinea-Bissau	.87
Guyana	.79
Haiti	5.18
Honduras	4.23
Hong Kong	5.40
Israel	4.16
Jamaica	2.30
Jordan	3.38
Kenya	19.54
Lesotho	1.47
Liberia	2.11
Madagascar	9.73
Malawi	6.84
Malaysia	15.19
Mali	7.72
Malta	.36
Mauritania	1.83
Mauritius	.98
Nepal	16.11
Nicaragua	3.16
Niger	5.94
Panama	2.13
Papua New Guinea	3.43
Paraguay	3.28
Peru	19.20
Portugal	10.16
Rwanda	5.87
Sao Tome and Principe	.11
Senegal	6.40
Sierra Leone	3.54
Singapore	2.52
Somalia	4.54
Sri Lanka	15.60
St. Christopher and Nevis	.06
St. Vincent and Grenadines	.12
St. Lucia	.13
Suriname	.38

Swaziland	.73
Syrian Arab Republic	9.93
Togo	2.87
Trinidad and Tobago	1.17
Uganda	14.96
Uruguay	2.99
Venezuela	16.85
Yemen Arab Republic	6.66
Yemen, PDR	2.23
Zambia	6.45
Zimbabwe	7.98

Source: International Monetary Fund, *International Financial Statistics Yearbook 1986* (Washington, D.C.: IMF, 1986).

NOTES

1. The World Bank, *World Development Report 1986* (New York: Oxford University Press, 1986), pp. 180–81, 243.

2. See S. Kuznets, ''Economic Growth of Small Nations,'' in *Economic Consequences of the Size of Nations*, *Proceedings of a Conference Held by the International Economic Association*, E. A. G. Robinson, ed. (London: Macmillan, 1960), pp. 14–31; Hollis B. Chenery and Moises Syrquin, *Patterns of Development 1950–1970* (London: Oxford University Press, 1975).

3. Daniel Landau, ''Government and Economic Growth in Less Developed Countries: An Empirical Study for 1960–1980,'' *Economic Development and Cultural Change*, 5: 35–37 (October 1986).

4. Kuznets, ''Economic Growth of Small Nations,'' pp. 27–31.

5. The International Monetary Fund, *International Financial Statistics Yearbook 1986*, Washington, D.C., 1986.

6. Kuznets, ''Economic Growth of Small Nations,'' pp. 27–31.

REFERENCES

Chenery, Hollis B. and Syrquin, Moises (1975). *Patterns of Development 1950–1970*. London: Oxford University Press.

International Monetary Fund (1986). *International Financial Statistics Yearbook 1986*. Washington, D.C.: IMF.

Kuznets, S. (1960). ''Economic Growth of Small Nations.'' In *Economic Consequences of the Size of Nations*, *Proceedings of a Conference Held by the International Economic Association*, E. A. G. Robinson, ed. London: Macmillan.

Landau, Daniel (1986). ''Government and Economic Growth in the Less Developed Countries: An Empirical Study for 1960–1980.'' *Economic Development and Cultural Change* 35.

World Bank (1986). *World Development Report*. Washington, D.C.: World Bank.

14

Values, Population, and International Responsibility

JOHN J. PIDERIT, S. J.

Economists are accustomed to ambiguous results and qualified conclusions. If considerations of equity are also incorporated into economic analysis, one can appreciate Aristotle's famous warning that one should not demand too much precision in ethical matters (*Nichomachean Ethics*, I, 3:1094,b12–14). Rather than an admission of failure, this warning should serve to keep expectations at a reasonable level when investigating ethical issues. The warning also suggests to economists a method for considering moral issues.

Standard procedure in economics is to build a model that replicates in a controlled manner certain limited aspects of a real economy. When applying the model to an actual economy, the economist claims that those aspects of an existing economy that have not been incorporated into the model are of secondary or tertiary importance.

Aristotle in his admonition concerning the type of accuracy one can expect in ethics was referring to principles that guide the actual ethical judgments one has to make. In deriving what he considered to be principles for correct action, Aristotle did not hesitate to use stylized facts and simplified examples, which brought across the point he was trying to make. Ultimately, however, examples do not suffice. One wants to say something concerning correct action that covers a range, narrow as it might be, of possible situations. However, ethical principles are to be applied to real life. Because real life is so wonderfully varied and because correct ethical decisions have to be made for particular instances, it is difficult to formulate principles that are, on the one hand, sufficiently general and, on the other hand, applicable to real-world situations.

In fact, it is far easier to do what economists do, namely, enunciate conclusions valid only for the type of economy currently being modeled. One then always qualifies the conclusions by harking back to the restrictive assumptions made in the model. This is certainly a cautious way of proceeding. When attempting to fuse economics with ethics, prudence dictates following this methodological lead of economists.

One way of achieving fusion is to limit by modeling the field of investigation. In this essay the approach is to take one of the standard models of international trade, as developed over the years by economists, and assume that this is the reality with which the ethically inquiring mind must deal. In the context of a specific economic model, the ethically inquiring mind in this study confronts a particular moral problem: excessive population growth. Even in this case, there will be sufficient fuzziness to worry any practical person oriented to action. Nonetheless, using a model offers a way of focusing on the important moral issues that occur in the context of international development and population growth.

Selecting a theoretical model does not mean that the primary concern is with envisioning the proper functioning of a just society, as in the tradition of Rawls (1971). Rawls is concerned with principles of justice and with institutions that promote justice. He sets himself the task of constructing a society that is completely fair and just. He wants to be realistic in that he considers the sometimes perverse inclinations and dispositions of individuals. For this reason, his institutions must engender adherence to just principles. However, this is not a theory which proposes remedies for past injustices.[1] In fact, however, casual observation, coupled with almost any conceivable principles of justice, indicates that our world is fairly rife with injustice. Hence, the rectification of injustice must be an important component in any plan to establish a just society.

When population growth is discussed in the context of economic development, the usual issue is whether population growth fosters or retards growth in GNP per capita. Careful attention is paid to measures of inequality within a country or across countries to ascertain whether high population growth is strongly correlated with heavily skewed income distributions or low growth in GNP per capita (Little, 1982: 195–200).

The concern in this chapter is rather the responsibility of wealthy countries towards less developed countries, especially in the formulation and implementation of population policies. The distribution of income in a country is, from this point of view, less important than the disparities in average income levels between two countries or groups of countries.

No economic model can substitute for a careful analysis of moral issues. This analysis will be undertaken in the following section, in which the moral principles of a primary values approach are developed. The third section briefly contrasts the primary values approach with the utilitarian approach, which is more frequently developed in the economic literature, and also briefly considers the Rawlsian alternative. A Heckscher-Ohlin model is examined in the fourth section to determine the range of ethical issues one can address in such a model. The actual range of issues turns out to be quite narrow. A Keynesian growth model has more factors which lend themselves to moral analysis, and it is developed in the fifth section. The concluding section draws out the implications of a primary values approach for specific policies.

ANALYSIS OF MORAL ISSUES

The primary values approach considers the obligations incumbent on men and women, inasmuch as they are born into a society of other human beings.[2] The starting point is one of the community of individuals, for whom, it is claimed, certain values are primary or fundamental. To nurture personal self-development, each person is called upon to foster the development of community and to foster the "flourishing" of all other individuals in the community.[3]

The goods or values that promote the human flourishing are related to community and also to the drives of every human being. Thus essential goods include life, friendship, knowledge, beauty, recreation, and practical reasonableness. The list is meant to be comprehensive. For that reason the values are intentionally general. Any good or value that is not listed, but that someone thinks ought to be included, can be considered either a particular instance of a more general good or a subgood under one of the categories. For example, health is certainly an important good for every individual. It is included under life. Both family and patriotism are also important values. They are included under friendship, which includes all relationships among individuals.[4]

Within this framework, justice can be divided into three areas: distributive, commutative, and social justice. Distributive justice refers to a fair allocation of goods. In any society there are roles, functions, goods, offices, and so on, collectively referred to as the common stock and the incidents of communal enterprise, which "do not serve the common good unless and until they are appropriated to particular individuals."[5] Commutative justice refers to fair relationships in the exchange between individuals (or other personal or corporate entities) of all goods, offices, and so on. Social justice is both the obligation of the individual to participate in society and the obligation upon society to foster participation by individuals in society through work, politics, and community action.

Equity in the context of economic development falls mainly under distributive justice. More important than the division of areas are the principles which give content to the meaning of "fair." The two guiding principles in the primary values approach are the common good and subsidiarity.[6]

The principle of the common good is that society is to be structured so as to foster the "flourishing" of all individuals. To flourish does not necessarily mean to be happy or content with one's material welfare. Likewise, maximizing utilities, as in the normal economic paradigm, of all individuals in society usually does not foster the flourishing of all individuals, although it may be a reasonable approximation under certain circumstances. Strict equality of income or wealth is also unlikely to lead to the flourishing of all individuals, since individuals have different capacities and make more or less effort in securing goods. The primary way in which this approach differs from a utilitarian one is that flourishing as a human being involves pursuing simultaneously many values or goods, which are not infrequently only distantly related to the economic goods traded in the marketplace.

Crucial to the principle of the common good is that, if maximization is indeed a legitimate concept in moral discourse, it must ultimately refer to a vector of goods. Happiness alone or simple utility do not suffice as characterizations of human striving and flourishing. Furthermore, there is no strong lexicographic ordering within the elements of the vector. There is a weak lexicographic ordering in the sense that life, since it is the *sine qua non* for the realization of the other goods, has priority over the other goods. The priority, however, is by no means absolute. Either truth or friendship, broadly conceived and depending on circumstances, may require surrendering one's life.

The second principle of justice is subsidiarity. Despite the obvious meaning of subsidiarity, the name does not mean that this principle is subordinate to the common good. Subsidiarity means that human organizations and associations should be structured in such a way that the smallest feasible unit has authority to make decisions affecting its own welfare. In a political and economic sense, small is beautiful, as long as the size is feasible.[7]

Private property, for example, is justified by the principle of subsidiarity. To pursue one's own flourishing one needs disposition over one's goods. Usually, both subsidiarity and the common good are principles that qualify each other without any general rule of subordination. For example, private property is not an absolute right, but a right that is conditional upon the common good.

Because the flourishing of human individuals and of the human community requires the use of the common stock and the incidents of communal enterprise, and because practical reasonableness is a human good, the waste of resources is to be avoided. In this sense, efficiency is an instrumental good for human flourishing. One ought not, however, to conclude that efficiency is a fundamental good. If inefficiency in a technical economic (Pareto) sense is necessary to foster human flourishing, so be it. Efficiency within reason is a human good. It is not an unqualified human good.

Equality of income is also not a primary good, though large disparities of incomes in a society usually indicate that society is not promoting the flourishing of all its members. Income is a necessary means to attain most of the primary goods. In this instrumental sense income is also a good. Because society is to promote the flourishing of all individuals, if all individuals were absolutely identical, equality of income would be just.[8]

Unequal incomes have to be justified by the differences among individuals. By their effort and talent people contribute different amounts. People need different amounts of income because of their health or infirmities. People have different capacities to enjoy certain goods. People take varying risks in seeking to achieve goals. Finally, some people take the rewards of their efforts immediately and others save to savor their rewards at a later date. Thus, effort, talent, need, capacity, risk, and savings are the primary factors that justify variations in income.

These factors should not be narrowly construed, especially if they are to be applied to an entire economy. For example, risk refers not merely to a person's willingness to enter a new field of endeavor. It also refers to a society's willingness to bear the cyclical effects of certain types of market arrangements. Saving, as applied to the entire society, refers to capital formation. Societies that have emphasized capital formation over consumption are justified in having higher levels of income. The common stock and the incidents of communal enterprise are scarce, but also capable of development. Since development of these goods enables the flourishing of the whole community of nations, those societies which promote the development of the common stock should be rewarded with higher levels of income.

PRIMARY VALUES APPROACH AND UTILITARIANISM

The utilitarian approach, in its different variations, assumes that individuals seek to maximize what is variously called their happiness, their utility, or their satisfaction. Furthermore, the means by which people maximize their satisfaction is through the consumption of goods and the efficient use of resources, such as labor, which are at their disposal. As long as the utility functions satisfy certain standard assumptions concerning the manner in which preferences for goods are formed, the actual form of the utility function is left unspecified. In this way one allows for different feelings and satisfactions among individuals. The vegetarian gets no satisfaction from chicken or beef but gets plenty of utility from peas and carrots.

In assessing the best economic policy that affects many individuals, the utilitarian prescribes that individual utilities should be added together and the economic policy that maximizes the sum of individual utilities should be chosen. In performing the summation, society may wish to weight the utilities of certain people more than others. But such a weighting is a political or ethical judgment, which the utilitarian eschews.

The essential difference between a utilitarian approach and the primary values approach, based on a person's orientation towards certain fundamental values, is twofold, corresponding to the level of the individual and the level of society. At the individual level, the approach of primary values denies the relevance of happiness or satisfaction as an ultimate goal. Instead, satisfaction is a by-product of the pursuit of the primary values.

Inasmuch as goods and the incidents of communal enterprise are necessary in order to pursue values, the primary values approach must also attend to meeting in an efficient manner the needs of individuals. The utility function with the income constraint is a step in the right direction. Something similar is also appropriate in the primary values approach. Yet it is not sufficient. Not only does it not address the question concerning which needs are "legitimate," but it also takes the income constraint as given. Certainly a theory of justice ought to examine how much income, resources, offices, responsibility, roles, and so forth are available to different individuals. Similarly, taxes and other burdens come within the purview of an ethical system. The utilitarian approach relegates these questions to politics or philosophy. In so doing, it relinquishes its claim to set a coherent ethical standard.

At the level of society the utilitarians believe that people can be compared based solely on their levels of satisfaction. The primary values approach rejects such comparisons based on satisfaction, no matter how it is conceived. The primary values approach does not claim that individuals are strictly incomparable. On the contrary, the primary values approach claims that human nature is sufficiently "natural" that we can indeed make valid comparisons among individuals. However, the basis of comparison must include the elements mentioned earlier: talents, effort, and—most important, because it relates to the fundamental value of life—need.

Let us turn now to the specific problem of "over" population. Population growth can be excessive for a number of reasons. The country experiencing rapid population growth may not be able to generate sufficient jobs to allow all people to be productive in their economy. Alternatively, sufficient jobs are being created but the world's essential resources, particularly those for which there are no markets, are being consumed with no reasonable hope that substitutes will be generated before the essential resources are depleted. A third possibility is that the developed world is simply frightened by having to assume the minority role after population growth has stabilized.

Though each of the reasons generates a host of ethical questions, the concern in this paper is the inability of the developing country to generate sufficient jobs. This results in low per capita income and poverty.

The primary values approach dictates that the entire community should be concerned with the welfare of all its members. This is qualified by the principle of subsidiarity, which relegates more responsibility to the social grouping more directly regulating the people in question. In this instance, the government of the developing country itself bears primary responsibility for formulating and implementing population policy. But, if the government is making serious efforts, and if, in general, the effort, talent, risk undertaken, and capacity are roughly the same in the developing country as in the developed country, need alone is sufficient to prompt a response, in the primary values approach, by the developed country.[9] Note that in this view the primary motivation is to assist people in the global community who are not able to flourish despite a similar array of talents, capacities, and so on, as in the developed country.

Utilitarians have no way of treating the population problem inasmuch as they have no way of evaluating the importance of more or fewer people in the world or in a particular nation. Utilitarians must appeal to philosophers or politicians to determine the optimal growth rate.

As indicated earlier there is a question whether the ills of the present society are capable of being treated within Rawls' system because he envisions a just society. If the present poverty of developing nations was foreseen in the original position, Rawls' difference principle offers a prescription. But to most people, his prescription will seem excessively austere. According to the difference principle, the resources of a society must be allocated in such a way as to assist the most disadvantaged group in society. This would mean that the resources of the wealthiest nation should pour into the most disadvantaged country until it is no longer the most disadvantaged. At that point the wealthy country would turn its spout to the next disadvantaged country. This is not a prescription with which many people in developed countries can live.

As will be seen in the concluding section, the primary values approach prescribes a policy that can be termed moderate. This is in strong contrast to the utilitarian approach, which, at least on this question, has no approach. This is also a criticism of the Rawlsian approach if the current situation of excessive population growth is considered the result of previous injustice. If it is not, the policy prescribed by Rawls is extreme.

THE HECKSCHER-OHLIN GROWTH MODEL

Before considering the Heckscher-Ohlin model of international trade, a casual comparison of the principles enunciated in the primary values approach with the real world (not the model!) is informative. One might think that a market economy fufills rather nicely the requirements of justice. Since, by and large, the free market laws of supply and demand reward higher effort, talent, capacity, risk, and savings with higher income, advocates of the free market system can claim that the market structures personal income in the proper relationship, even if the gaps between different classes of economic actors seem excessively large.

A few caveats are in order. First, such claims for the fairness of the free market can only be made for situations in which the free market exists and functions according to the laws of supply and demand. There are sufficiently many examples of economic realities for which there is no market. The best known examples are those of public goods and externalities.[10] Second, even when a free market exists, for various reasons it may not function with a Walrasian auctioneer, as imagined by economists. Involuntary unemployment seems to be a feature of a number of labor markets. More telling are the situations when the quality of a good offered is affected by the price in the market. This interdependence has ramifications in insurance markets, capital markets (loans), labor markets, and technological change. The effects can be noticed on the macro level as well as on the micro level.[11] Of course, the nonexistence of certain markets or their imperfect functioning due to a dependence of quality on price is not of concern in this discussion, since ethical principles are being applied not to real economies but to an economic model, in which all pertinent markets are assumed to exist.

More troublesome in international trade are the large discrepancies in wages between developed countries and less developed countries. Such discrepancies are real. It is difficult for a free market enthusiast to claim that such discrepancies are justified by need, effort, talent, and so on.

Consider the following two-sector Heckscher-Ohlin growth model.[12]

$$Y_i = F^i(K_i, L_i) \qquad \text{where } i = 1, 2 \qquad (1)$$

F_i is homogeneous of degree one in capital and labor and Y_i is the output of good i. Therefore, equation 1 can be written as

$$\frac{Y_i}{L_i} = F^i(r_i, 1) \qquad \text{where } r_i = \frac{K_i}{L_i} \qquad (2)$$

Let ^ indicate a growth rate. Then equation 2 can be written as

$$\hat{Y}_i - \hat{L}_i = \hat{F}^i \qquad (3)$$

In a Heckscher-Ohlin world, technology is shared throughout the world. In this instance this is taken to mean that F^i ($i = 1, 2$) is the same both at home and abroad. The equation corresponding to equation 3 for the foreign country, whose values are denoted by asterisks, is

$$\hat{Y}_i^* - \hat{L}_i^* = \hat{F}^i \qquad (4)$$

The home country is the developing country and the foreign country is the developed country.

Both countries are assumed to have perfectly functioning markets in goods and factors without any dominant firms or unions. Labor units and capital are homogeneous as is the quality of the goods. At all times trade is balanced, that is, the capital account is always zero. Under these assumptions and with some additional regularity conditions, the country which is relatively abundant in capital exports the capital-intensive good and the other country, which is relatively abundant in labor, exports the labor-intensive good. Furthermore, factor prices are equated between countries, even though there is no trade in capital goods. In equilibrium, the capital-labor ratio in the developing country is the same as the capital-labor ratio in the developed country.

The Heckscher-Ohlin growth model presented above severely constricts the field of ethical considerations. The only difference between the developing country and the developed country in this model is that the developed country is relatively capital abundant. In fact, when using such a model it makes very little sense to use the term developing country. Since nations share technologies and since factor price equalization induces the use of identical capital-labor ratios in the production of a good in the home country as well as in the foreign country, the significance of "developing" evanesces. In short, neither country has a problem of unemployment, underutilized capital, or poverty, either absolute or relative.

THE KEYNESIAN GROWTH MODEL

If a population problem is to emerge theoretically in the model, one must allow for less than perfect markets. Using the same notation and the Hicksian strategem of a composite good, however, one can easily move from the Heckscher-Ohlin model portrayed in the previous section to a more Keynesian model of interdependent countries.

If the international price of commodities remains fixed, then one can form the composite good Y. For simplicity, and without loss of generalization assume that $P_1 = P_2 = 1$. Thus,

$$Y = Y_1 + Y_2 \tag{5}$$

Taking growth rates, one obtains

$$\hat{Y} - \frac{Y_1}{Y} \hat{Y}_1 + \frac{Y_2}{Y} \hat{Y}_2 \tag{6}$$

Assume both economies are moving along their steady-state growth paths.[13] These paths are designated by the subscript zero and all values are calculated as deviations from the steady state growth paths. For notational purposes, let lower case letters refer to deviations from steady state growth paths:

$$y \equiv \hat{Y} - \hat{Y}_0 \quad \text{where } Y \text{ is GNP}$$

$$n \equiv \hat{L} - \hat{L}_0$$

$$x \equiv \hat{X} - \hat{X}_0 \quad \text{where } X \text{ is the balance of trade} \tag{7}$$

$$e \equiv \hat{E} - \hat{E}_0 \quad \text{where } E \text{ is expenditures}$$

Growth in capital occurs, but behind the scenes. It grows in the two countries at the rate necessary to maintain prices constant.

Excessive population growth is assumed to have a detrimental effect on per capita income. At the same time, each country's growth is linked to the other country through the trade account. A linear approximation (around the steady state growth paths) to this relationship is given by the following equation:

$$y - n = \beta e - \gamma n + \delta x(y, y^*, s) \tag{8}$$

where β, γ, and δ are greater than 0.

On the left hand side is the growth in per-capita income. Above average growth in expenditures is captured by the first term.[14] The deleterious effects of an overly rapid growth in population is represented by $-\gamma$.[15] Finally, rapid growth in net exports has a positive effect on growth. (The initial level of the trade balance is assumed to be positive for the developing country.)

Through the balance of payments accounts, the balance of trade in one country has an effect on the balance of trade in the other country. Above-trend income growth in the home country causes a deceleration in trend growth for the balance of trade as the country begins to import more. In a similar fashion, above-trend growth in foreign income causes a surge in exports and a positive effect on the trend growth rate for the trade balance. Thus, the derivatives for the trade balance function have the following signs:

$$\partial x / \partial y \equiv x_y < 0$$

$$\partial x / \partial y^* \equiv x_y^* > 0 \tag{9}$$

$$\partial x / \partial s \equiv x_s = -1$$

The last argument, s, is a shift parameter. Since the shift results in below-trend growth in the balance of trade, the shift represents an exogenous inflow of resources into the country.

In a similar manner the growth equation for the foreign country is

$$y^* - n^* = \beta^* e^* - \gamma^* n^* - \delta^* x(y, y^*, s) \tag{10}$$

Because they are coefficients of growth rates, all the parameters which appear in equations 8 and 10 are between zero and one. Note the last term in the above equation. It appears with its own quasi-elasticity δ^*, but there is no asterisk on the x-function, the balance of trade. The reason is that the home country and the developed country are the only two countries in the world. Therefore, the trade surplus of one country is the trade deficit of the other country.

In (y^*, y) space, as depicted in Figure 14.1, the equilibrium growth line for the developing country is the steeper of the two, with a slope greater than one, while the line for the developed country has a slope less than one. Increased productivity of any sort shifts the lines to the right. Even if the productivity increase only occurs in one country, the other country benefits through the trade sector.

A population problem for the developing country means that $n\ (= \hat{L} - \hat{L}_0)$ is positive. Suppose n can be decreased by a comprehensive program of family planning. In other words, a transfer of goods to the "population sector" will decrease the excessive growth rate, that is, $\partial n / \partial s \equiv n' < 0$, where ∂s refers to a permanent transfusion each year of ds percentage points of the composite good.

Figure 14.1
Interdependent Growth

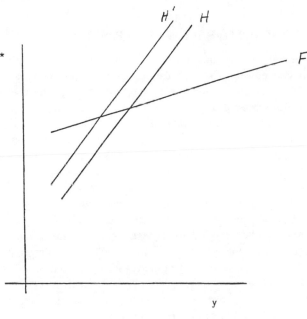

The developed country obtains this annual infusion by decreasing its own annual consumption:

$$\beta^* \, de^* \; = \; - \; \delta^* \, ds \tag{11}$$

Thus, the flatter curve in Figure 14.1 does not shift. The steeper curve shifts to the left; on the diagram it is indicated by H'. This shift causes lower equilibrium growth rates for both the developing country and the developed country.

That the growth rate in the developing country should fall is not surprising since population growth is one of the components of growth in GNP. More important is the question whether GNP per capita rises in the developing country. It does provided

$$- \; \gamma \, n' > \delta \tag{12}$$

This means that the positive effect of the decrease of population growth rate on the growth rate in GNP per capita is larger than the negative effect which the transfer has on the balance of trade. There is, of course, no guarantee that the condition in equation 12 will be fulfilled. An ill-conceived or ill-executed program of population control will have a negligible effect on n and thus n' will be small negatively, and $-\gamma\, n' < \delta$.

IMPLICATIONS OF THE PRIMARY VALUES APPROACH

The developed country that transfers resources to the developing country suffers a loss in consumption per capita. They therefore have the legitimate expectation that such a loss should be productive. In the primary values approach efficiency within reason is a value.

Efficiency can clash with the value of subsidiarity. In the population problem postulated in this paper, there is no problem with overconsumption of the world's nonrenewable resources. Thus, subsidiarity gives freedom to the smallest feasible group. In this instance, barring no difficulties, the smallest feasible group for deciding the number of children to have is the married couple. If the excessively high population growth rate generates poverty within a country, the appropriate group to handle the problem is the country itself.

When a developed country offers its assistance to a less developed country to help reduce its population growth, does the developed country have the right to impose conditions? Yes, if this is the only feasible way to insure that the program will be effective. The more the program can be entrusted to the direction of the developing country itself, the more this accords with the flourishing of the human person, even in a situation of poverty.

The direct way of handling a problem may not be the most effective. Many studies have shown that population growth attenuates as per capita income increases. Efforts to increase per capita income may be more productive than programs in family planning. In particular, many developing countries lack developed markets. Developed countries can fulfill their obligations, as conceived by the primary values approach, in a number of different ways. Since the expertise of developed countries is in markets, to alleviate overpopulation it might make more sense for the developed countries to offer to assist less developed countries in establishing markets or in improving the functioning of already existing ones.

NOTES

1. Rawls explicitly excludes treatment of how one moves from an actual society to his just society, grounded in a social contract. Furthermore, he does not consider what happens if individuals break a contract to which they, at least implicitly, agreed. See Rawls, 1971: 7–11.

2. Various terms are used to designate this approach. The traditional term is "natural law." Since this lends itself to misinterpretation and since "teleological" is abstruse and unfamiliar, "primary values" is being used as a surrogate. Although the primary values approach has a long tradition in the United States as well as in Europe, in both Protestant and Catholic circles, its most recent systematic formulation is to be found in the U.S. Bishops' Pastoral Letter on the U.S. Economy, Section 2B, 61–95.

3. Rawls considers the primary values approach to be a form of intuitionism, since

there is an irreducible group of first principles, which must be balanced, in an intuitive way, against each other. See Rawls, 1971: 34–40.

4. Other taxonomies are clearly possible by using either more general or more particular concepts. For a more complete justification of the six goods listed in the text see Finnis, 1980: 85–97.

5. Finnis, 1980: 166.

6. In the bishops' letter the term "solidarity" is more frequently used to refer to every person's obligation to promote the common good.

7. Subsidiarity is a requirement of efficiency. The smaller the group, the better able the group is to determine the practical means to foster the flourishing of individuals within the group.

8. In a society in which all individuals were absolutely identical, it would be hard to conceive of community or society as we normally understand it, since the reason people share thoughts, goods, and emotions with one another is precisely because people are different. For this reason it is very difficult to analyze in moral terms economic models that presuppose that all individuals have identical preference functions and offer homogeneous labor.

9. The question of savings is difficult since the developing country is much poorer. In Aristotlean fashion, one can claim that savings are the same if they are proportional, given the income level in each country. Alternatively, if the developing country is saving at approximately the same rate at which the developed country saved when it was in its developing stage, then one can conclude that there is no significant difference in savings.

10. See Mischan, 1981: 125–52, for a thorough discussion of the economic difficulties associated with externalities. Also Cowen (1985) questions the surgical distinction between private goods, on the one hand, and public goods, on the other.

11. See Stiglitz, 1987.

12. This model is the general equilibrium model of Heckscher-Ohlin theory. For an exposition see Jones, 1965.

13. The growth model is an adaptation of Dornbusch's static model of interdependent countries (Dornbusch, 1980).

14. Expenditures are affected by y, the growth in GNP. However, for simplicity this relationship has not been included. None of the results are changed if y is included as an argument of e.

15. Normally one considers growth in population to have a positive effect on supply. In this type of Keynesian model, however, the economy is driven by effective demand. Excessively rapid population growth puts a drag on effective demand.

REFERENCES

Aristotle. *Nicomachean Ethics*, trans. by Martin Oswald. Indianapolis: Bobbs-Merrill Educational Publishing.

Cowen, Tyler (1985). "A Public Goods Definition and Their Institutional Context: A Critique of Public Goods Theory." *Review of Social Economy* 43(1): 53–63.

Dornbusch, Rudiger (1980). *Open Economy Macroeconomics*. New York: Basic Books.

Finnis, John (1980). *Natural Law and Natural Rights*. Oxford: Clarendon Press.

Jones, Ronald W. (1965). "The Structure of Simple General Equilibrium Models." *Journal of Political Economy* 73: 557–72.

Little, Ian M. D. (1982). *Economic Development*. New York: Basic Books.

Mischan, E. J. (1981). *Economic Efficiency and Social Welfare*. London: George Allen & Unwin.

Rawls, John (1971). *A Theory of Justice*. Cambridge, Mass.: Harvard University Press.

Stiglitz, Joseph E. (1987). ''The Causes and Consequences of the Dependence of Quality on Price.'' *Journal of Economic Literature* 25 (1): 1–48.

U.S. Bishops' Pastoral Letter (1986). ''Economic Justice for All.'' *Origins* 16(24):409–55.

Author Index

Ahlburg, D., 40
Ahn, Peter, 172, 184
Ali, S. A., et al., 116–17, 120–21, 127, 130, 134, 137
Allan, William, 60, 172, 174, 184
Allen, J., and Barnes, D., 36, 42
Alonso, W., 95, 105
Anker, R., and Knowles, J., 41
Aristotle, 211, 223
Arnold, F., and Shah, N. M., 117, 123
Arnold, F., et al., 39

Bairoch, P., 26, 42
Barnett, H., and Morse, C., 32, 42
Barnett, H. J., 41
Basmann, R. L., 152, 159
Becker, G. S., 83, 92
Behrman, J., and Birdsall, N., 40
Beller, A., 195, 197
Bernard, F. E., and Thom, D. J., 72–73, 75
Bernheim, B. D., and Stark, O., 135, 137
Bhagwati, Jagdish N., 7, 121, 123, 139, 142
Bhagwati, J. N., Schatz, K. W., and Wong, K., 113–14, 123
Bilsborrow, R. E., 39, 62, 75
Binswanger, Hans P., 179 80, 184
Binswanger, Hans P., and Ruttan, Vernon, 177–78, 185

Binswanger, Hans P., and Shetty, S. V. R., 180, 185
Birdsall, Nancy, 7, 40, 64, 75
Blau, F., and Hendricks, W. E., 195, 197
Bloom, D. E., and Freeman, R. B., 7, 38, 92
Bloomestein, H., and Nijkamp, P., 102, 105
Bohning, W. R., 140, 159
Boserup, Ester, 15, 19, 22–23, 35, 42, 62, 75, 166, 175, 185, 188, 197
Boulding, E., 188, 197
Brown, A. A., and Neuberger, E., 102, 105
Brown, G., and Field, B., 41
Brown, L., 41
Buringh, P., van Heest, H., and Staring, G., 34–35, 42
Buvinic, M., 188, 197

Cain, M., 29, 39, 42
Caldwell, J. C., 19–20, 22–23, 39
Cameron, G. C., and Wingo, L., 95, 105
Campano, Fred, and Salvatore, Dominick, 7, 93
Cassen, R. H., 39
Chenery, Hollis B., and Syrquin, Moises, 210
Chesnais, Jean-Claude, 15, 22–23, 27–28, 42

Choucri, N., 40, 115, 123
Chourci, N., and Lahiri, S., 120, 123
Christensen, L. R., Jorgenson, D. W., and Lau, L. J., 48, 57
Clark, Colin, 34, 42, 108, 123
Cleland, J., and Sathar, Z., 40
Coale, Ansley J., 7
Coale, Ansley J., and Hoover, Edgar M., 14–15, 22–23, 25, 42
Coleman, D., and Schofield, R., 21, 23
Corden, W. M., and Findlay, R., 90, 92
Cowen, Tyler, 223

David, Martin, and Menchik, Paul L., 54, 57
Davis, C., Haub, C., and Willette, J., 114, 123
Deardorff, A., 40
Deaton, Agnus S., and Muellbauer, John, 54–55, 57
Demeny, P., 8, 107, 123
Denison, E., 38
Denison, E., and Chung, 38
De Sweemer, C., 40
De Wilde, John C., 173, 185
Dornbusch, Rudiger, 223

Easterlin, Richard A., 26, 42
Ebiri, K., 127, 130–32, 134–35, 137
Eckholm, E., 36, 42
Eizenga, W., 54, 57
Engelhardt, Thomas, 173, 185
Espenshade, Thomas J., 54–57
Evenson, R., Popkin, B., and King-Quizon, E., 41

Fair, R. C., 148, 159
FAO, 34, 36, 42, 44, 62–63, 65, 75
FAO, and International Institute for Applied Systems Analysis, 35
FAO, and UN Environmental Programme, 36, 44
Fearnside, P. M., 60–61, 75
Fei, J. C. H., and Ranis, G., 82, 92
Fields, G. S., 143, 159
Finnis, John, 223
Fogarty, M. S., and Garofalo, G., 105
Fréderickson, P., 41

Frenzen, D., and Hogan, D., 40
Fry, Maxwell J., 55, 57
Fry, Maxwell, and Mason, Andrew, 55, 57

Garn, H. A., 105
Garofalo, G., and Fogarty, M. S., 96, 105
Gilani, I., Khan, M. F., and Iqbal, M., 121, 123, 130, 133, 135, 137–38
Gilbert, A. G., 105
Gilland, Bernard, 35, 42, 59, 75
Gleave, M. B., and White, H. P., 172, 174, 185
Glover, D., and Simon, J., 41
Goldfarb, R. S., 112, 123
Golladay, F., and Liese, B., 41
Gorse, J., et al., 69–72, 75
Gosh, P. K., 8, 92
Greenwood, M. J., 8, 92, 140, 159
Greenwood, M. J., and Hunt, G. L., 159–60
Greenwood, M. J., et al., 143, 160
Gregory, P., 39
Grossman, J. B., 113, 123
Grove, A. T., 170, 185
Gupta, Kanhaya L., 57

Hall, D., and Hall, J., 32, 42
Hammer, J., 39
Harrington, W., and Fisher, A., 36, 42
Harris, J. R., and Todaro, M. P., 8, 83, 85–86, 92, 125, 138
Harrison, Paul, 61, 66, 76
Hart, R. A., 87, 93
Harvey, A. C., 159–60
Hausman, J. A., 147, 160
Hayami, Yuhiro, and Ruttan, Vernon W., 37, 42, 177–78, 185
Haynes, R., and Adams, D., 41
Heller, P., and Drake, W., 41
Henderson, Vernon J., 8, 33, 42, 93
Heyneman, S., and Loxley, W., 40
Higgins, G. M., et al., 68, 76
Ho, T. J., 69, 76
Hobcraft, J., McDonald, J., and Rutstein, S., 40

IBRD, 59, 62, 65, 70, 72, 76, 184–85
ILO, 110, 123

Kelley, Allen C., 22–23, 39, 55, 57
Kelley, Allen C., and da Silva, L., 41
Kelley, Allen C., and Williamson, J.,
    89, 93
Kerven, C., 118, 123
Keyfitz, N., 34, 43
Khan, J., and Ofek, H., 96, 105
Kim, S., 115, 123
King, T., and Kelley, A. C., 8
Kirchner, J. W., et al., 61, 76
Knowles, J. C., and Anker, R., 137–38
Krazenbuehl, T., 40
Kubat, D., 135, 138
Kuznets, Simon, 19, 22–23, 26, 43, 200,
    203, 210

Johnson, M., Bell, F., and Bennett, J.,
    41
Johnston, J., 147, 160
Jones, Ronald W., 223

Laber, G., and Chase, R. X., 86, 93
Lam, D., 8
Landau, Daniel, 200, 210
Lau, Lawrence J., Feder, Gershon, and
    Slade, Roger, 183, 185
Lee, Ronald, 18–19, 23, 40
Leff, Nathaniel, 29, 39, 43, 54, 57
Leontief, Wassily, 32, 43
Lewis, W. A., 8, 82–83, 93
Lindert, P., 39
Linn, J., 41, 93
Lipton, M., 127, 138
Little, Ian M. D., 212, 223
Lowry, I., 87, 93
Lucas, Robert E. B., 114, 117 18, 123,
    125–26, 128–32, 137–38
Lucas, Robert E. B., and Stark, Oded,
    126–28, 137–38
Ludwig, H. D., 185

McGranahan, D., Pizarro, E., and Pi-
    zarro, Richard C., 193, 198
MacKellar, F. Landis, and Vining, Dan-
    iel, Jr., 32, 43

McNamara, R., 39
McNicoll, Geoffrey, 8, 13–14, 22–23,
    27–28, 39–40, 43
Malthus, Thomas, 59–60
Mason, Andrew, 8, 39, 47, 54–55, 57
Mason, K. O., 187, 198
Mayer, E., 40
Meerman, J., and Cochrane, S., 65, 76
Mellor, J., 35–36, 43
Mellor, J., and Johnston, B., 36, 43
Mera, K., 96, 105
Mera, K., and Shishido, H., 105
Merrick, T. W., 8
Mills, E. S., and Hamilton, B. W., 104–
    5
Miracle, Marvin P., 174, 185
Mischan, E. J., 223–24
Modigliani, Franco, 47, 57
Modigliani, Franco, and Brumberg, Rich-
    ard, 47, 57
Montgomery, Mark R., 33, 43
Morgan, W. B., 172, 185
Mosley, H., 41
Mueller, E., 39
Muth, R. F., 140, 160
Myrdal, Gunnar, 139

Nagi, M. H., 110, 123
National Academy of Sciences, 30, 33,
    35–36, 38, 44
National Research Council, 2–4, 7–8,
    22–23, 59, 76, 93
Nijkamp, P., 102, 105
Norman, M. J. T., 185

Oberai, A., 39
OECD, 140, 147, 160, 193, 198
Okogbo, B. N., 172, 185

PADCO, 96, 98, 105–6
Paine, S., 113, 116–17, 120, 123
Palmer, I., and von Buchwald, U., 188,
    198
Paulino, L. A., 64–66, 76
Pindyck, R. S., and Rubinfeld, D. L.,
    147–48, 160
Pingali, Prabhu L., and Binswanger,

Hans P., 35, 43, 63, 76, 174, 176, 185

Pingali, Prabhu L., Bigot, Yves, and Binswanger, Hans P., 63, 76, 176, 185

Powers, Mary G., 187, 197–98

Preston, S., 35, 41, 43

Qutub, S. A., and Richardson, H. W., 97, 106

Ram, R., 39, 55, 57

Rau, R., 39

Rawls, J., 212, 217, 222–24

Rempel, H., and Lobdell, R. A., 137–38

Revelle, R., 35, 43

Reynolds, L., 37, 43

Richards, A. I., 174, 186

Richardson, Harry W., 93, 95, 98–101, 106

Robinson, W., 39

Rodgers, A., 8, 26, 39

Rodgers, G., 39, 43

Rodgers, G., Hopkins, M., and Wery, R., 39

Rogers, A., 87, 93

Rosenzweig, M., and Wolpin, K., 31, 44

Rounce, N. V., 172, 186

Russell, S. S., 129, 138

Ruthenberg, H. P., 63, 173, 186

Ruttan, Vernon, 181–83, 186

Sabot, R. H., 102, 106

Safilios-Rothschild, C., 188, 198

Sahota, G. S., 87, 93

Salvatore, Dominick, 8, 87–89, 93, 140, 142–43, 159–60

Sanders, John H., and Ruttan, Vernon, 178, 186

Sanderson, W., 40

Sapir, A., 158, 160

Schapera, I., 186

Schultz, T. Paul, 31, 44

Schultz, T. W., 40, 83, 93

Sedjo, R., and Clawson, M., 42

Serageldin, I., et al., 124, 159–60

Shaw, R. P., 143, 160

Shyrock, H., and Siegel, J., 195, 198

Simmons, G., et al., 41

Simmons, J., and Alexander, L., 40

Simon, Julian L., 8, 15, 22–23, 30–31, 44, 59, 76

Simon, Julian L., and Khan, H., 32, 38, 44

Simon, Julian L., and Steinman, G., 34, 44

Simon, Julian L., and Wildawsky, A., 36, 44

Sinclair, S., 39

Sjaastad, L. A., 8, 83, 93, 126, 138

Slade, M., 32, 44

Smart, J. E., Teodosio, V. A., and Jimenez, C. J., 116–17, 124

Smith, Adam, 139

Smith, V. K., 41

Solow, R., 38

Somermeyer, W. H., and Bannick, R., 54–57

Squire, L., 39

Srinivasan, T., 35, 44

Stahl, C. W., 140, 160

Standing, G., 30, 44

Stark, Oded, 93

Stark, Oded, and Lucas, Robert E. B., 126, 138

Stiglitz, Joseph E., 223–24

Straubhaar, Thomas, 139, 142, 146, 160

Sveikauskas, L., 97, 106

Swamy, Gurushri, 110, 113, 115–19, 121, 124, 140, 160

Talbot, L. M., 72–73, 76

Tan, J., and Haines, M., 40

Todaro, M. P., 8, 83, 86, 90–91, 93–94, 125, 138, 142, 146, 157, 160

Toulmin, Camilla, 174, 186

Trapnell, C. G., and Clothier, J. N., 186

Turnham, D., 9, 81, 94

UN, 1, 3–4, 7, 9, 25, 27–28, 30, 33–34, 36–38, 41, 44, 70, 80–81, 92, 94, 109, 111, 124, 189, 193, 197–98

UNDP, 98, 105

U.S. Council on Environmental Quality, 32, 44

U.S. Department of Agriculture, 60, 76

Vanderkamp, J., 94
Vanek, J., 192
Venieris, Y., and Gupta, G., 40
Vlassoff, M., 39
Vlassoff, M., and Vlassoff, C., 39
Von Rotenham, D., 186
Von Tunzelmann, G. N., 18, 22–23

Ware, H., 188, 191–92, 198
Warren, R., and Passel, J. S., 111, 124
Weiner, M., 119, 124
Wheaton, W. C., and Shishido, H., 97, 106

Williamson, J. G., 112–13, 124
World Bank, 3–4, 7, 9, 38, 44, 59, 94, 140, 159–60, 184, 201, 210
World Resources Institute, 70, 76
Woytinsky, W. S., and Woytinsky, E. S., 109, 124

Yap, L., 86, 94
Youssef, Nadia H., 197–98

Zachariah, K. C., and Conde, J., 110, 124
Zolbert, A. R., 108, 124

Subject Index

African agriculture, recent evolution of, 64–66

Aggregate savings in relation to population growth, 29–30, 45, 47, 54–57

Agricultural innovations: farmer-based, 170–76, 182; science- and industry based, 177–82

Argentina, worker migration into, 110

Australia, migration into, 108–10

Bangladesh, 98–101, 111, 115–16, 119–21, 127–28, 130–32, 134, 137, 183

Basic needs approach, 187–88

Belgium, migration into, 110

Botswana, 111, 126, 129, 131

Brain drain, 121–22, 128, 139

Brazil, 63, 65, 82, 178, 181–82

Burkina Faso, 60, 64, 69–72

Burundi, 168, 172

Cameroon, 63, 65, 168, 170, 172

Canada, migration into, 108–9

Chad, 64, 68–72

Childrearing expenditures, 45–48, 53–57

China, 173–74

Composite attractivity index, 6, 142, 154, 157

Dependency effect, 29, 45–46, 54–55

Egypt, 96, 98–101, 111, 118–21, 173

Ethical issues of population growth, 216–17; Heckscher-Ohlin growth model, 217–19; Keynesian growth model, 219–22; primary values approach, 213–17, 222; utilitarian approach, 214–16

Ethiopia, 60, 65, 168, 173

Farming systems, 33–37, 62–64, 74, 165–70, 182

Food production and food supply, 33–38, 59–60, 64–65, 67, 69, 75, 182

France, 110, 113, 154, 157

Free market system, 217–18

Gambia, 69–72

Germany, 110, 113–14, 116, 129–30, 154–55, 157

Ghana, 65, 110, 116

Greece, 111, 115, 146–47, 154–57

Guest worker migration. See International Migration; Worker Migration

Guest worker programs: Germany, 114, 129–30; Middle East, 115, 128–29, 133; South African mining houses, 114, 126–30

Harris-Todaro migration model, 83, 85

Heckscher-Ohlin model of international trade, 217–19

Holland, migration into, 113
Human carrying capacity, 5, 34–35, 59–62, 66–74

Illegal migration, 110–11, 130
Immigration policies, 111–14
Index of occupational segregation, 195
India, 65–66, 109, 111, 115, 121, 127, 172–74, 178–81, 183
Indonesia, 63, 66, 98–101
Induced innovation hypothesis, 177–79
International migration: costs and benefits to countries of origin, 118–21, 131–37, 155–58; determinants of migration, demand side, 111–14, 128–31, 140–44, 154, 157–58; determinants of migration, supply side, 114–16, 125–28, 136–37, 140–44, 154, 157; effects of migration, 116–20, 131–35, 143–45, 155–58; illegal migration, 110–11, 130; immigration policies, 111–14; permanent migration, 108–10; worker migration, 110, 112–22, 125–37, 139–59
Italy, 109, 111, 146–47, 154–57, 159
Ivory Coast, 110

Japan, 173–74, 177–78, 181

Kenya, 65, 69, 72–73, 90–91, 168, 170, 172, 178
Keynesian growth model, 219–22
Korea, 115, 121, 173
Kuwait, 110, 129

Land Resources for Populations of the Future Project, 67, 69
Land use intensity: determinants of, 166–70; innovations in response to, 170–77
Lesotho, 111, 126, 129, 131
Lewis two-sector model, 82–83
Life cycle savings model, 45–51
Luxembourg, migration into, 110

Malawi, 129, 131–33
Mali, 59–60, 69–72, 110, 173–74
Mauritania, 69–72
Mexico, 81–82, 111, 119

Middle East, migration into, 110, 113, 115
Migration. See International Migration; Rural-Urban Migration; Worker Migration
Mozambique, 129, 132–33

National urban policy, 90–92, 95, 97, 99–101, 104–5
Nepal, 59–60
New Zealand, migration into, 108–10
Niger, 69–72
Nigeria, 63, 65, 69, 168, 170–72, 174

Optimal population growth, 14

Pakistan, 97–99, 111, 115–16, 118–19, 121, 128, 130–32, 134, 137
Philippines, 115–17, 121, 172–73, 178–79
Policy implications of: agricultural growth requirements, 180–84; child-drearing expenditures-aggregate savings relationship, 55–57; international labor migration, 121, 132–33, 136, 155; international responsibility of developed to less developed countries, 222; urbanization and internal migration, 90–92, 99–100, 104–5
Population and its relationship to: aggregate savings, 29–30, 45, 47, 54–57, 107; agricultural output and farming systems, 33–37, 62–64, 74, 165–70, 182; availability of resources, 2, 31–34, 37; capital formation, 15, 28–31, 107; economic development, 2–5, 14–16, 25–27, 37, 208; economies of scale, 32–33, 37; environmental concerns, 2, 35–36, 70, 73, 75; food production and food supply, 33–38, 59–60, 64–65, 67, 69, 75, 182; health, 31, 36–37; human carrying capacity, 34–35, 59–62, 66–74; income distribution, 2, 30; international migration, 5–6, 108–11, 135, 139–44; international responsibility of developed towards less developed countries, 212, 216–17, 222; investment, 30–31, 107; per cap-

ita income, 2–3, 15–18, 25–28, 107, 219–22; role of family, 19–20; rural-urban migration, 79–82; technological change, 32–34, 37, 60–61, 74, 165, 177–82; unemployment and underemployment, 29, 80–82; urban growth and urbanization, 2–3, 5, 79–82, 91–92, 96–97

Population estimates, 1, 59, 65, 80, 182, 208–10

Population policy, 21–22, 91, 105

Population theories, 3, 15–21

Portugal, 109–11, 146–47, 154–57

Poverty threshold, 61–62

Rural-urban migration, 79–90, 92, 99

Rwanda, 168, 172

Sahelian and Sudanian Zones, 69–72, 74

Senegal, 69–72, 168, 172

Small nations: definition, 199–200, 208–10; determinants of growth rates, 201–7; export orientation, 202–3

South Africa, 117, 126–30, 132–33

Spain, 109–11, 146–47, 154–57, 159

Sri Lanka, migration into, 108

Stationary population, 59

Status of women: indicators of the, 191–97; measuring the, 189–91; rise of "women in development" issues, 187–89

Sub-Saharan Africa, population and carrying capacity of, 64–75

Swaziland, 126

Switzerland, migration into, 110, 113

Taiwan, 173, 178

Tanzania, 59–60, 65, 168, 170, 172, 174

Technological changes in agriculture, 177–82

Temporary migration. See Worker Migration

Thailand, 171, 179, 184

Todaro migration model, 85–90, 92, 125, 142–43, 157–58

Trinidad and Tobago, 189–91

Turkey, 110–11, 114–17, 119–20, 127–28, 130–32, 134, 137, 146–47, 154–57, 159

Two-sector model, 82–83

Uganda, 59–60, 65, 69, 168, 172

United States, 108–10, 112, 177–78

Urban minimum wage policy, 90–92

Urban population growth, 80–82, 92

Urban unemployment and underemployment, 79–81, 83, 90–92

Urbanization: economic benefits, 95–97, 100–101, 104; qualitative benefits and costs, 101–3; urban investment costs, 97–101, 104–5; urban settlement patterns, 97–199, 104–5; urban unemployment and underemployment, 79–81, 83, 90–92

Venezuela, migration into, 110–11

Women in development, 187–89

Worker migration: characteristics of migrant workers, 115–16, 122, 128–29, 131; costs and benefits to countries of origin, 118–21, 131–37, 155–58; costs to migrant workers, 126–27, 137; determinants of labor migration, demand side, 112–13, 128–31, 142–44, 154–55, 157–58; determinants of labor migration, supply side, 114–16, 125–28, 136–37, 142–44, 154–55, 157–58; difference from internal migration, 126–27; effects of worker migration, 116–21, 137, 143–45, 155–58; extent of worker migration, 110–11, 113; model of worker migration, 140–48, 159; remittances, 116–20, 126–28, 132–37, 144, 155

Yemen Arab Republic, 111, 119, 121

Yugoslavia, 110–11, 114–15, 158

Zaire, 174, 183

Zambia, 60, 168, 173–74

Zimbabwe, 69

About the Editor and Contributors

HANS P. BINSWANGER is Chief of the Agriculture Operations Division for Mexico and Central America of the World Bank. His published work deals with a broad spectrum of agricultural development issues including the following: induced innovation, research resource allocation, and income distribution consequences of technical change; decision theory; the measurement of risk and risk aversion; econometric studies of supply response, factor demand and consumer demand; rural labor markets and contractual choice; rural nonfarm activities and employment; agricultural mechanization and mechanization policy; the evolution of farming systems in Sub-Saharan Africa; and the impact of population growth on agricultural technology and production relations.

CLIVE DANIEL holds a Ph.D. from Fordham University. Dr. Daniel, a former journalist in Barbados, West Indies, now teaches economics at Fordham University and does research in development economics. His primary area of interest is the impact of growth on the welfare of the poor in underdeveloped countries.

DAVID E. HORLACHER, Ph.D. in Economics, Pennsylvania State University, is Chief of the Population and Development Section of the United Nations Population Division. Prior to joining the United Nations, he held professorships in Economics at Bucknell and Susquehanna Universities. Author of articles on the cost benefit analysis of family planning and application of economic-demographic models to planning, he has engaged in numerous consultancies concerning the implications of population trends in developing countries.

ROBERT E. B. LUCAS was born in the United Kingdom and was educated at the London School of Economics and Massachusetts Institute of Technology. He is currently Professor of Economics at Boston University and was a recipient of the Chanan Yavor award for his work with Oded Stark on motivation to remit.

His research interests include human resources, industry and trade in developing countries, with special reference to South Asia and Southern Africa.

F. LANDIS MACKELLAR is Assistant Professor of Economics at Queens College of the City University of New York. Prior to this appointment, he was economist at Wharton Econometric Forecasting Associates in Philadelphia, Pennsylvania. He holds graduate degrees from Cambridge University and the University of Pennsylvania.

DENNIS J. MAHAR is currently an Advisor on the Economic Advisory Staff of the World Bank. He holds a Ph.D. from the University of Florida. Dr. Mahar previously served as Deputy Division Chief in the World Bank's Population, Health, and Nutrition Department and as Senior Economist in both the Latin America and Caribbean and Africa Regional Offices. He was also one of the authors of the Bank's 1984 *World Development Report*, which focused on the relationships between population growth and economic development. Before joining the World Bank in 1978, he worked as an economist at the Institute of Economic and Social Research (Rio de Janairo) and the Ford Foundation, and taught at the University of Florida and Pikeville College. Dr. Mahar is the author of numerous books, monographs and articles on economic development issues.

ANDREW MASON is Assistant Director for Professional Education of the East-West Population Institute, East-West Center, and Professor of Economics at the University of Hawaii. His recent research includes papers on population growth and saving appearing in the National Research Council's *Population, Growth and Economic Development* and in a forthcoming issue of *Population and Development Review*; a monograph published by UNFPA, *Population Growth and Economic Development: Lessons from Selected Asian Countries*; and several studies on the economic impact of changing demographic characteristics of households in developing countries.

GÖRAN P. OHLIN, Professor of Economics at the University of Uppsala, Sweden, and since 1985 Assistant Secretary General of the United Nations. He was one of the founders of the Development Center of OECD and has been a consultant to the World Bank and the United Nations on issues of international economic relations.

JOHN J. PIDERIT, S. J., is Assistant Professor of Economics at Fordham University and Master of one of the residential colleges at Fordham. He obtained his M. Phil. in economics from Oxford University and his Ph.D. from Princeton University. His interests and training are in international trade and finance. More recently he has focused on the way in which ethical norms can be incorporated into standard models of international trade and finance.

PRABHU L. PINGALI is an economist with the International Rice Research Institute. He has been associated with the Agricultural and Rural Development Department at the World Bank in a series of studies dealing with the evolution of farming systems in Sub-Saharan Africa and the impact of population growth on agricultural technology and the institutions. He has also worked on economics of pest control.

MARY G. POWERS is the Dean of the Graduate School of Arts and Sciences at Fordham University. She received her Ph.D. at Brown University. She has produced numerous books and articles in the area of social demography and social stratification. Her current research involves the study of life histories of Puerto Rican women with particular attention to education, labor force, and family formation activities. Her professional activities include election to several offices in the American Statistical Association, the American Sociological Association and the Population Association of America, as well as holding consultant and advisory positions with the U.N. Statistical Office and Population Division, at the U.S. Bureau of Census, and in the Department of Health and Human Services.

HARRY W. RICHARDSON is Distinguished Professor of Economics and Regional Planning at the State University of New York at Albany and Professor of Economics and Urban and Regional Planning at the University of Southern California at Los Angeles. He is the author of nineteen books and more than 110 papers and has worked extensively for international and bilateral agencies such as the World Bank, the United Nations, and U.S. Agency for International Development. His current research interests include the application of policentric models to metropolitan regions and policy issues in megacities.

DOMINICK SALVATORE, Chairman and Professor of Economics at Fordham University and Consultant to the United Nations, is the author of ten books, among which are *International Economics*, 2d ed. (1987) and *Microeconomics: Theory and Applications* (1986) and the editor of four books, one of which is *The New Protectionist Threat to World Welfare* (1987). He is co-editor of the *American Economist* and is on the board of editors of the *Journal of Policy Modeling*. His research has been published in leading journals and presented at the Annual Meetings of the American Economic Association, the United Nations, the New York Academy of Sciences, the Vienna Institute of Comparative Economic Studies, New York University, University of Rome, and others.

THOMAS STRAUBHAAR is a Lecturer at the University of Berne and was a Postdoctoral Fellow at the University of California, Berkeley. He has written several articles on problems of international economics and economic development and the forthcoming book *On the Economics of International Labor Migration* (1988).

GURUSHRI SWAMY is an economist with the Africa Region of the World Bank, and holds a doctoral degree from the Delhi School of Economics, India. She was a member of the staff team that produced the *World Development Report 1984* on Population Change and Development. She has also worked in the areas of workers' remittances and food demand and distribution.